Martin Luther, German Saviour
German Evangelical Theological Factions and
the Interpretation of Luther, 1917–1933

The Protestant ruling classes of the pre–First World War German Empire took for granted that Martin Luther was the greatest of all German men. In the early twentieth century, however, Luther came under attack from Catholics, liberals, and socialists, groups who became the governing coalition of the Weimar Republic after Germany's defeat in the First World War. Protestant conservatives struggled to win back power in the Weimar years – and one object of their battle was to restore the veneration of Martin Luther.

Theological trend-setters after the war were dogmatic or systematic theologians. Whether men of the right like Karl Holl or men of the left like Karl Barth, they wanted to return to Luther's fundamental Reformation theology and to justification through faith alone. In the mid-1920s, however, Barth saw the dangers of Lutheran theocentrism wedded to German nationalism and moved towards a more Reformed Christology and a greater critical distance from Luther. The other six major Weimar-era theologians discussed – Karl Holl, Friedrich Gogarten, Werner Elert, Paul Althaus, Emanuel Hirsch, and Erich Vogelsang – connected their theology to their Luther studies and to their hopes for the rebirth of Germany after the humiliation of the Versailles order. To differing degrees, they presented Martin Luther as the German saviour, and all except Karl Holl, who died in 1926, worked out specifically theological reasons for supporting Hitler when he came to power in 1933.

JAMES M. STAYER is professor of history at Queen's University.

McGILL-QUEEN'S STUDIES IN THE HISTORY OF RELIGION

Volumes in the McGill-Queen's Studies in the History of Religion have been supported by the Jackman Foundation of Toronto.

SERIES TWO   In memory of George Rawlyk
Donald Harman Akenson, Editor

Martin Luther, German Saviour

German Evangelical Theological Factions and the Interpretation of Luther, 1917–1933

JAMES M. STAYER

McGill-Queen's University Press
Montreal & Kingston · London · Ithaca

© McGill-Queen's University Press 2000
ISBN 0-7735-2044-9

Legal deposit second quarter 2000
Bibliothèque nationale du Québec

Printed in Canada on acid-free paper

This book has been published with the help of a
grant from the Humanities and Social Sciences
Federation of Canada, using funds provided by the
Social Sciences and Humanities Research Council
of Canada.

McGill-Queen's University Press acknowledges the
financial support of the Government of Canada
through the Book Publishing Industry Development
Program (BPIDP) for its activities. We also
acknowledge the support of the Canada Council for
the Arts for our publishing program.

Canadian Cataloguing in Publication Data

Stayer, James M.
    Martin Luther, German saviour: German evangelical
    theological factions and the interpretation of Luther,
    1917–1933
    Includes bibliographical references and index.
    ISBN 0-7735-2044-9
    1. Luther, Martin, 1483–1546. 2. Theology,
    Doctrinal – Germany – History – 20th century.
    3. Evangelicalism – Germany – History –
    20th century. I. Title.
    BX8065.2.S83 2000   230'.4143'09041   C99-901193-6

This book was typeset by Typo Litho Composition Inc.
in 10/12 Palatino.

To Hans-Jürgen Goertz and Werner O. Packull

Contents

Preface

(

The usual mark of genuine quality in English-language works in German history is an affirmative answer to the question "Will the Germans find this study significant?" Not to make that requirement would amount to conceding that non-German scholarship on German history can only be second-rate, a kind of para-scholarship for those who do not read German.

In this case, however, my intended readership is in the first place the English-language Protestant communities. Germans tend to know – or at least, be unsurprised by – the viewpoint expressed here. But in the English-speaking Protestant world, the idea lingers that, in the last years of the First World War and in the Weimar Republic, Martin Luther was "rediscovered." According to this view, Germans had continuously revered Luther as a national hero, but only in the years following the fourth Reformation centenary in 1917 did they once more understand that he was above all a theologian, both in his self-understanding and in his historic importance. This new understanding arose, it is said, because the terrible crisis of the war jolted German Protestants out of the complacent superficialities of "cultural Protestantism," which upheld an easy identification of Protestant religiosity and secular culture – the whole modern way of life. "Cultural Protestantism" was closely identified with theological liberalism, with the theological heritage of Albrecht Ritschl and the writings of noted contemporaries such as Adolf von Harnack and Ernst Troeltsch. Persons of liberal persuasion lacked both respect for Martin Luther and the capacity to understand him. The return to

Luther and the Reformation and the rejection of superficial liberalism was the achievement of two movements – the Luther Renaissance and the Dialectical Theology. The Luther Renaissance, led by Karl Holl and Emanuel Hirsch, was a purely scholarly recovery of the Reformer's place in the history of theology, a place that had not been properly understood even by confessional Lutheran churchmen, let alone by "cultural Protestants." The Dialectical Theology, led by Karl Barth and Friedrich Gogarten, rejected the dominant tradition of nineteenth-century German cultural Idealism, which had corrupted Protestant theology. In its place, it provided a new foundation for Protestant faith with a revival of the theology of the Word of God as proclaimed by the Reformers. Since Barth was Swiss Reformed, this renewed Reformation theology was not exclusively Lutheran but appealed to both Luther and Calvin, who were almost the same – at least when compared to the characteristic beliefs of modernity.

The deformation of German life under the Third Reich does not at all detract from the significance and worth of the insights of the Luther Renaissance and the Dialectical Theology. It is true that Emanuel Hirsch was a Nazi Party member (and even developed an academically presentable argument that Jesus was not Jewish "in a racial sense") and that Friedrich Gogarten became an avowed supporter of Hitler. But to detract from the sound scholarly and religious insights of an earlier period on the basis of these personal details is but an appeal to national and political prejudice of the sort that would turn Martin Luther into an ancestor of Hitler. Furthermore, it is well known that Karl Barth was an enemy of the Nazi regime and an inspirer of the Confessing Church – fundamentally, Hitler was an enemy of Christianity, and Martin Luther an inspiration for Germany to recover its authentic Christian foundations.

I suspect that theologically sophisticated German Protestants would smile at the naïveté of the position espoused above; at least, they would not advance it so baldly. They are aware of the way that Luther scholarship became a battlefield of opposing currents of systematic theology in the years following the First World War, a situation that continued at least until the 1960s.[1] They almost certainly also share the insight of the *Spiegel* cover that coloured Luther black, white, and red, the colours of the imperial (and Nazi) flag and of the German conservative nationalist tradition. Toward the end of his life, Emanuel Hirsch reminisced with a confidant that in 1917 and 1918 "the opposition between black-white-red and black-red-gold really set the tone for the Protestant church and theology, not the previous theological groupings."[2] This is something that Germans tend to know but not to write about, partly because it is obvious and partly because it is embarrassing. A German professor of my acquaintance told of a conversation with another professor who wanted to lecture on the continuities between the Luther Renaissance and the German Christian movement, a radically pro-Nazi grouping that strayed far outside Christian orthodoxy. The professor preparing the lectures wanted to know where he could read about the topic. The answer was "You can't read about it; you have to know it." Germans tend to know, but the contents of this study are, I think, something that English-speaking Protestants will need to read about. A broader point is that, at least since the nineteenth-century period of Ritschl's dominance, academic Protestantism in Great Britain and North America has been a passive consumer of German theological styles. In the twentieth century, Harnack was succeeded by Barth, Rudolf Bultmann, and perhaps Jürgen Moltmann. It is time for non-Germans to become more sophisticated about the way that a particular German environment – *Sitz im Leben*, to use the fashionable phrase – entered into the production of each piece of writing associated with these great names.

There is something else: a lot of scholarship, unfortunately, is a defaming of the last generation, if only because of the truncated summaries in which it is presented, as a foil or backdrop to one's own "findings." The third generation, that of the grandchildren, is called to rectify the one-sidednesses of its immediate predecessors. I confess to reading Ernst Troeltsch and Albert Schweitzer with an appreciation that I cannot bring to Karl Holl or even to Karl Barth, let alone Emanuel Hirsch or Friedrich Gogarten. These latter seem to me antimodern modernists – modernists who rant against modernity as Friedrich Nietzsche did.[3]

We in the late twentieth century have, one hopes, survived the once-trendy and always arrogant rejections of liberal democracy associated with fascism and communism. Perhaps our grandfathers' generation of liberal theologians deserves another look too. They have been denounced as the spokesmen of a superficial optimism. They would probably prefer to be remembered for their *Wahrhaftigkeitsbedürfnis*, their need to tell the truth as best they could understand it. Albert Schweitzer wrote: "It is the task of Protestantism to be absolutely genuine and honest. If it loses that need for fearless integrity, then it is only a shadow of itself and it becomes unsuited to fulfill its calling for the Christian religion and for the world."[4] Schweitzer applied that maxim to his efforts to understand Jesus and Paul, but I think that it has its application, too, to "understanding Luther."

Seven men are the protagonists of this study: Karl Holl, Karl Barth, Friedrich Gogarten, Werner Elert, Paul Althaus, Emanuel Hirsch, and

Erich Vogelsang, to name them in the order of their appearance. Why them especially? The attempt to produce knowledge involves focus – a degree of sovereign choice on the part of the researcher or writer. However, there is a rationale behind the choice of these specific people. All were significant Evangelical theologians; all were prominent figures in the life of the German Reich during the Weimar Republic; and the intellectual and spiritual life of each was preoccupied with *Ringen mit Luther* (wrestling with Martin Luther), to cite the title of a recent study of Barth. Hence this is not a survey of Luther studies generally in the Weimar period. In Germany, not to mention Scandinavia, significant contributions were made by others: Otto Scheel, Gerhard Ritter, and Heinrich Boehmer come to mind. It is not a study of the entire Holl school, nor of all participants in the Dialectical Theology. However, the common concern with Evangelical theology, with Luther, and not least, with Germany created a lively discourse, sometimes friendly, sometimes polemical, among these seven men. The contention of this study is that it was significant both for Luther studies and for the twentieth century.

Acknowledgments

Thanks are due to the staffs of the libraries of Queen's University, Heidelberg University, Münster University, and Marburg University for their assistance in the location of sources for this study. Likewise, I am grateful to Professor D Dr Robert Stupperich, Münster, for allowing me to work with his collection of the correspondence of Karl Holl. Professor Dr Gottfried Seebaß and Professor Dr Taira Kuratsuka of Tokyo helped me to orient myself in Heidelberg, as did Professor Dr Martin Brecht in Münster. Thanks also to the staff of the Theologischen Studienhaus, Heidelberg, and to my long-time friends the Böttcher family of Telgte for providing accommodation during my German research. The manuscript has particularly benefited, both in style and in content, from the critical reading of friends and colleagues: Klaus Hansen, the late George Rawlyk, Harold Mah, Marguerite Van Die, and Clyde Forsberg of Queen's University, Werner Packull and James Reimer of Conrad Grebel College, and Hans-Jürgen Goertz of Hamburg University. The project was supported by a research grant from the Social Sciences and Humanities Research Council of Canada. I am particularly grateful to my cheerful and highly competent co-workers in preparing the manuscript, Cindy Butts, Sharon Judd, and Norma St. John. This is my second book with McGill-Queen's University Press. I am honoured to be in the company of such fine scholars of the history of religion as the late George Rawlyk and Donald Akenson. Diane Duttle, Roger Martin, Joan McGilvray, Heather Ebbs, Curtis Fahey, and Elizabeth Hulse have been pleasant and helpful associates in the preparation and production of the books.

Martin Luther, German Saviour

1 Luther Scholarship before the Great War

The notion that the Reformers were "newly discovered,"[1] that Martin Luther experienced a "Renaissance" in Germany in 1919–21 with the end of the First World War and the beginning of the Weimar Republic, is a very paradoxical one. This rediscovery of the historical Reformation and its theology supposedly occurred at the precise moment that the historical method lost the pre-eminence that it had enjoyed in German theology throughout the nineteenth century. Particularly between the two wars, dogmatic theology replaced history as the dominant approach that shaped the other areas of Protestant theological study.

Wolfgang Trillhaas, a student of many of the prominent theologians of the 1920s, explains the broad contours of Protestant theology in twentieth-century Germany as a successive domination of historicism, dogmatics, and, following the Second World War, biblical studies: "The change of epochs of theological development was directly manifested in the change of the leading specialty, which imposed its principles upon the other theological specialties."[2]

The great names of German Protestant theology (and to a considerable degree of world Protestant theology) before the First World War were Albrecht Ritschl (1822–89) and Adolf von Harnack (1851–1930). The followers of Karl Holl and Karl Barth claimed that they had made a new beginning – abandoning liberalism and "cultural Protestantism" and returning to the theology of the Reformers. In fact, despite their attacks on the liberal world of their fathers and teachers, they were its heirs. From the standpoint of Protestant orthodoxy, despite some orthodox rhetoric which they used as camouflage, the men of the Luther Renaissance and the Dialectical Theologians were all "modernists." The anti-modern modernist who cuts a striking figure among the sophisticated has been a recognizable type, at least from Friedrich Nietzsche onward. To understand Holl and Hirsch and the various Dialectical Theologians when they set up the standard of "understanding Luther," it is requisite to have some understanding of those figures whose reputations they attempted to bury.

Albrecht Ritschl did not think of himself as a liberal but as someone who had made a synthesis or found a middle way between orthodoxy and liberalism. In one sense he was right – an austere intellectual, he lacked the moralizing ethical piety of more authentic liberals such as Harnack, Albert Schweitzer, and Ernst Troeltsch. However, the liberals, and their successors, fed on his intellectual substance.[3]

Ritschl was a theological positivist working with the history of dogma with the aim of showing how speculative metaphysics had encroached upon Christianity from the middle of the second century onward. The original religion of Jesus and Paul (he did not set them against each other in the manner of some later liberals) was in this way replaced by Catholicism, with its legalistic approach to sin, its authoritarianism, and its monastic enmity to the world. The Reformation began the half-conscious project of restoring the religion of Jesus and Paul. "The Reformation ideas are more hidden than open in Luther's books"; and Philipp Melanchthon, the real founder of the Lutheran church, reverted to scholasticism and brought the Reformation project to an abrupt halt. In this light, Ritschl saw his historical detective work on the accumulation of doctrine as a return to the Reformation's original reductionist task. Trillhaas articulates the program of Ritschl and the Ritschlians in a lapidary formula: "The task of current dogmatics is to put aside all extra-biblical notions and return to biblical theology and to make a system of it, using general academic categories."[4] Harnack and Reinhold Seeberg wrote histories of dogma in order to pursue that Ritschlian objective.

However, Ritschl the positivist and enemy of metaphysics had some concealed metaphysical baggage of his own. Although he avoided the Hegelian framework of his teacher, Ferdinand Christian Baur, a vulgarized Kantianism was central to his outlook. It informed the conception of Christian liberty that he took to be the forward-looking, positive quality of the Reformation. In the tracts of 1520, *On Christian Liberty* and *To the Nobility*, Luther accentuated the ethical energies of justification by faith. Freedom from the obligations of works righteousness and merit theology was freedom for Christian work in worldly callings. In this manner, God had revealed himself in Christ:

"The permanent significance of Jesus Christ for his church is based upon the fact that he, exclusively, had the ability to carry out his calling, the introduction of the Kingdom of God."[5] This "job" of Jesus Christ, the Kingdom of God, was the central principle of Ritschl's theology. The beginning of the Kingdom would come in the spirit of Luther's unfulfilled legacy, through work in the world, prayer, and submission to the will of God. This was no utopia, said Ritschl. In fact, it was the very special utopia of the upper middle class of the Bismarckian Reich, here proclaimed as the revelation of God transmitted through Jesus, Paul, and Luther. Here we have the classic statement of "post-millennialism," a neo-Kantian Christ pointing the way to the evolutionary realization of the Kingdom of God through human historical progress.

Ritschl regarded Luther as a hopelessly unsystematic theologian of genius caught in a historical transition between medieval and modern that he had helped to create. This interpretation gave Ritschl full licence to rummage about in Luther's theology, rejecting the traditional, "medieval" elements that he disliked. For instance, De Servo Arbitrio (On the Bondage of the Will), which Luther thought his best work, should in Ritschl's view never have been written. Its dualistic stress on the wrath of God and its image of Christ's contention with the devil for the souls of men were most uncongenial to his sunny, monistic theology of the Kingdom. Ritschl was concerned to discover Luther's "original line"; hence he made the very important assumption that the Reformer was more "himself" in the beginning of his theological career than later on when he asserted that the distinction between law and gospel was the litmus of a proper theology. One of the ironies of the encounter between Luther and Ritschl was that where Luther was most systematic he was least appealing to Ritschl, who was full professor for systematic theology at Göttingen for the last quarter-century of his life.[6]

Ernst Troeltsch observed that German Protestantism was, among other things, "a half-academic cultural religion."[7] Trillhaas comments that liberal Protestantism "was, and wanted to be, the religion of the cultured ... The whole world of culture, religious history just like literature, took a position beside the biblical Scriptures and became a series of 'parables' of divine truth."[8] The effect was a mixture of the sacred and the profane – there was one historical-critical method, and everything that was knowable was mediated through history. As Kant revealed, we cannot know "the thing in itself"; what we can know are historical phenomena. Putting that reservation aside, Adolf von Harnack could make an appeal to truth against Karl Barth that makes the English-language reader think of Thomas Huxley and

Bishop Wilberforce: "An academic presentation of theology can inflame and edify because of its object. But an academic theology whose purpose is to inflame and edify brings alien fire to its altar. As there is only one academic method, so there is only one academic task – the pure knowledge of the object."[9] Thomas Aquinas had once taught that any philosophical assertion which contradicted dogma must be faulty philosophy. The half-academic cultural religion of Protestant Germany asserted that anything which contradicted or denied real *Wissenschaft* must be faulty religion.

This view meant, however, that the search for the religion of Jesus which Ritschl had announced was a historical problem, an academic matter to be settled by academics. This kind of encroachment of historicism upon religious faith was denounced in 1892 by Martin Kähler in an influential talk, "The So-Called Historical Jesus and the Historic, Biblical Christ."[10] The gospels, he warned, were not proper sources for a historical reconstruction of the life of Jesus but a proclamation of the historic good news that Christ is Lord. Kähler came from outside the circle of academic theology. The professors soldiered on. In the same year as Kähler's talk, Johannes Weiß wrote *The Preaching of Jesus on the Kingdom of God*.[11] Weiß was Ritschl's son-in-law. He pointed out that Jesus thought of the Kingdom as an eschatological event, a new age brought about by God breaking into history, and that the gradual, ethical realization of the Kingdom of which Ritschl had written was a historical anachronism. It projected nineteenth-century liberal and Kantian ideals upon Jesus and the New Testament. Despite such a central objection, however, the momentum of the Ritschlian project was not broken. Luther continued to be interpreted as an involuntary groper towards the religion of Jesus and modernity.

Historicism brought with it a sense of one's place in history. Sigmund Freud greeted the new century with his *Interpretation of Dreams*. Adolf von Harnack, celebrated as the leading Protestant theologian of his day, can be excused for thinking that his own *Essence of Christianity* (1900) was the beginning of twentieth-century religious thinking instead of what it was, an expression of the expiring piety of the nineteenth century. Paying no heed to Kähler or Weiß, Harnack radicalized Ritschl's project of the reduction of dogma in a way that would no doubt have astonished and dismayed his predecessor.[12] The book is best understood as a radical assault on theology generally and Christology specifically. It aims to level the distinction between the layman in the pew and the pastor in the pulpit, which it views as a carry-over from Catholicism, by a radical reduction of doctrine.

The Essence of Christianity reflects northern European Protestant ethnocentrism. Its scorn for the Latin Catholic and even more for the Greek and Eastern churches is one of its underlying notes. Presumably the evangelical churches have truly recovered a great deal of the original gospel message by de-emphasizing tradition, ceremony, an external church, and doctrinal orthodoxy.

The Harnack notion of the gospel is heavily dependent on a New Testament biblical positivism that was a part of the Ritschlian tradition. It involves a sovereign selectivity as applied to the New Testament, according to which the three synoptic Gospels and the Pauline letters are reliable historic traditions. The fact that these gospel narratives centre in Galilee is a mark of their authenticity. Everything before Jesus' ministry (the Virgin Birth, Christmas stories, etc.) is dismissed as legendary accretion, but the New Testament accounts of the relation between Jesus and John the Baptist are taken quite literally. The Gospel of John is drawn on liberally where it fits Harnack's outlook, but its theology is rejected. Pauline Christianity is accepted more or less in the terms in which it appears in the New Testament – basically, the idea is that Paul won over and assumed the initiative among the disciples. The notion of an original Jewish Christianity led by James "the brother of the Lord," which was displaced by Paul's neo-Christianity, is implicitly rejected. Rudolf Bultmann's introduction to the 1957 English translation of Harnack[13] faults his view of the original gospel of Jesus as being unhistoric on two grounds. The first, with a quotation from Albert Schweitzer, is that Harnack minimizes and smooths over Jesus' eschatological proclamation of the Kingdom of Heaven, making it rather innocuous. The second, which explains the first, is the objection that Jesus' gospel à la Harnack is ahistoric. Again like Ritschl, Harnack is always distinguishing between the "husk" and the "kernel" of all his protagonists' beliefs – what was merely traditional in their outlooks and what was original and essential (a distinction unknowable to the historical figures and accessible only to the historian). The eschatological content of Jesus' message can be largely dismissed by referring to the long tradition of Jewish eschatology. Jesus' sayings affirming the law can be put aside as mere tradition, so that something like a Lutheran law-and-gospel distinction can be imposed on the New Testament. By this device, Harnack can make a priori distinctions between the Jewish, the Hellenistic, and the authentically Christian.

He summarizes Jesus' gospel under three headings: the Kingdom of God and its coming, God the Father and the infinite value of the human soul, and the higher righteousness and the commandment of love. For the reasons mentioned, the second and third themes

overpower the first. The idea of an internalized Kingdom ("the Kingdom of God is within you") is played off against the eschatological
meaning of the Kingdom. Knowing God as one's Father, trusting
that the world is in his hands, and abandoning all selfishness to
serve God through the neighbour turn out to be the kernel of the gospel. All else is husk. The Passion narrative is not rejected, even
though it is placed in Jerusalem rather than in Galilee. Jesus' entry
into Jerusalem on the ass and his cleansing of the Temple from the
money-changers are clear evidence of his Messianic self-understanding. He had rethought the Jewish Messianic traditions and purified
them of their political, warlike trappings. His conception of the Messiah as the suffering servant was original and non-Jewish, Isaiah 53
notwithstanding. Indeed, Jesus did come to understand himself as
the Son of God. What he meant when he called himself the Son of
God is "nothing but the practical consequence of knowing God as
the Father and as his Father. Rightly understood, the name of Son
means nothing but the knowledge of God ... Jesus is convinced that
he knows God in a way in which no one ever knew Him before, and
he knows that it is his vocation to communicate this knowledge of
God to others by word and deed – and with the knowledge that people are God's children."[14] Harnack's account of the Resurrection narratives is of a piece with his view of the miracle narratives. This was
a pre-scientific age and people saw things differently then. Ancient
literature is full of the marvellous. Jesus lives eternally, and the faith
and hope of Christians is that they will live eternally with him. This
faith and hope is one that cannot be either confirmed or denied by
the knowledge of the senses.

The apostolic church supposedly dispensed with Jewish law and
ceremony. It was an entirely spiritual community of charismatic inspiration, ethical purity, and brotherly fellowship. Harnack did not honour all apostolic traditions equally: "The Acts of the Apostles tell us
that in Jerusalem they went so far as to have a voluntary community
of goods. Paul says nothing about it; and if we are to accept this obscure report as really trustworthy, then neither Paul nor the Christian
communities among the Gentiles took pattern by the enterprise."[15]

From there on, the history of Christianity was marked by descent
into doctrine, ceremony, and organization. Catholicism about 200 CE
made its accommodation with Greek philosophy by identifying Jesus
with the Logos. Even so, the Logos principle was only equivocally divine; thus later Greek Catholicism worked out an elaborate theology
of the God-man, of Trinity and Christology. "The idea of the God-
Man nature, the idea of God becoming a man, is what is new in the
new, nay, is the only new thing under the sun,"[16] as Harnack quoted

one of the Greek fathers. But this Christianity centred on the doctrine of the Incarnation is not *"a Christian product in Greek dress, but a Greek product in Christian dress."*[17] The orthodoxy of the Greek councils was assumed intact by Roman Catholicism, which continued an ecclesiastical version of the Roman world-empire. *"The Roman Church ... pushed itself into the place of the Roman World-Empire, of which it is the actual continuation;* the empire has not perished, but has only undergone a transformation."[18] This church, true to the Roman genius, is a "legal institution," administering salvation by specific legal processes, the sacraments. The genius of St Augustine, with his quirky recovery of Paulinism, was the chief force for preservation of the gospel in the Roman communion. The Reformation, by its revolution against the priests and hierarchy, opened the way for a return to the gospel. Luther was its hero, but of course he was not perfectly equipped to restore the gospel: "any trustworthy knowledge of the history of [traditional] dogmas was as yet an impossibility, and still less was any historical acquaintance with the New Testament and primitive Christianity attainable. It is marvelous how in spite of all this Luther possessed so much power of penetration and sound judgement."[19] "And just as Eastern Christianity is rightly called Greek, and the Christianity of the Middle Ages and of Western Europe is rightly called Roman, so the Christianity of the Reformation may be described as German, in spite of Calvin. For Calvin was Luther's pupil, and he made his influence most lastingly felt, not among the Latin nations but among the English, the Scotch, and the Dutch. Through the Reformation the Germans mark a stage in the history of the Universal Church. No similar statement can be made of the Slavs."[20]

Obviously, in interpreting Luther, Harnack had more to work with than in his expressions about Jesus. The preoccupation of Germans with Luther had become stronger in the late nineteenth century than previously. In 1875 Julius Köstlin produced an important biography. The complete scholarly Weimar Edition of Luther's works began with the fourth centenary of his birth in 1883 and provided continuing grist for scholarship's mills as volume succeeded volume in the late nineteenth and early twentieth centuries. And as Adolf von Harnack acknowledged, if a complete picture of Luther's theology was required, there was no better place to go for it than the two-volume study by his orthodox father, Theodosius, which appeared in the 1860s.

The younger Harnack made no secret of his aversion to notions of returning Protestantism to the "whole Luther," with his massive medieval superstitions, the contradictions of his theology, the errors of his biblical exegesis, and the injustice and barbarity of his polemics.[21]

Lacking all sense of history, Luther was an alien spirit to Harnack: "History in the strict sense was a closed book for [Luther]. He showed no perception either of historical relativity or of the growth and development of knowledge within history. Under these circumstances how could he have been capable of properly conveying the content of the Bible as a historical document? And how can a *pure* expression of the essence of Christianity be expected from someone who does not fulfill this requirement?"[22]

Harnack's view of Luther was not dominated by such negative tones, however. He was both too much of a Protestant church historian and a Protestant establishment figure for that. Luther was an archetypical "great man in history": "he became a hero through his joyful faith."[23] For a moment, from 1519 until 1523 more or less, he rose above his personal limitations and became the very embodiment of the Reformation, "both the return to Pauline Christianity and the grounding of a new age."[24] Basically, Luther was a divided figure: a restorer of ancient dogma and the harbinger of the new undogmatic Christianity (which was, of course, for Harnack the religion of Jesus). Luther restored the dogmas of the early ecumenical councils, and thus, in his concentration on the abuses of the Roman church and Latin scholasticism, he restored Hellenistic philosophical elements that were an alien growth on the body of original Christianity.[25] But at the same time he brought something new: "he redefined the ideal of religious perfection as no Christian had done since apostolic times."[26] Since Luther rejected the notion of attaining merit in the sight of God, the real testing ground of faith was doing one's duty in "the natural orders of life" – marriage, family, state, and vocation. "What the medieval period looked at with distrust, the job and the duty of the day, was for [Luther] the real sphere of a life pleasing to God." Compared to medieval religion, his amounted to an "enormous reduction": "the humble and assured trust in God's fatherly providence and faithfulness in one's vocation (in love of neighbour) – these he made the main thing, in fact the only thing."[27] Harnack stated that he had learned much from Ritschl in his approach to Luther[28] – in fact, his was a more nuanced and historically enriched repetition of the Ritschlian framework.

Harnack observed that there were problems inherent in a method that "brings Luther into conflict with himself."[29] His reply to this quandary was that, among biographers and historians, only theologians were so obsessed by system that they missed the point that there is no surer way to distort the perception of a great man than to force everything he said into an artificial unity.[30] So Harnack's Luther embodied the conflict between the restorer of the creeds of the ancient church and the modernist who reduced Christianity to dutiful work in the world.

Many themes of the Luther research of the 1920s were anticipated in Harnack's *History of Dogma*. The "spiritual struggles" of the monastic period are registered. He can even use the term *Anfechtung*,[31] but he does not use it to draw a psychological sketch of Luther in the manner of later interpreters. Nor was Luther's theology of law and gospel lost on Harnack. But like most Luther scholars of his day, he paid special attention to the early theological lectures, particularly the lecture on Romans of 1515–16, which had recently appeared in the Weimar Edition.[32] A peculiarity of Harnack's approach to Luther was the way in which he treated the topic of faith. True to Ritschlian aversion to dogma, faith was almost entirely *fiducia* (trust), hardly at all *fides* (belief). Against the orthodox Lutherans and anticipating the Luther Renaissance, Harnack forged a tight connection between justification and regeneration; very much in the spirit of Luther's early Romans lecture, salvation was both "being righteous" and "becoming righteous."[33]

Perhaps the most distinctive mark of German Luther scholarship in the early twentieth century (in contrast to both earlier and contemporary Luther studies) was its insistence on removing Augustine from the "evangelical succession": Paul-Augustine-Luther. Of course, this revision was preordained by the Ritschlian perspective, according to which "original Christianity" had disappeared by the second century. The disposition to minimize and disparage Augustine and to give Luther credit for leaping over him and returning directly to St Paul makes Harnack a link in a chain connecting Ritschl and Holl. For him, Augustine was a less-sober, less-disciplined thinker than Luther. He lacked the Reformer's perception of the profundity of sin, and thus he took God's saving grace to be something mysterious and obscure, not the assurance of forgiveness of sin through faith in Jesus Christ that it was for Luther.[34] Fundamentally, Augustine and the predestinarian theologians of medieval scholasticism were all synergists who regarded divine grace as an *auxilium* on the road to salvation.[35] The rupture with this synergism was "perhaps Luther's greatest contribution to theology and therefore, in *one* respect, *De Servo Arbitrio* was his greatest writing."[36] Erasmus's statement on free will, which provoked Luther's expressions on the bondage of the will, was "an entirely worldly writing, in the deepest sense irreligious."[37] (How the quintessential modernist could preach!) The self-sufficiency of divine grace was to Harnack "the basic fact of Christian experience." In stressing God's will as the cause of everything else, Luther "gave religion back to religion, grounded the knowledge of faith in its self-sufficiency: thereby he set forth the generation of faith, the experience of the revelation of God in the heart, as an undiscussable axiom, to the Jews a stumbling block, to the Greeks foolishness. But who understood him!"[38] Here we have the hidden theme of German Protestant modernism – from the perpetually misunderstood Jesus to the perpetually misunderstood Luther.

It must seem odd, outside the sphere of German and Scandinavian Protestant theology, to find Harnack, the self-declared modernist, waxing rhapsodic over religious determinism, just at the time that predestination was losing its hold even among traditional Calvinist denominations in the English-speaking world. This was the working out of Wilhelminian Kantianism in Protestant theology. (Of course, Kant's name was taken in vain – he was, after all, the philosopher of freedom and autonomy.) Harnack wrote approvingly of Wilhelm Dilthey's notion that the essence of Lutheranism was breaking free from egoistic motivation, such as was to be found "even in the highest and most delicate Catholic religiosity."[39] It was an axiom of the Kantian-educated Protestant governing classes of Prussia that "duty" trumped the "pursuit of happiness" in ethics, even when, or especially when, the pursuit of happiness presented itself as the pursuit of personal blessedness. (One of the most characteristic and peculiar notions of this Luther literature was the so-called sin of eudemonism – Augustine's sin in aspiring to eternal salvation!)

In breaking free from the inferior religiosity of medieval man, Luther had prepared the way for the Wilhelminian Reich (indeed, for the Nordic master peoples in Britain, America, and Germany), in which Protestants were morally superior to Catholics, Jews, and freethinkers. In Harnack's view the Reformation was the time when "the covenant between Protestantism and Germanness was sealed. (To be sure, evangelical Christianity was a gift to all humanity, and, conversely, today the German spirit is by no means subjected to Protestantism and has not been for a long time.) Nevertheless, Protestantism and Germanness belong together indivisibly. Just as the Reformation saved the German Reich in the sixteenth century, so today the Reformation is still the Reich's strongest power, continuing principle, and highest goal."[40]

Just as in early-twentieth-century America, Protestants believed that they were more American than "others," so Protestants had a similar attitude in the Wilhelminian Reich. The majority was Protestant and so was the ruling family, the Hohenzollerns, with their tradition of enforced merger of Lutheranism and Calvinism. Father Hartmann Grisar, SJ, the most eminent German Catholic Luther scholar of his day, complained that at the Reformation anniversary of 1917, in the midst of the war, Germanness was so much connected with Luther that German Catholics' lack of enthusiasm for the Reformer seemed to cast doubt on their patriotism.[41] Here, too, Harnack fathered the Luther Renaissance of Karl Holl. Both Ernst Troeltsch and Holl, the major contenders in early-twentieth-century Protestant Luther scholarship, contributed to the Harnack festschrift of 1921.[42] Indeed, Holl wrote a respectful introduction to that volume, and Harnack a generous appreciation of Holl's scholarly achievements after the latter's death in 1926. Whatever their differences, the academics in the "half-academic cultural religion" of German Protestantism were "insiders." Catholics, whatever their academic accomplishments, were "outsiders." And Social Democrats with opinions on the Reformation lacked status entirely; they were not eligible to become professors, and therefore they could not produce *Wissenschaft*, only political propaganda.

If the Protestant insiders did not always love one another, they observed the civilities. But in 1904, civility underwent a spectacular collapse in Luther scholarship, with the appearance of the book on Luther and early Lutheranism by Father Heinrich Denifle, OP.[43] Throughout Harnack's treatment of Luther in his *History of Dogma*, the footnotes give hostile attention to Denifle, his "raging against and insulting" of Harnack, his attempts to turn Luther into an "evil demon," his "distortions and slanders."[44] Interconfessional polemics had been quiescent for a long time; the Protestants were not amused.

Denifle, a Vatican archivist, had a well-established scholarly reputation as an expert on medieval manuscripts, German mysticism, and medieval universities. It would have been better for that reputation had he left Luther alone. Clearly, it was his intention to do the church a real service in the evening of his life by destroying the Luther legend. Too much of his long book was mere scolding and denunciation. In the tradition of the sixteenth-century polemic of Johannes Cochläus, Luther's character was described as a product of pride, unchastity, and falsity. Behind this bombast, however, was some substance. On the micro-level, Denifle made numerous critical comments on the Weimar Edition which more often than not turned out to be justified. More important was the debate he initiated over the Autobiographical Fragment in Luther's introduction to the 1545 edition of his Latin works. This document became a point of recurring importance in Luther scholarship for more than fifty years. (Whether the issue is now exhausted is currently answered in different ways, depending upon the scholar's perspective.) In brief, Luther's reminiscence seemed to say that he had had an evangelical experience in 1519 when he was preparing his second lecture on the Psalms. The substance of his experience was his insight that the "divine justice" (*iustitia dei*) referred to in Romans 1:17 was not a justice which God demands of people but a justice which he bestows on them (when he justifies them). Denifle pointed out that the insight which Luther claimed for 1519 was one that permeated his lectures on Romans of 1515–16, whose manuscript had been newly recovered, one version by Denifle himself in the Vatican archives. He concluded that Luther was lying, that his evangelical experience was a fabrication. A broader point was that the medieval church had, according to Denifle, always taught what Luther claimed to have discovered. Hence the notion of Catholic belief in justification by works was a Protestant slander and distortion.[45] Denifle, of course, devoted considerable attention to the vulgarity and violence of Luther's polemics – this was a matter that Protestant scholars could not deny, but preferred not to dwell on. As to Protestant glorification of Luther's teaching on justification, that the righteous God justifies sinners, from Denifle's perspective this was the doctrine of the "self-deluding god" – a God who saw the same people differently, even though they had not changed.

It is idle to speculate whether Denifle would have been more convincing had he expressed his arguments with greater moderation and better manners. Father Albert Maria Weiß, who edited Denifle's incomplete work after his death in 1905, acknowledged that his predecessor "doubtless too often gave free rein to his heart, that powerful Tyrolean heart."[46] It remains to add that Hartmann Grisar, who wrote the next major Catholic study of Luther, although he moderated Denifle's tone and withdrew some of the moral judgments that his predecessor had made against Luther, did not calm the interconfessional hostility in Luther scholarship when he produced a three-volume study on the Reformer in 1911–12.[47] For one thing he began the tradition of psychological research on Luther, which usually suggested that there was at least something the matter with the man. In this spirit he dropped into the discussion the citation from one of the versions of the *Table Talk* which seemed to say that the Holy Spirit had given Luther his evangelical experience while he was on the toilet.[48] This tradition of renewed Catholic polemic was certainly one factor that aroused Karl Holl and the Luther Renaissance.

Troeltsch's *The Significance of Protestantism for the Beginning of the Modern World* (lecture of 1906, published in 1911)[49] is credited, equally with the attacks of Denifle and Grisar, with goading Karl Holl into starting the Luther Renaissance. It is an odd little book, more a pundit's essay than professorial research, which is probably what Holl meant when he complained that Troeltsch based himself exclusively on secondary sources.

It contains an almost unqualified celebration of modern pluralistic society, with its free competition of ideas and cultural styles and its expanding personal freedom, based on a healthier and more numerous population organized into monogamous families and those two great motors of progress, science and technology.[50] Since its beginning in the Enlightenment, this modern world has been more compatible, says Troeltsch, with Protestantism than with Catholicism. However, at the same time, modernity has transformed Protestantism into an intellectually receptive, unauthoritarian "neo-Protestantism" that is a world apart from the authentic "old Protestantism" of Luther and Calvin which dominated parts of Europe in the confessional age of the sixteenth and seventeenth centuries. At that time, Europe still lived in a rigidly authoritarian culture in which church and state sought in their different but complementary ways to manage society according to biblical percepts, with the purpose of leading their subjects to eternal salvation. Truly, the state had greater theoretical independence of the church than in Catholic countries – in fact, it had practical dominance – but the main difference of the confessional age from the Middle Ages, according to Troeltsch, was that instead of one hierarchical society seeking its authoritarian, ascetic otherworldly goals, you now had three such societies (Catholic, Lutheran, and Calvinist), each pronouncing anathemas against the other two. The outcome was to weaken the pre-modern estate-based society and to prepare the way for a new world-affirming modernity.[51]

Perhaps what most irritated German Protestants about Troeltsch's *obiter dicta* was his disposition to disparage Lutheranism, not only by comparison with Calvinism, from which he distinguished it sharply, but also in contrast to nonconformist sects and mystical religious individualism. Here, of course, we encounter the preoccupations of Troeltsch's *Social Teachings of the Christian Churches and Groups*, which appeared about the same time. The persecuted "stepchildren of the Reformation" (he may have been the first to use this phrase), the sectarians and individualists, first found refuge in Holland under the religiously tolerant regime of William of Orange. Here they entered into a relation of mutual influence with Calvinism, and this kind of Reformation truly came into its own in mid-seventeenth-century England under Cromwell. There puritanism first initiated toleration as a matter of religious principle, which later amalgamated with secular forces in the Enlightenment and set the tone for the religious pluralism of the modern world.[52] Compared with Calvinism, Lutheranism tended towards withdrawal into an individualistic piety that lent itself well to subjection to temporal power and was at home in the stagnant economy of the pre-modern world.

Troeltsch gave his original lecture on Protestantism and modernity at Stuttgart in 1906, substituting for Max Weber, who was unable to accept the invitation. On capitalism and the "spirit of capitalism," without which such an untraditional and inhuman economic system as capitalism could not have taken hold, Troeltsch proclaimed the entire Weber thesis[53] (without those methodological qualifications about "ideal types" that make Weber's exact meaning so hard to nail down).

Certainly, Troeltsch's essay illustrates the view, powerful in pre-1914 Germany, that Britain and America had gotten the more effectual, more forward-looking part of the Protestant heritage. The essay really only came to deal with Luther seriously in its last section, which, he explained, had not been included in the 1906 talk.[54] The real significance of Protestantism for the modern world of Europe and America did not lie in its indirect (and only partially effectual) transmissions to society and culture, both of which were doubtless more secular than in the confessional age. Rather, its real significance lay in its contribution to modern Euro-American religiosity. Among the Anglo-Americans an amalgam of muted Calvinism and sectarianism dominated religion and set the tone in ethics. In the German-Scandinavian cultural area something that Troeltsch characterized as Lutheran idealism, which was not entirely Lutheran but had absorbed the German Enlightenment and the greats of the cultural pantheon (Kant, Goethe, Hegel, etc.), was in the ascendant; and it was not without impact on England and America.

Luther's personal contribution to this German religiosity appeared not too different to Troeltsch than to Ritschl and Harnack. Luther's goal was the traditional medieval one of supernatural salvation, but his means to that goal was very personal and pointed to the religiosity of the German Enlightenment. He sought saving faith by striving for inner freedom and inner certainty. His new means of doing religion eventually transformed the goal so that, unintentionally, he became the father of the modern religious sensibility. Like Harnack before him, Troeltsch described Luther's faith as *fiducia*, rather trust than belief. And he broke ground in alluding to Luther's early struggle for this trust. In this way, for all their resentment of psychological probings in the manner of Grisar, the German Protestant scholars hunting for the modern in Luther shifted the focus from his ideas (which were surely not modern) to a psychology which they imagined to be modern. It is unclear whether Holl, who made total opposition to Troeltsch's interpretation into a principle, was aware that Troeltsch had preceded him in the area of Luther's (psychological) struggle for faith (psychologically defined).

In the first years of the twentieth century, scholarly critique vaguely unsettled the traditional German Protestant reverence for Martin Luther. Moreover, this critique came from Roman Catholics and Protestant liberals who opposed confessional, orthodox Lutheranism and whose contemporary agendas certainly influenced their scholarship. Nevertheless, the reaction against Denifle, Grisar, and Troeltsch would probably have remained a matter for professors only, without wide public resonance, had it not been for the First World War and the subsequent overthrow of the monarchy in 1918. Only then did the enemies of Luther and Lutheranism – Catholics, liberals, and Socialists – appear to be enemies of Germany. Against the background of war and defeat the academic enterprise of rehabilitating Luther became the search for a German saviour. Walter Bodenstein, Karl Holl's biographer, gives us a good insight into how changes in the German world transformed Luther research: "At stake here was something more than academic problems of Luther research. An inner unease about the accuracy of the traditional image of Luther collided with the attempt of the Catholic spirit, as well as radical socialism and skeptically educated moderns, to destroy the view previously accepted by the German people that Luther was the greatest German man ... Therefore, behind the enmity towards Luther of the various groups there arose the deeper question *of whether the German people would in the future remain the people of Martin Luther.*"[55]

The Evangelical theological tradition of Wilhelminian Germany asserted both Luther's modernity and his penetration to the core of the religion of Paul and Jesus. It presented his as the uniquely German voice in the choir of historical Christianity. Both Catholic and liberal Protestant dissent from this prevailing viewpoint made it necessary to put it on a sounder scholarly foundation. The wartime embattlement of German culture made Karl Holl's project of fortifying Luther scholarship into an expression of national patriotism.

2 Karl Holl and the Origin of the Luther Renaissance

Karl Holl attended Ernst Troeltsch's lecture of 1906 in Stuttgart.[1] Up until then he had written one slight essay on Luther.[2] Since Troeltsch afterwards added the part of the published 1911 pamphlet that treated Luther in substance, it cannot have offended Holl in 1906, but Holl was nevertheless offended. The point at issue was that Troeltsch's notion of modernity seemed inspired by a politics that wanted Germany to pattern itself on Anglo-American democracy. Undoubtedly, the institutions of related northern European Protestant peoples were modern and worthy of respect – Holl studied Calvin and British religious figures, and with his allegiance to the *Unierte* church of Prussia he never was really a "Lutherocentrist." But could not Germany have its own "special path" into modernity, more in accord with its own traditions?

It is significant that Holl's stronger traditional nationalism first separated him from the more cosmopolitan views of Troeltsch about the relation of Protestantism and modernity. Until the First World War, Holl was not known primarily as a Luther scholar. He was above all an expert in the intricate and arcane business of establishing the texts of two lesser Greek church fathers, John of Damascus and Epiphanius of Salamis.[3] In the process he practised conventional philological scholarship, seeking out the *Sitz im Leben* of these documents, and occupying himself with relevant literary currents, dogmatic developments, liturgical and institutional history, prosopography, and so on.[4]

Holl's background in German Protestant theology was conventionally liberal. It is true that by the time of his death in 1926 the eulogies found him impossible to classify as either liberal or orthodox,[5] but that was due to his celebrity late in life as the founder of the "Luther Renaissance." (This was a term initiated by Holl's professorial successor at Berlin, Erich Seeberg, not by Holl himself.) Earlier, Holl had written approvingly of David Friedrich Strauss and Ralph Waldo Emerson in a way that only a liberal theologian could do.[6]

Born in Tübingen, the son of a teacher, Holl had studied theology in his home city under the direction of the liberal professor Carl von Weizäcker. He served briefly in a pastorate and earned a licentiate in theology in 1890.[7] His academic and pastoral beginnings were difficult. On the one hand, having to explain himself to ordinary people and children as a vicar gave him a lesson in clarity and directness that he never forgot: "If I cannot explain something to a twelve-year-old, it is a sign that I do not understand it myself."[8] However, he felt that he was lacking in the sense of elevation by an outside power that was essential to a pastoral calling.[9] Moreover, his first venture into Greek patristic research, a study of Polycarp of Smyrna, was not well received. Although he got a degree, his supervisor, Weizäcker, pronounced the devastating assessment: "better no Polycarp than Holl's Polycarp."[10] In 1892 Holl was further alienated by the controversy surrounding the defrocking of Christoph Schremp, one of his former teachers, by the Württemberg Protestant church. Schremp was dismissed because he could not in good conscience repeat the Apostles' Creed. Holl's comment was that a congregation could expect any sacrifice from a pastor except the sacrifice of his conscience.[11] The Schremp controversy occasioned the organization of the Friends of the *Christian World* (Verein der Freunde der Christlichen Welt), centred around the liberal theological journal published at Marburg University. Holl joined the Friends and maintained his membership until the final phase of the First World War.[12]

Lacking a calling for the pastoral ministry and without the backing to compete for a professorship, Holl considered a change of careers. Here his liberal friendships, going back to a study trip in 1889–90, came to his rescue. Marburg and Berlin were the university centres of Protestant liberalism. At Marburg he had begun a lifelong friendship with Adolf Jülicher, professor of New Testament and early church history, who provided unofficial guidance with the Polycarp research,[13] as well as Martin Rade, perennial editor of the *Christian World*. More important was Adolf von Harnack at Berlin, already world renowned and a welcome figure at the imperial court. Harnack had originally pointed Holl towards research in early Greek patristics. His continuing confidence and his procurement in 1893 of a position for Holl in the work on editions of the church fathers under the auspices of the Prussian Academy of Sciences probably rescued the younger man's academic career. In 1900 Holl obtained an associate professorship at Tübingen and in 1906, again through Harnack's good offices, a full professorship at the University of Berlin. In the pre-war years he remained virtually unknown, largely hidden in Harnack's shadow.[14]

Whatever his early disinclination for the pastorate, Holl continued to be a man of religion, caught between the critical outlook of liberal academic theology and a personal struggle for faith. In 1900 he published an article in the *Christian World* which he described to his friend Rade as a sort of personal confession:

I am perhaps not the only one among the "liberals" who seeks edification for the most part at orthodox sermons. Not because powerful personalities impress me, but because it is amongst these ranks that one generally finds the courage to assert the strongest religious claims, to call a sin a sin, to speak of the living, present God instead of human religious claims. I can seldom think of a time when I have not been "offended" in the course of such sermons. I hear an exegesis in which the historical sense of the text has not been correctly explained; claims presented as fact which to me are only legends; statements passing for Christian truths in which I perceive remnants of Jewish or Catholic beliefs ... Nevertheless, I continue to attend these sermons faithfully ... The sense of power outweighs that which is offensive.[15]

At the time that Holl made his final move to Berlin, the patristic scholar began to write systematic theology. His focus was the doctrine of justification (according to Luther, "the doctrine on which the church stands or falls"). These Pauline texts from Romans and Galatians, so central to the Reformation, had been the object of critique in the nineteenth century. Paul de Lagarde and, more recently, Wilhelm Dilthey contended that the Protestant doctrine of justification could not be simply equated with St Paul's doctrine of justification, and the latter with the gospel of Jesus. In those same years, Albert Schweitzer was coming to very similar conclusions. He insisted that Paul must be understood within the religious framework of first-century Judaism, its apocalypticism, and its body mysticism. The Pauline teaching on justification, however, was a polemical tool against Jews and Christian Judaizers, an explanation of the providential necessity of the Jews' substantial refusal to accept Jesus as Messiah. The Epistle to the Romans and its special emphases are but a "secondary crater" within the main crater of "eschatological mysticism" on the Pauline moon.[16] In opting for a rehabilitation of the traditional Lutheran doctrine of justification, Holl had very excellent liberal theological antecedents. No less a figure than Albrecht Ritschl had insisted on the centrality of the doctrine of justification, styling it the major expression of God's love for humankind.[17] Adolf von Harnack's father, the very orthodox Theodosius, had replied to Ritschl by stressing the wrath of God, and Holl, as we shall see, strove for a paradoxical union of the outlooks of Ritschl and the elder Harnack.

In another sense, he undertook to correct both Adolf von Harnack and Ritschl. In one of his sermons, Holl said that Ferdinand Christian Baur was his "true and only teacher in historical research."[18] Baur, the founder of critical church history among German Protestants, was dead well before Holl was born. He had been Ritschl's teacher, and Ritschl broke away from him because he preferred a more positivist approach to church history over the vestiges of Hegelianism that he detected in Baur. Adolf von Harnack's historicism was more pronounced than Ritschl's, so it was with a certain justice that, in the festschrift for Harnack in 1921, Ernst Troeltsch suggested that *Harnack was Baur's intellectual successor.*[19] There was a touch of deliberate ingratitude towards his patron, Harnack, spiced with political differences, in Holl's tribute to Baur.

Nevertheless, Holl had something very specific in mind, something very central to his theological outlook, when he made his reference to Baur. In 1919 he wrote to Jülicher:

You are well aware that my work on Luther is forcing me to engage myself seriously with the New Testament. I really cannot avoid coming back to Baur. The antithesis between Paul and the original Christian community, the relationship between Paul and Peter-James, is actually the fulcrum upon which the history of the New Testament turns, and the key to understanding the New Testament writings. How otherwise does one come to set the names of Paul and James over certain books? And the "Ebionite" [Jewish Christian] characteristics of Luke's Gospel are absolutely undeniable. It now seems to me as if much valid knowledge has been buried by Ritschl and Harnack. But will anyone be believed who disinters it? Perhaps – God willing and I am granted life, and I say this honestly – I will yet do it sometime.[20]

Baur believed that the struggle between Pauline Christianity and the original Jewish Christianity of the first apostles was mirrored in the New Testament writings. He thought that the Epistle of James and the two Epistles of Peter were efforts at mediation between Pauline Christianity and the Judaizers, the group who insisted that Christians must observe the Jewish law. Baur also held the Pauline letters to be the most historically authoritative writings in the New Testament, closest to the spirit of Christ.[21] Ritschl regarded all of this as too speculative and denied that such a sharp dichotomy between Pauline and Jewish Christianity was to be found in the New Testament. For him, all New Testament Christianity, whether it went under the name of Paul, Peter, or James, rested in Jewish traditions. The great rupture between the early church and the gentile church came with the application of Greek philosophy to the construction of Christian doctrine. Harnack basically continued Ritschl on this point.[22] It was contrary to the portrait of Jesus that he drew in *The Essence of Christianity* to privilege the Pauline epistles in Baur's manner, as opposed to the synoptic Gospels. But what Harnack regarded as the weakness of Baur's approach Holl saw at the high point of his development as a theologian, as its particular strength. The tight linkage of the theology of Jesus, Paul, and Luther had been an article of faith for him since 1905.

His paper of that year, "The Doctrine of Justification in Light of the History of Protestantism," delivered in Marburg to the Friends of the *Christian World*, was a personal dogmatic statement, made, of course, with reference to his Lutheran-Calvinist *Uniert* Protestant tradition. He insisted against Lagarde and Dilthey that, rather than being the special creation of the Reformers, the Protestant doctrine of justification went right back to Paul and Jesus:

The nerve of the whole outlook is the concept of God with which Luther operated: the paradox of a God who is unbendingly serious in his moral demands, yet creates salvation and life for the evildoer. In the boldness of this conception of God Luther reaches back to Paul and Jesus; and their agreement on this decisive point gives us the right to view the Reformation as a renewal of the primitive Christian standpoint. The doctrine of justification of Paul is nothing else than the dramatic presentation of the inner conflict into which the genuine Christian concept of God must necessarily cast a human being. Luther felt this conflict more personally, more concretely than Paul and therefore regarded it as permanent.[23]

Besides the permanence of the justification process and a "deepening of religious individualism ..., which distinguishes Luther from Paul and raises him above Paul," the main peculiarity of the way in which Holl understood Luther's doctrine of justification was that it bestowed not only God's mercy but also moral regeneration: "For God does not accept the person whom he draws into a relationship with himself in order to let him as he is, but in order to transform him into someone who is really righteous ... Thus we can say, when God declares the sinner, in the moment in which he is only a sinner, as righteous, he is anticipating the outcome to which he himself will lead the person."[24] In 1906 Holl insisted that Luther had a robust monotheism which was lost both to subsequent generations of Lutheran orthodoxy and to Pietism. Concerning orthodoxy, "the fanatical polemic against the Reformed doctrine of predestination misled the Lutheran dogmatists into an ever-increasing attenuation of the idea of power in their concept of God."[25] "Pietism aimed to renew the Lutheran doctrine of justification, but like orthodoxy, it lacked Luther's concept of God. Its concept of God was weak, quietistic."[26]

Following these intuitions, which Holl presented as a systematic theologian, he began the serious study of Luther. This undertaking was launched in 1910 with the publication of an article on the doctrine of justification in Luther's lecture on Romans of 1515–16 – that newly recovered manuscript which Denifle had made the object of bitter confessional controversy. The contemporary interpreter Dietrich Korsch puts the matter succinctly: "We are confronted by the fact that Holl's detailed historical research on Luther followed the development of the systematic structure of Holl's own doctrine of justification, but that these ideas got their persuasiveness because they were transmitted through the historical figure of Luther."[27]

Certainly, another factor conditioning Holl's interpretation of Luther was his research on Calvin for the four hundredth anniversary of the Geneva Reformer's birth in 1909.[28] He believed that Calvin's doctrine of double predestination, according to which God created and sustained evil as well as good, was an improvement upon Luther's belief that God, for reasons hidden from the faithful, permitted evil to occur.[29] Holl regarded Calvin as a loyal, if independent-minded, continuer of Luther's theology – a position, certainly, that could be verified from Calvin's own statements. This viewpoint went well with the Protestant ecumenism of the Prussian Evangelical Church, as well as with the post-Ritschl suspicions against Melanchthon as the figure who had abandoned the unique greatness of Luther's theology. The outcome was the strong ethical coloration of Holl's Luther interpretation. Current interpretation indeed affirms that, beside the unmerited imputation of righteousness to the believer, Luther maintained a secondary emphasis on moral regeneration throughout his career. This theme was not separable from his soteriology, and into the 1530s he could promote the idea of a "natural," although not a "legal," connection between the righteousness of works and salvation.[30] Nevertheless, Holl's stress on a Lutheran soteriology that connected *Rechtfertigung* (justification) with *Gerechtmachung* ("making righteous") sounds very much like the undialectical affirmation of the law characteristic of Calvin and his mentor Martin Bucer, the fathers of Reformed Christianity.[31] Because of his admiration of

Calvin and his unguarded receptivity to Luther's earliest theological writings, Holl missed the tension between law and gospel in Luther's theology following the break with Rome. Of course, such a view of Luther fitted well with the ethic of service and duty inculcated in the elites of turn-of-the-century Wilhelminian Germany.

In the years of his early affirmation of the justification theology, Holl expressed it in terms of a personal leap of faith that were reminiscent of Søren Kierkegaard. His student Emanuel Hirsch, later a major authority on Kierkegaard, remembered that in 1908 Holl had taught the Danish theologian in a way that was "brilliant, given the grasp of Kierkegaard at that time."[32] Increasingly, however, Holl moved away from the extreme individualism of Kierkegaard and developed a justification theology that emphasized the community equally with the person. Because of his excessive individualism, wrote Holl in late 1914, "with the passing of years Kierkegaard becomes increasingly unpleasant to me."[33] The war had already begun, but the idea of community was best developed in Holl's essay "The Development of Luther's Concept of the Church," on which he was at work before the start of hostilities, although it was published only in 1915.[34]

Hence Holl's theology was developing on the same tracks before 1914 that it continued during the war and in the wrenching period of defeat and revolution in 1918–19. For this reason one must be cautious about attributing too much to these external factors in attempting to understand Holl and his post-war presentation of Luther. However, the notion of a "tectonic shift" in his justification theology occasioned by the war is asserted firmly by Holl's two major modern interpreters, Johannes Wallmann and Heinrich Assel.[35] Holl himself wrote to an academic friend that he considered that bringing his research on Luther to a conclusion was a "contribution to the war effort" (*ein Kriegswerk*).[36] In the course of the war and afterward, he increasingly took a conservative nationalist standpoint that separated him from his earlier associates in liberal theology, and he developed new ties with orthodox or "positive" theologians. The idea that the Reformation was a special world-historical contribution of the Germans to Christianity that enabled them to lead Protestantism back to the genuine gospel by stripping away the accretions of Roman Catholicism and Greek Orthodoxy was not really foreign to Ritschl and Harnack.[37] But in the conditions of the First World War, with its mutual alienation of German and Anglo-American Protestants, the notion of the justification theology as a historic revelation to the Germans shifted from signifying a German contribution to the common civilization to providing a foundation for a German national religion.

The key community in Luther's ecclesiology was the invisible assembly of those with genuine faith, an inner leaven in the external, visible church where the Word was preached.[38] In the circumstances of the First World War, Holl wrote about how during the wars of the nineteenth century the *Volk*, the nation, had come to replace the church as the more vital external community.[39] The true believers continued their leavening influence. They were identified with the Pauline conception of the strong in faith. But the strong personalities who provided vitality to their communities became something rather different from the Corinthian Christians, whose faith would not be undermined by eating meat sacrificed to idols, but who for the sake of the weaker brethren refrained from doing so.[40] They partook of the Goethean notion of the daemonic, of Hegel's world-historical individuals, of Max Weber's charismatic personalities who counterbalanced the gray rationality of an increasingly disenchanted world. They were *Führergestalten*, to be sure, just so long as we keep in mind that Karl Holl, no more than Max Weber, had any inkling of how *Führer* figures might turn out in practice. Still, Holl's tendency to mix notions such as heroes sacrificing, if need be, their own salvation for that of their people with references to the special spiritual charisma of Hindenburg and Ludendorff illustrates how the Pauline conception of the strong was vulnerable to political debasement.[41]

The respect in which the post-1914 Holl quite consciously went "a step beyond Luther" was in conceiving the Kingdom of God as the organic product of the struggle for "living space" of nation-states.[42] This was not Luther so much as Hegel coarsened by a touch of Social Darwinism. Individuals had no claim to pursue personal happiness, but they were credited with doing their higher duty when they subjected themselves to the (often cruder) collective egoism of nation-states.[43] Holl believed that "reality, the coarse events of history, is also a revelation of God,"[44] and he attributed religious meaning to German war aims and tactics such as unrestricted submarine warfare (like the slingshot with which David eluded Goliath's conventional armour). And this communitarian application of justification theology was no mere corollary for Holl; it stood at the centre of things. In his view, without its communitarian significance the Reformation's *Rechtfertigungslehre* was simply incomprehensible to modern man. As Heinrich Assel said, "The prior experience of spiritual community became [in Holl's eyes] the hermeneutical precondition of the understanding of justification."[45]

The erosion of Karl Holl's liberalism was no sudden thing. The stress on the theology of justification from 1905 onward amounted to a rejection of the broader findings of liberal New Testament studies on the apostle Paul. Particularly in the form in which Holl expressed it, with its considerable stress on the wrath of God, this *Rechtfertigungslehre* represented a conservative turn connected with his own search for religious certainty. The stress on community, which emerged just before 1914, lent itself well to a contrast of German Lutheran Christian community and the excessive religious individualism of Anglo-American Protestantism. So the idea of a distinctive, even superior, German way of entering the modern world lay ready for use in 1914. It was one theme in the war propaganda about the superiority of German culture to the superficial civilization of the Western Allies.

After 1914 Holl developed a political conservatism that became only more pronounced after 1918. He shared the nationalist enthusiasm for the beginning of the war, when class divisions seemed to be put aside in devotion to the common cause. By 1917, Protestant liberals such as Troeltsch had abandoned the early wartime euphoria and joined the movement for a compromise peace without annexations and indemnities. This was the substance of the famous peace resolution of July 1917, in which the parties that held the majority in the Reichstag – the liberal Progressives, the Catholic Centre Party, and the Social Democrats – called for "a peace of understanding and permanent reconciliation of nations."[46] Holl took the other side, joining the Vaterlandspartei movement of 1917, which sought a victorious German peace. He was a firm, if not prominent, supporter of the Vaterlandspartei and resented liberal attacks on it.[47] So in the last months of the war Holl assumed a political position supported primarily by conservative theologians and rejected in the main by liberal ones. This stance led in 1918 to his withdrawal from the Friends of the *Christian World*.[48] Almost plaintively he had written in 1915 to that journal's editor, Martin Rade, wondering why it should be impossible to hold liberal theological opinions at the same time as an entirely different political standpoint.[49] He still liked Rade's devotional writings, but he could not tolerate the growing ambivalence about the German war effort and war aims that suffused the pages of the *Christian World*.

The defeat and socialist revolution of the winter of 1918–19 were a particularly severe trial for Holl. On the one hand, his firm belief that God's will was revealed in the historical day-to-day enabled him to say things such as "In the world war we have collided with Calvinist powers and we lost. Wouldn't it perhaps be better if we received a small transfusion of Calvinist blood? I regard it as fortunate that in Germany we have Reformed territory as well as Lutheran."[50] But the blood transfusion must be "small." Holl nurtured a distaste for figures such as Troeltsch and his former mentor, Harnack, who went over to affirmation of a democratic republic as a future government for Germany.[51] This position amounted to wholesale abandonment of the German political tradition and mere replication of Anglo-American structures. Particularly suspect for Holl was the emergence of the black-red-gold coalition as the governing power of the new Weimar Republic. It was a continuance of the defeatist majority that had passed the peace resolution of 1917 – Socialists, political Catholics, and middle-class Democrats. Holl and his students, particularly the extreme nationalist Hirsch, saw here the victory of the disparagers of Luther.[52] The Catholic Centre Party was to politics what Denifle and Grisar were to scholarship. Social Democratic founders Friedrich Engels and Karl Kautsky had written popular historical tomes glorifying Thomas Müntzer and the Peasants' War rebels, and accusing Luther of selling out the German people to the princes. And in the Democratic Party lurked Ernst Troeltsch, with his ironic detachment from Martin Luther.

So, as Karl Holl's Luther research of 1914–18 was a contribution to the war effort, the collection of his essays into a big, 450-page Luther book that appeared with Siebeck in 1921 was a blow against the anti-Lutheran parties of the Weimar coalition. In, with, and under its scholarly substance it was a reassertion of the aristocratic, conservative Protestant forces – the displaced peoples of state of the Wilhelminian Reich.

Holl's collection of essays on Luther imposed itself for decades upon scholarship about the Reformer. A collection of eight essays (enlarged by a ninth, "Luther und die Schwärmer," in 1923), it was extensively annotated in the manner of German scholarship of the time. Holl's book was the first to rely primarily on the critical Weimar Edition, which had been in progress since 1883 – a point that he was most willing to make in his annotations to score points against other scholars. The notes were full of attacks on enemy scholars, above all the three whose irreverent treatments of Luther had helped to cause the Luther Renaissance – Heinrich Denifle, Hartmann Grisar, and Ernst Troeltsch – with more limited attention to Max Weber, Walther Köhler, Paul de Lagarde, Wilhelm Dilthey, et al.

The major themes are stated and returned to from different points of view as the topics succeed one another. "What Did Luther Understand by Religion?" sounds the main theocentric tone of the God of wrath and love, the God whose Yes was hidden under his No. The second essay, "The Teaching of Justification in Luther's Lecture on Romans, with Special Reference to the Issue of Certainty of Salvation," had been the opening gun of the Luther Renaissance when it was published in the *Zeitschrift für Theologie und Kirche* in 1910. It highlights

special themes of the 1515–16 lecture – namely, the connection of justification and regeneration, illustrated from the parable of the Good
Samaritan, and total submission to the will of God, including resignation to one's own damnation. Next, "The New Construction of Morality" assesses the selfless, uncompromising morality that Holl sees
Luther to have advanced in place of the self-regarding, flexible morality of Catholicism. Essays 4 and 5 explore, more or less chronologi-
cally, the early emergence of Luther's idea of an invisible church and
his changing attitudes to the external, visible church. According to
Holl, he never wanted the external church to be turned over to the
princely government to the extent that it actually was in the Protestant
princely territories. Essay 6, "Luther's Judgment of Himself," originally the first paper by Holl on Luther, coordinates Luther's self-assessment with his soteriology: he was at the same time a sinner
standing under the wrath of God and the world-historical instrument
of God's love to humankind. Essay 7, "The Cultural Significance of
the Reformation," follows the diffusion of Luther's conceptions of
personality and community through modern German culture. The last
essay of the 1921 collection, "Luther's Importance for the Progress of
Exegesis," argues that the Reformer created the foundations of modern Protestant hermeneutics, and that through it he established the
principles of interpretation for historical and literary texts.

The seemingly technical concluding essay sheds a particularly
clear light on Holl's theological identification with Luther – or, to put
the matter more bluntly, his identification of Luther with his own
theology. According to Holl, Luther's genius instinctively grasped
that exegesis or interpretation was the application of inspired intuition to the literal, grammatical sense of a text. The exegete could not
depart from the literal meaning, but the literal reading was not sufficient to grasp an author's intention. In interpreting the Bible, one
needed grammar plus the inspiration of the Holy Spirit, the source of
inspiration for the biblical authors. One needed not merely to read a
text but also to transpose oneself into the mind of its author: "Exegesis is never anything else than a constant jumping out of oneself into
an alien subject."[53] Luther constantly lived his life as a man of religion in the study of Scripture; the Spirit inspired him through the
Word. (Thomas Müntzer seemingly presumed to be one "who spoke
with authority, not as the scribes and Pharisees." He correctly observed that, unlike him, Luther was a scribe, fundamentally skeptical
of claims to direct inspiration.)[54] Luther went so far as to portray the
prophets of the Old Testament as persons who got their inspiration
through study of the writings of Moses and their predecessors.[55]
Luther inhabited the mind of God by inspired study of the Word of

God; Karl Holl inhabited the mind of Luther through intuitive absorption of his writings in the Weimar Edition. Through Holl's influence, Reformation studies became for a time pre-eminently an exegetical study of Martin Luther.

According to Holl, "Luther began from the Pauline gospel in the full confidence that this gospel was Christendom – indeed, religion itself."[56] But as he engaged in serious, thorough biblical scholarship, he became increasingly aware of "the multiplicity of the contents of the Bible, the differences among its parts."[57] He gained a critical sense of what he read – that the predictions of the Old Testament prophets were not always correct, that the accounts of Jesus' Resurrection clashed with one another, that the theology of James's epistle contradicted the Pauline theology, that the book of Hebrews, attributed by tradition to Paul, must have been written by someone else. The human authors of the biblical books were inspired by the Holy Spirit, but not in such a way as to efface their individual differences. Indeed, if as Luther continued to insist, the Bible was clearly understandable and unified in matters pertaining to salvation, then there must be a centre of authority within it.

Unapologetically, Holl portrayed Luther as ordering the Bible by returning to his starting point. If he was now both too well informed and too honest to read Paul into the rest of the Bible, he would assert Paul's primacy over the rest of the Bible. Paul conveyed the gospel message more clearly than the four Gospels, with their preoccupation with the acts and miracles of Jesus. Indeed, the written New Testament was only an instrument to serve the preaching of the gospel, needed to prevent erroneous preaching; but if the need to put the gospel into written form was indisputable, the outcome was not entirely desirable. The gospel, the Word of God, was to be found within the Bible, but it was not to be identified with the Bible. In fact, it went too far even to identify the gospel with the whole corpus of Pauline epistles (whether the writings that tradition attributed to Paul or the smaller group that modern scholars assign to him). This was a matter that Holl approached indirectly, but he was surely aware that contemporary New Testament scholarship was disputing the centrality within Paul's message of the special theological issues of Romans and Galatians. He called Luther's lectures on Romans (1515–16) and Galatians (1519) "his most brilliant, an achievement (I weigh these words carefully) not surpassed up to the present day."[58] As his sympathetic contemporary Paul Althaus commented, when Holl sought Luther's teaching of justification, he made no distinction between that teaching and the right one (that is to say, his, since systematic theologians were not in the business of presenting wrong ones).[59] And as we have seen in the foregoing, for Holl, and Holl's Luther, the *Rechtfertigungslehre* was the gospel, "Christendom, indeed, religion itself."

Holl commented, seemingly in passing, that "Luther was one of those professors who eliminated the freshest and most direct of their oral presentation when they published their lectures."[60] This assertion was a justification for devoting more attention to Luther's lectures than to his publications. And since only the early lectures had received a critical editing in the new, Weimar Edition, they deserved the most precise attention. The problem was that, in the introduction to the edition of his Latin works of 1545, to which Denifle had directed the attention of twentieth-century scholarship, Luther himself seemed to dismiss as immaterial all of his theological writings before 1518/19. In a three-page note[61] Holl examined the issue. For him, Luther's expressions of 1545 were of secondary importance, for reasons to be noted; but given the continuing prominence of the issue in modern Luther scholarship, it is good to examine carefully Holl's discussion of the subject.

There follows the text of Luther's Autobiographical Fragment of 1545 with parallel translation. Since it became increasingly central to the Luther Renaissance's interpretations, it will be rendered in full.

Interim eo anno iam redieram ad Psalterium denuo interpretandum, fretus eo, quod exercitatior essem, postquam S. Pauli Epistolas ad Romanos, ad Galatas, et eam, quae est ad Ebraeos, tractassem in scholis. Miro certe ardore captus fueram cognoscendi Pauli in epistola ad Rom., sed obstiterat hactenus non frigidus circum praecordia sanguis, sed unicum vocabulum, quod est Cap. 1: Iustitia Dei revelatur in illo. Oderam enim vocabulum istud "Iustitia Dei," quod usu et consuetudine omnium doctorum doctus eram philosophice intelligere de iustitia (ut vocant) formali seu activa, qua Deus est iustus, et peccatores iniustosque punit.

Meanwhile in that year [1519], I had returned to interpreting the Psalter again, confident that I was better equipped after I had expounded in the schools the letters of St Paul to the Romans and the Galatians, and the letter to the Hebrews. I had certainly been overcome with a great desire to understand St Paul in his letter to the Romans, but what had hindered me thus far was not any "coldness of the blood" so much as that one phrase in the first chapter: "The righteousness of God is revealed in it." For I had hated that phrase "the righteousness of God" which, according to the use and custom of all the doctors, I had been taught to understand philosophically, in the sense of the formal or active righteousness (as they termed

Ego autem, qui me, utcunque ir-
reprehensibilis monachus vivebam,
sentirem coram Deo esse peccatorem
inquietissimae conscientiae, nec mea
satisfactione placatum confidere pos-
sem, non amabam, imo odiebam ius-
tum et punientem peccatores Deum,
tacitaque si non blasphemia, certe in-
genti murmuratione indignabar Deo,
dicens: quasi vero non satis sit, mise-
ros peccatores et aeternaliter perdi-
tos peccato originali omni genere
calamitatis oppressos esse per legem
decalogi, nisi Deus per euangelium
dolorem dolori adderet, et etiam per
euangelium nobis iustitiam et iram
suam intentaret. Furebam ita saeva
et perturbata conscientia, pulsabam
tamen importunus eo loco Paulum,
ardentissime sitiens scire, quid S.
Paulus vellet.

Donec miserente Deo meditabun-
dus dies et noctes connexionem ver-
borum attenderem, nempe: Iustitia
Dei revelatur in illo, sicut scriptum
est: Iustus ex fide vivit, ibi iustitiam
Dei coepi intelligere eam, qua iustus
dono Dei vivit, nempe ex fide, et esse
hanc sententiam, revelari per euangelium iustitiam Dei, scilicet passi-
vam, qua nos Deus misericors
iustificat per fidem, sicut scriptum
est: Iustus ex fide vivit. Hic me pror-
sus renatum esse sensi, et apertis
portis in ipsam paradisum intrasse.
Ibi continuo alia mihi facies totius
scripturae apparuit. Discurrebam
deinde per scripturas, ut habebat

it), by which God is righteous, and-
punished unrighteous sinners.

Although I lived an irreproachable
life as a monk, I felt that I was a sinner with an uneasy conscience before
God; nor was I able to believe that I
had pleased him with my satisfaction. I did not love – in fact, I hated –
that righteous God who punished
sinners, if not with silent blasphemy,
then certainly with great murmuring.
I was angry with God, saying "As if
it were not enough that miserable
sinners should be eternally damned
through original sin, with all kinds of
misfortunes laid upon them by the
Old Testament law, and yet God adds
sorrow upon sorrow through the
gospel, and even brings his wrath
and righteousness to bear through
it!" Thus I drove myself mad, with a
desperate disturbed conscience, per-
sistently pounding upon Paul in this
passage, thirsting most ardently to
know what he meant.

At last, God being merciful, as I
meditated day and night on the connection of the words "the righteousness of God is revealed in it, as it is
written: the righteous shall live by
faith," I began to understand that
"righteousness of God" as that by
which the righteous lives by the gift
of God, namely by faith, and this
sentence, "the righteousness of God
is revealed," to refer to a passive
righteousness, by which the merciful
God justifies us by faith, as it is written, "The righteous lives by faith."
This immediately made me feel as
though I had been born again, and as
though I had entered through open

memoria, et colligebam etiam in aliis vocabulis analogiam, ut opus Dei, id est, quod operatur in nobis Deus, virtus Dei, qua nos potentes facit, sapientia Dei, qua nos sapientes facit, fortitudo Dei, salus Dei, gloria Dei.

gates into paradise itself. From that moment, the whole face of scripture appeared to me in a different light. Afterwards, I ran through the scriptures, as from memory, and found the same analogy in other phrases such as the "work of God" (that which God works within us), the "power of God" (by which he makes us strong), the "wisdom of God" (by which he makes us wise), the "strength of God," the "salvation of God" and the "glory of God."

Iam quanto odio vocabulum "iustitia Dei" oderam ante, tanto amore dulcissimum mihi vocabulum extollebam, ita mihi iste locus Pauli fuit vere porta paradisi. Postea legebam Augustinum de spiritu et litera, ubi praeter spem offendi, quod et ipse iustitiam Dei similiter interpretatur: qua nos Deus induit, dum nos iustificat. Et quamquam imperfecte hoc adhuc sit dictum, ac de imputatione non clare omnia explicet, placuit tamen iustitiam Dei doceri, qua nos iustificemur.

And now, where I had once hated the phrase "the righteousness of God," so much I began to love and extoll it as the sweetest of words, so that this passage in Paul became the very gate of paradise for me. Afterwards, I read Augustine, *On the Spirit and the Letter*, where I found that he too, beyond my expectation, interpreted "the righteousness of God" in the same way – as that which God bestows upon us, when he justifies us. And although this is expressed somewhat imperfectly, and he does not explain everything about imputation clearly, it was nevertheless pleasing to find that he taught that the "righteousness of God" is that, by which we are justified.

Istis cogitationibus armatior factus coepi Psalterium secundo interpretari.

Made more excited by these thoughts, I began to interpret the Psalter for the second time.[62]

Holl has not the shadow of a doubt that Luther is referring to his second treatment of the Psalms, the *Operationes in Psalmos* of 1519, as the time when he arrived at a satisfactory understanding of Romans 1:17, which "immediately made [him] feel as though he had been born again and as though [he] had entered through open gates into paradise itself." Later scholars would hint that such an unsubtle interpretation of the Latin verb *captus fueram* (had been overcome) made the 1519 dating a "superficial" reading of the text.[63] This argument was especially used to impress English speakers, with their notoriously weak linguistic skills and doubtful Latinity, but Holl's Latinity seems to have been beyond reproach. His explanation is that 1519 and the *Operationes* were looked back upon by the Luther of 1545 as the completion of his theological development. The Reformer asked the readers of his Latin works to bear in mind "that he, too, like others had made progress in the course of his writings. This progress continued – that is the point – until the second interpretation of the Psalms. But then it was finished." Holl flatly rejects interpretations of the Autobiographical Fragment of 1545 which try to read Luther as saying that he had made his evangelical discovery at the time of the *Dictata*, the first lecture on the Psalms of 1513–15, or the lecture on Romans of 1515–16. He parts company with his favourite student, Emanuel Hirsch, on this matter. Luther is clearly referring to 1519 and the *Operationes*, *but he is wrong*: "[The Autobiographical Fragment of 1545] is indeed an assertion which contradicts the public record: the content of the *Dictata* and the Romans lecture. But the old Luther conceived of himself in this way." Holl's approach, then, is to *agree* with Denifle that Luther's reminiscence made no sense, except as the older man's effort to indicate the completion of his theological development.

His own notion of Luther's development puts the strongest emphasis on his earliest theological writings, particularly the *Dictata*, an especially difficult text whose editing came under fire in the later Luther Renaissance. Holl argues that Luther's theology of justification was worked out before he began the *Dictata* – that is, before 1513. It must have taken some time for him to evolve the ideas that he presented in his first lecture on the Psalms: "By then Luther had not only arrived at a precise understanding of the Pauline gospel but independently derived a teaching of justification from it, firmed up and deepened his views of morality with reference to his theology of justification, and finally shaped a new concept of the church based upon it."[64] The "discovery" of the *Rechtfertigungslehre* could be assigned to 1512 or 1511, and "prior to this turning point – thus approximately between 1509 and 1511 – Luther must have broken through to his new moral insight."[65]

It was one of the most controversial stresses of Holl's interpretation – attacked, for instance, by the theologians of the Dialectical Theology – that a moral insight preceded Luther's soteriology. But given that Holl had dismissed Luther's own appraisal, that his theological writings prior to 1519 were immature and less reliable, the stress on the ethical content of his theology was well grounded. Particularly, Luther's use of the story of the Good Samaritan in the Romans lecture illustrates that God, in saving sinners, also set about to heal them from their sinfulness:

In the same way our Good Samaritan Christ took the half-dead invalid into the inn and undertook to cure him of his sickness, and began to heal him with the promise of most perfect health in the future life, and not imputing sin to death, but in the meanwhile in hope of the promise of the cure forbidding him to do or not to do those things which would hinder that cure and increase sin, i.e. concupiscence. Is he not therefore perfectly just? No, but at the same time he is a just man and a sinner, a sinner in very deed, but just by the sure promise and reckoning of God that he would free him from it, until he is made perfectly whole. And in this way he is perfectly whole in hope, but in fact a sinner, yet he has the beginning of righteousness, in that he always seeks more, and always knows himself to be unjust.[66]

The conclusion that Holl drew from this passage in his essay on the Romans lecture was that "To declare righteous and to make righteous are inwardly connected as means and end"[67] – in other words, the object of the justification of the sinner was the formation of the holy person. Holl could point to the continuance of such statements into Luther's later years, but the Dialecticians thought that such an interpretation of Luther bore the mark of Kant and the moralism of liberal theology.

Luther's high morality appeared to Holl as a total rejection of Catholic casuistry, with its distinctions between mortal and venial sins, between commands obligatory for all Christians and counsels of perfection, the higher standard for Christians who had retired from the world into monastic communities. "The fundamental error of the Catholic conception of morality was that it was based on what it was possible for human beings to achieve, instead of simply asking what was the will of God."[68] All of this was supposedly brought into focus by the complicated quarrel within the Augustinian order in 1509 and 1510, which led to Luther's trip to Rome in the latter year. He took the side opposed to his superior, Johannes von Staupitz, of whom he otherwise wrote and spoke with great reverence. Staupitz, as the leader of an Observant movement for monastic reform, tried to force a supposedly higher standard on Luther's chapter in Erfurt. Luther, as late as the *Dictata*, was constantly denouncing *singulares*, persons who disturbed their communities by self-righteously aspiring to an unusually high morality or standard of observance. Holl attributed a special importance to this quarrel – it supposedly exploded for

Luther the prevailing Catholic approach to morality, based on moral athleticism and works of supererogation. The real morality was universal, based on the absolute commands of God. It had to be accepted as obligatory and carried out with a joyful will, with none of the medieval distinctions between "semi-merits," in which divine commands were met "according to the substance of the deed," and "full merits," which involved the pure motive prescribed by the divine Lawgiver.[69] The idea of a prior moral discovery before the theological discovery associated with the Experience in the Tower fell flat in later Luther historiography. It seemed to signal an unseemly moralism in Holl's entire approach. The prevalent view now is that Luther's embroidering of the theme of human unworthiness in the sight of God, rather than being the first expression of his anti-Catholicism, grew naturally from the late-medieval monastic piety of self-abasing humility. In this matter, as on the topic of the general character of the *Dictata*, the view of Denifle and Grisar that "Luther stood entirely on Catholic ground," although scornfully rejected by Holl, is now widely accepted.[70]

Holl did not completely deny that many medieval scholastic theological concepts were to be found in the *Dictata*. Luther continued to use ideas such as "semi-merits" or "doing your very best" which were seemingly in contradiction to the absolute morality that Holl attributed to him. The explanation for this discrepancy that continued in the Luther Renaissance tradition (e.g., Gordon Rupp) was that "the new wine was poured into old skins": "Luther still used these formulas in his lecture on Romans, when he had already objectively outgrown them by far."[71] The most striking medieval quality of the *Dictata* was Luther's use of the four-fold approach to Scripture, the Quadriga, which distinguished the literal sense and three figurative senses: the allegorical, the tropological or moral, and the anagogical or eschatological meanings. Holl noted this characteristic[72] and also Luther's primary reliance on two interpretations of the Psalms: the Christological literal one, which read the Psalms as pertaining to Christ, and the tropological one, which applied them to oneself. In the tight integration of these two approaches, Holl found evidence that, before beginning the *Dictata* in 1513, Luther had already worked out his doctrine of justification. "Christ was first understood when one experienced his effect, his judgment and his mercy on oneself, as conversely Christ opened up the meaning of the Scriptures."[73]

Although Holl placed Luther's moral insight before his preserved Wittenberg lectures, he allowed for its development. In the Romans lecture, under the influence of mystics such as Tauler and Suso, Luther identified self-assertion and pursuit of happiness as the root of wickedness. Matthew 19 showed Jesus commanding a questioner to love his neighbour as himself. Augustine developed the traditional interpretation of these words, as affirming one's natural self-esteem and using it as the measure of the love owing to one's fellow human beings. Luther taught instead that love of neighbour should replace love of self. One must look into the heart of one's personal darkness and despise oneself and become towards one's neighbour the vehicle of the creative, redemptive love of God. For Luther, personal religion was outgoing in service of the community. If personal religion was focused on self-centred works of piety rather than on service to the neighbour, it was at base proud and self-righteous. Certainly, the abandonment of cultic acts in search of one's personal salvation, and their replacement by outward-directed acts of service, was a Reformation ideal early and widely understood, a major source of the Reformation's appeal to the theologically unschooled.[74] For Holl this was based on a consciously anti-Augustinian ethics: "On the matter of love of God, [Luther] opposed to the formula accepted since Augustine, that people are permitted to love themselves in God, the opposing principle that loving God amounts to hating oneself."[75] "It must be said that, in spite of his high reputation, Augustine was one of the corrupters of Christian morality."[76] Luther's attitude toward the founder of his order, if not uncritical, was fundamentally reverent. In May 1517 he wrote: "Our theology and that of St. Augustine are going ahead, and they reign in our university and it is the Lord's doing. Aristotle is gradually going down, perhaps into eternal ruin. It is wonderful how out of favour are the lectures on the Sentences. Nobody can hope for an audience unless he professes this theology, i.e. the Bible or St. Augustine or some doctor of real authority in the church."[77] Holl's anti-Augustinianism was in the final analysis not owed to Luther but to Harnack and Ritschl with their hubris about leaping over Greek and Latin Catholicism and returning to Paul and Jesus.

On the matter of the character of the morality that Holl found in Luther and the way in which it compared to the morality of the Protestant governing circles of the Wilhelminian Reich, it is easy to see both the basis of the widespread criticism that Holl had created a Kantian Luther[78] and of his own repudiation of that idea. Luther, he said, rejected the impulse toward an autonomous morality that scholastic theologians derived from Aristotle.[79] In this most important respect, Luther stands in the tradition of Kant's opponents, not his forebears, and Luther's (and Holl's) morality was a morality derived from and dependent on religion. On the other hand, Holl saw in Kant's ethics "submission under an unconditional law" and "the rejection of ideas of happiness and welfare" that distinguished German culture from the values that France and England owed to the Enlightenment.[80] To Holl's way of thinking, these statements were not an admission that he had Kantianized Luther but an illustration of how much Kant, like other German cultural greats, owed to the Reformer.

Luther's ethics, his soteriology, and his psychology were unified in a most impressive way by Holl, with the outcome that the theme of *Anfechtungen* became very important for Luther studies from Holl's book of 1921 through the influential Luther books of the 1950s.[81] The power of Holl's work lay in its integration of Luther's ideas and his biography, and its psychological content permitted secular men of letters such as Lucien Febvre and Erik Erikson[82] to translate it out of theology into terms that were evocative for a wider, secular public. Hence notions such as God's Yes hidden under his No had an emotive resonance among persons who were in other respects unbelievers.

Luther's statements about himself contained bewildering oscillations between the darkest self-repudiation and the most exaggerated self-glorification. Holl saw here two personal styles highly characteristic of the age: "the absolute self-rejection of the monk" and "the equally absolute self-affirmation of the Renaissance power man."[83] But in Luther his soteriology welded the monk and the Renaissance man into a harmonious synthesis. In himself he was a poor sinner standing under the wrath of God, but since he was at the same time an instrument of God's love and power, his achievements and his cause were deserving of hyperbolic – indeed, reverent – praise. But the balance weighed towards Luther condemning himself as a sinner in the sight of God. In reality, he was exceptional among religious men in his lack of self-satisfaction and sustained inner peace.[84] "Luther was never able to feel entirely fulfilled in the way this was possible for others. Not even when he found firm ground to stand on with his justification teaching. An attack from the outside always only strengthened him in his conviction. Here he had the feeling that whatever his enemies asserted was something that he had thought through and inwardly overcome long ago. But in his own interior he constantly found it necessary to start his thinking, his search for God, all over again from the beginning."[85] Since the person who was justified in the sight of God was always at the same time, and quite accurately, a sinner in his own eyes, he was always repenting, always beginning anew. Luther's incapacity to enjoy the peace of a completed conversion was something that the Catholic polemicists jumped up and down upon. For Holl it was the mark of his special religious depth. "He was more or less aware that he could not do without his inner conflicts [*Anfechtungen*]. He had to admit that Staupitz was right to say that they were as necessary to him as food and drink."[86] These *Anfechtungen* were for Luther gracious expressions of the wrath of God, an *ira misericordiae*, the No that concealed the hidden Yes.

Holl presented the *Anfechtungen* as a lifelong recurrence of Luther's struggle for awareness of a gracious God in his monastic years.[87] However, they could only with difficulty be connected with 1511 and 1512, the years when Holl believed that Luther had worked out his soteriology. The evidence that they occurred in his later years was clear enough, but linking them with his formative insights was much more difficult.[88] In the *Table Talk* Luther referred to the *tentationes* as starting only in 1521. To which Holl responded, "Luther was obviously then referring only to *Anfechtungen* related to his conception of calling," that is, whether he had committed an awful crime in leading so many people to disbelieve what their ancestors had believed time out of mind. And Holl was able to find a reference to *tentationes* from a statement of 11 November 1517.[89] But this discovery was far from establishing a convincing connection between the *Anfechtungen* and the emergence of the *Rechtfertigungslehre*. As with the Autobiographical Fragment of 1545, Holl was quite willing to dismiss Luther's reminiscences when they conflicted with the systematic theology in support of which he invoked Luther's theology. Parallelling Holl's assertion of his *Verstehen* of Luther was his bold insistence on Luther's *Verstehen* of Paul: "The true creator of this distinctive self-understanding is not Luther himself. As everywhere, here Luther walked in the footsteps of someone greater. He learned from Paul to feel at one and the same time that he is nothing in the sight of God and nevertheless 'foolishly' to boast in God. That Luther was able to recreate this most personal quality of Paul confirms the degree to which he had taken Paul's whole essence into himself, indeed, sucked it in."[90] But current New Testament scholarship is very skeptical about whether Paul had anything like *Anfechtungen*; it challenges whether he shared "the introspective conscience of the West," to which Augustine is acknowledged to have sounded the keynote.

If sometimes Luther praised God for his *Anfechtungen*, at others he responded to them as afflictions to be treated with psychological homeopathic remedies. He had the sense that these *Anfechtungen* were connected with his physical condition. Therefore he sought to counteract them by means of appropriate care of his body. When he felt one coming on, he would eat and drink more heavily than usual – without appetite, in the consciousness that this, too, was a kind of fasting.[91] If the sympathetic Protestant tradition was disposed to be so open about the great man's psychological states, its supporters had no real grounds to close this area of interpretation to psychologizing priests and Freudian analysts.[92]

The area in which Holl focused upon Luther's intellectual development was in his view of the church, and his eventual standpoint about church and state, through to the time when Protestant territorial churches emerged. In this area from the time of the *Dictata* (1513–15) to the period following the Peasants' War of 1525, Holl showed Luther's ideas to be in constant movement. It was a matter of great importance for him that Luther's conception of the church was not a product of the external controversy of 1518–21. In such a case "the suspicion could hardly be fended off that it was more the expedient grasped in an emergency, a weapon in battle, than a product of Luther's distinctive inner development."[93] In fact, Luther's ecclesiology was not a product of the indulgence controversy but was directly derived from his *Rechtfertigungslehre*. It was a pure idea, unsoiled by external historical process. In Holl's eyes, "Luther's magnificently logical development was admirable."[94] The *non plus ultra* of idealist historiography was to imagine an individual's biography determined by his gradual discovery of the logical consequences of his ideas. This notion became the leitmotif of the Luther Renaissance.

In the *Dictata* Luther recognized that many outward Christians were not true Christians. These were the self-righteous, those who did not condemn themselves in the sight of God. Inside the external church there was a narrower circle of true Christians, who alone deserved the title of the church of Christ.[95] The external church was the place where the Word of God was proclaimed, and according to God's promise, the preaching of the Word could not go without fruit. So some believed and were saved. "If the church of Christ is invisible to corporal eyes, it can be seen with spiritual eyes, that is, with faith."[96] This invisible church is "a real community – indeed, the only true community because the most interior community."[97] Obviously, these ideas of an invisible church emerged from the tradition of St Augustine, but for Holl, here as elsewhere, Luther's ideas were a great improvement over Augustine's. "Indeed, he found in Augustine's thought the distinction between the visible Catholic church and the true church of the 'spiritual' or 'converted.' But for Augustine the deeper conception of the church was tied only to the timeless decree of election, while for Luther the Word of God effective in history was the foundation. That had the advantage that Luther was able to establish a connection between the visible and invisible churches, which Augustine despite all his efforts never succeeded in doing."[98] Holl saw Luther's church idea as a place where his twin stresses on the person and the community came into harmony: "all religious, and ultimately all moral life, can grow and sustain itself only within an encompassing community."[99] The true Christians loved and served their neighbours as instruments of God; therefore there could be no thought of restricting the external church to a spiritual elite; it had to be an open, "people's church" (*Volkskirche*).

The outbreak of the indulgence controversy confronted Luther with apparent abuse on the part of external church authority. So he studied the historical development of papal power, able to put himself at a critical distance from it because he knew that the true church was not the historical church of Rome but a spiritual assembly of persons united in God. After the Leipzig disputation he gradually became aware that true, spiritual Christian priesthood belonged to all believers, rather than being restricted to the external first estate. If all believers were priests, in times of emergency believing Christians from outside the external priesthood might be called upon to reform the church. Of these lay priests, who could be better placed to execute the reforms than the political class? Commenting on the reform proposals that emerged with Luther's *Address to the Nobility* (1520), Holl wrote, "The more precisely Luther grasped the essence and limits of the spiritual power, so much the more clearly did the distinct right of the state emerge for him."[100]

According to Holl, "Luther's concept of the church and the significance he assigned the government [*Obrigkeit*] fit tightly together. The topic was very clearly and consistently thought out."[101] Whether in a Reformation-era *disputatio* or in a volume of twentieth-century systematic theology, if you fell into self-contradiction, you lost your credit.

The relation of church and state was not for Holl subsumed in the concept of *corpus christianum*, the interpretive device applied to Luther by Ernst Troeltsch and his scholarly predecessors. This idea assumed that the Middle Ages believed in a Christian society with church and state as its two arms. Holl showed very convincingly that, whether applied to "the Middle Ages" or to Luther, the concept was an anachronism. Used fairly rarely, the term simply meant "church," not "Christian society." Both the external church and the temporal power were, to be sure, instruments of God's plan and at the service of the true, invisible church. On the other hand, "spiritual and temporal power are distinct in their character; the one rules only through the Word, the other through compulsion."[102] In ideal or even normal circumstances the two had different tasks, only indirectly coordinated, say, through the government's keeping order. The majority of people in temporal society were not true Christians, but then that was the way that Luther conceived the external church too.

However, to Luther's way of thinking, the Reformation was a great religious emergency in which genuine Christians had to do what they could to reform the external, institutional church without compromising its independence. As a matter of historical fact, even Holl realized that such an enterprise was doomed to failure; but it was important to him to show that Luther never intended to turn the church over to the governments of the territorial princes and urban magistrates.

The governments had some fundamental responsibilities, as Luther conceived them, pertaining to the external life of the church. They should act against "robbery," by which he meant papal annates at the installation of bishops and similar Roman financial impositions. They should suppress "blasphemy," of which the most glaring instance was the mass. They should maintain public order, which could only be achieved by seeing that there was but one religion tolerated in a territory. Beyond that, matters such as appointing preachers, calling church councils, and structuring visitations, which inspected the religious life of parishes, fell to the rulers only to the extent that they were Christian brothers – "emergency bishops" – filling the role in the church that would normally fall to the bishops. Luther always conceived of the church as independent, each parish at least concurring in the appointment or removal of its pastor. And of course, the prince and his officials had no place in specifically church matters such as the preaching of the gospel, the administration of the sacraments, and the formulation of confessions.

To Holl's way of thinking, there was considerable disorganized freedom for the evangelical churches committed to the Reformation in the years prior to the Peasants' War. But with the Electoral Saxon instruction to the Visitation of 1527, the prince presumed to take responsibility for the spiritual, as well as the physical, well-being of his subjects. Holl presents Luther as adopting an attitude of "silent protest"[103] against this development and says that he grudgingly accepted princely authority in the evangelical churches only as a provisional necessity. From a longer historical perspective, "the price that evangelical Christianity had to pay for [the territorial established church] was too high"[104] and contrary to Luther's intentions.

The central themes of Holl's Luther book are best expressed in the lead essay, "What Did Luther Understand by Religion?" and in the one additional essay that he felt it imperative to add to the 1923 second edition, "Luther and the Schwärmer." "What Did Luther Understand by Religion?" was originally a Reformation anniversary lecture entitled "Luther's Conception of Religion," delivered by Holl at the University of Berlin in 1917. Greatly enlarged and heavily annotated, it became the first, flagship piece in the 1921 book. In his introduction to the English translation, Walter F. Bense credited Holl with "going back – more effectively than anyone else before him – beyond Lutheran Orthodoxy and Melanchthon to Luther himself."[105] In the estimation of Holl's friend Hans Lietzmann, the book brought together the divided factions of German Lutheranism, "overcoming much long-standing conflict and awakening once again in many hearts the awareness of the uniform foundation of all our religious and churchly life in the gospel recovered and interpreted by the genius of Martin Luther."[106] It would perhaps be too much coincidence if Holl's opus were at the same time a monument of scholarship and of ecclesiastical statesmanship. The improbability of such an achievement becomes all the greater when we remind ourselves how exactly Holl's *Luther* followed the structure of his early essays on the doctrine of justification (1906–07).

The strength and weakness of Holl's opening essay was that it was a work of systematic theology. He thought that Luther should be credited with being a systematic theologian: "If by a systematic theologian one means someone who is capable of surveying vast contexts of ideas, then Luther was a systematic theologian to much greater degree than Calvin, not to mention Melanchthon."[107] One here suspects Holl of being carried off into Luther's style of incautious hyperbole, although the disparagement of Melanchthon is typical.

The somber tone of the opening essay was well suited to the great European tragedy of an immensely destructive war which it seemed beyond the resources of generals and statesmen to bring to an end. As noted earlier, Holl tried to harmonize Albrecht Ritschl's justification theology, which stressed God's love, and Theodosius Harnack's emphasis on the divine wrath. Technically, Ritschl had the last word, in that God saved sinners, but the tone of Holl's presentation is closer to that of Theodosius Harnack.

God's requirements of human beings are absolute, "Nothing short of perfection satisfies him. It must be thus, if God is really the Holy One."[108] Luther's great insight was that the existing Catholic path to holiness was a snare and a delusion; true self-knowledge leads to confession of one's utter sinfulness, most of all when one is trying to please God. Holl's Luther prized his bad conscience, heightened by terrifying moments of intense psychological insight, as the foundation of his relation to God: "Luther's conscience had led him to recover the Pauline doctrine of the wrath of God which had been suppressed in the West, mainly by Augustine."[109] "At no moment do we will anything other than ourselves; we are compelled by a natural constraint to do so. This is what we dimly perceive when we are terrified by

God's holiness. It dawns upon us that we always instinctively want something different from our prescribed duty."[110] This insight is described as Pauline, renewed in the nineteenth century by Søren Kierkegaard ("and [by] Nietzsche, too, in his way"[111]). The moment of heightened self-despair is the one when the sinner is closest to God.

But this wrath of God is an act of love – an *ira misericordiae* – a wrath which is really compassion. Holl describes the wrath of God as a sort of patriarchal tough love: "Strength of will and wholesome severity give to love a pedagogical dimension. Love now is understood as a power that does not hesitate to inflict hurt in order to liberate its object from itself and to raise it above itself."[112] The wrath of God is his "alien" or "strange" work, with reference to Isaiah 28:21, masking his "proper" work of love. The will that has been broken by bad conscience is now prepared to accept the miracle of the love of God. It has the duty to accept his declaration in the first commandment that he is its God, although the human person is completely lacking in intrinsic worth. The sinner's forgiveness is "an incomprehensible miracle,"[113] but refusal to accept it would be the ultimate blasphemy. Holl crowns his soteriology with language destined to echo in Luther research from his day to ours: "Luther was able to peer through the gloom and fury of the divine wrath into the loving will of God. As he wonderfully expressed it, he now hears 'below and above the "Nay" the deep and hidden "Yea"' which God was speaking to him."[114]

For Holl, Luther, like Jacob in the Old Testament, was wrestling directly with God. Interposing Christ would have been an evasion, because it would have deprived him of direct confrontation with the one holy and wrathful God. Here the high monotheism of turn-of-the-century liberal Protestantism flirts with heresy. Continuing that tradition, Holl insists that Luther's Christology was heterodox, *despite his orthodox intention*. Luther was "convinced that this conception merely expresses the true meaning of the ancient dogma ... In this respect he was mistaken ... From the standpoint of the ancient councils, he skirted the borders of heresy all along the line."[115] Holl insists that Luther ("unintentionally") taught the subordination of the Son to the Father, so that Christ "does not his own will but the will of the Father. Such a doctrine accords well enough with Paul and John, but poorly with the Nicene dogma."[116]

Holl's presentation of Luther's Christology is intertwined with his own anathemas against Catholic medieval mysticism. On its face, mysticism was the ultimate proclamation against self-centred religiosity, but it posited that within the self there was a quality which enabled the person to couple with God. Its pretensions of utter self-abnegation reversed into self-deification; its practice of mortification tended to reverse into the "genuine masochistic passion"[117] of which Holl accused Heinrich Suso. Yet Luther in the years of his early theological lectures had clearly carried on a dalliance with mysticism. He manifestly thought that "Christ as spirit can be present in the believer";[118] but if Christ was not exactly God,[119] then Luther's "Christ-mysticism" would not have been the full-blown, self-deifying mysticism that would have introduced destructive contradiction into his soteriology. Clearly, Holl's theocentric soteriology trumped his Christology. When Friedrich Gogarten, polemicist from the Dialectical Theology, raised the issue of Holl's unorthodox Christology, Holl's response was a gruff "against such accusations I do not care to defend myself."[120] What it came down to was that, like the younger Harnack, Holl believed that he had penetrated behind the Greek philosophical categories of Nicea and Chalcedon to the biblical religion of John and Paul (and Jesus). The problem was that, in the tradition of Ritschl and Adolf von Harnack, he went on to insist that Luther agreed with him – if only implicitly. At a time when dogmatic or systematic theology was eclipsing the previously reigning church history in the theological disciplines, good dogma seemed worth a lot more than good history.

Holl's theocentrism insisted that in a strict sense there could be no human agency. To affirm human free will was tantamount to denying God's rule of the world. Holl's theocentrism insisted upon a "divine monergism" (*Alleinwirksamkeit*). The one limitation to the divine omnipotence, in this way of thinking, was the kind of covenanted self-limitation that the scholastic theologians had speculated about. Human beings, and the devil too, were ultimately puppets of God. He works all in all – he did, does, and will do it all. And he does everything with perfect justice, although Luther conceded that that is a matter of faith, beyond human understanding. "It is part of God's majesty that there is much we do not know about him. If his being were completely transparent to us, he would really no longer be God."[121]

Even more than Ritschl, Holl had been touched by the diffuse Kantianism that permeated German Protestant culture at the turn of the century. His insistence that duty was the only acceptable motive, that happiness – even happiness with God – was an unworthy goal, was very Kantian, as well as congruent with the wartime ethos of self-sacrifice. "For [Luther] everything depended on the purity of the ultimate motives,"[122] or as Kant would have it, there is nothing truly good except a good will.

This Kantian, culturally Germanic, insistence that genuine religion can be only "service to God, and the fulfilment of a duty to him ... divorced from the desire for salvation or happiness,"[123] was the key to the ethnocentric classification of Protestantism as the sole true religion, with Catholicism bunched together with all the other lower religions. "With primitive Christianity as his source, [Luther] reaffirmed the powerful motives that distinguish Christianity from all other religions."[124] The notion that Protestantism had reached back beyond Roman authoritarianism and Greek metaphysics to grasp the authentic gospel was not new with Holl; if anything, it was more blatant in Harnack's *Essence of Christianity* (1900). But Holl focused this cultural arrogance more exclusively upon a heroic, ahistorical Luther. Whatever Luther took from his medieval predecessors he thoroughly transformed, and what he passed on to Melanchthon and his successors was completely botched. The error of liberal church historians such as Troeltsch was to fail to see "Luther's unique greatness,"[125] to assert his fundamental continuance of medieval religiosity and to miss how much he "towers above his successors."

If "What Did Luther Understand by Religion?" expressed a high theocentrism that connected Holl with his liberal forebears, particularly Adolf von Harnack,[126] "Luther and the Schwärmer" surely bore the stigmata of imperial Germany's military defeat and the Wilsonian project of making Western democracy the universal way forward for progressive humanity. Here Holl was on the scent of the distinctive Protestant religiosity of England and America, hell-bent to expose its inferiority to German Lutheranism.

He wrote to his publisher, Paul Siebeck, in 1922 that he wanted the "Schwärmer" essay among his collected essays on Luther: "It is so necessary to rounding out the historical picture in that book that it absolutely must be included."[127] This was a curious comment because the "Schwärmer" essay was not primarily about Luther but about Thomas Müntzer and to a lesser extent George Fox and Sebastian Franck. What was particularly Luther's was the polemical packaging of the essay. Before this, no one since the Enlightenment, including Holl himself, had ventured to use Luther's denunciatory label "Schwärmer" as a serious description in academic historical theology.[128] For Luther it denoted all pro-Reformation groups of which he disapproved – which meant all that did not adopt his entire theology. Zwingli, for instance, was a "Schwärmer" to Luther, but not to Holl, given the Prussian Evangelical Church's fusion of Lutheran and Reformed congregations. "Schwärmer" were for Holl the ancestors of nonconformist Protestantism, vanishingly small in Germany but a characteristic element in ecclesiastical life in England, Wales, and North America.

The figure to whom Holl devoted himself most thoroughly was Thomas Müntzer, "the Satan at Allstedt," who engaged in polemical broadsides with Luther and who invited the Electoral Saxon princes to lead an apocalyptic crusade on behalf of the Reformation. In what Luther regarded as a judgment of God, Müntzer was executed after being involved on the rebel side in the Peasants' War of 1525. The fact that the revolutionary socialists[129] had singled him out as the hero of a popular Reformation, as opposed to Luther, the princes' lackey, led Holl to focus on him in the aftermath of the aborted German revolution of 1918–19.

Holl, together with Heinrich Boehmer, stands at the beginning of serious Müntzer scholarship,[130] he collected the basic source materials, with the strategic omission of most of the Müntzer correspondence, soon afterward gathered and published by Boehmer. Holl set about organizing Müntzer's thought in the manner of a systematic theologian, demonstrating that a mysticism of suffering was the connecting thread in his soteriology and that he complemented and partly undermined biblical authority by a strong belief in the continuing revelation of the Holy Spirit to God's elect.[131] Much less convincingly, Holl presented Müntzer as the founder of a voluntary, free-church tradition in the Reformation that continued with the Anabaptists.[132] His weak grasp of the details of Müntzer's career in Allstedt and Mühlhausen led him to present Müntzer as the carrier of anti-Lutheran ideas rather than as another, competing Saxon pastor with an alternative program of Reformation to Luther's.

Holl took for granted that Müntzer was an original follower of Luther who spoiled the Wittenberg theology through his mysticism and belief in direct revelation. In Holl's view this selfish, individualistic soteriology was mixed quite illogically[133] with a program of democratic revolution based on older Germanic traditions. This anti-Lutheran mystical religiosity (Holl denied the mystical element in Luther's theology through what appears to the contemporary observer as a series of intellectual contortions) underwent a three-stage devolution. The revolutionary mystics were succeeded by suffering sects who rejected violence, participation in government, and activity at law. The sects in turn gave way to religious individualists such as Sebastian Franck, whose ideas were later easily absorbed into the rationalist currents of the Enlightenment.[134] Because of their mystical self-deification these Reformation counterplayers of Luther's lacked any stable sense of community. Hence the nonconformists' bequest to England and America (illustrated by the substantial attention that Holl gave to George Fox)[135] was an excessive religious individualism. While Lutheran Germany with its sound sense of community was prepared to counter the future excesses of capitalism with social legislation, Anglo-American Protestantism stood helpless in the face of capitalist exploitation.[136] "The Schwärmer can pass as the true bearers of progress, as the men of the current hour, only if one accepts that the Anglo-American conception of state and society is the only correct one. But it was not the Schwärmer, who merely stirred things up, but Luther who articulated the substantive, creative religious truth. And his concept of the state, which stresses community in the nation [*Gemeinschaft im Volk*] stands closer to the final meaning of Christendom than the other, to which 'freedom' is everything."[137] So "Luther and the Schwärmer," and with it Holl's great book on the Reformer, ended with an invocation of Luther's name and "the final meaning of Christendom" against Wilsonianism and its progeny – the Weimar Republic, the Treaty of Versailles, and the League of Nations.

Karl Holl made a massive exegetical contribution to the understanding of Luther's voluminous writings. Like all knowledge creation it was driven, and limited, by the personal purposes of its progenitor. In Holl's case these were a powerful monotheistic faith, reverence for the historical Lutheran teaching on justification, and belief in the moral superiority of German culture. Although he came out of the midst of the pre-war liberal theologians, Holl implied that they had misunderstood Luther and had failed Germany in its moment of crisis. Immediately after the war his rejection of the pre-war theologians would be joined by the more explicit, abrasive, and bumptious ones of Karl Barth and Friedrich Gogarten.

3 The Dialectical Theology and Luther Studies

Walter von Loewenich, looking back at the previous decade of Luther studies from the vantage of 1948, singled out the excellence of a book by Otto Wolff, *Die Haupttypen der neueren Lutherdeutung* (The Main Types of Recent Interpretation of Luther; 1938). He called it "the best and most substantial study of this topic that we have in Germany."[1] Loewenich noted Wolff's disparagement of the Dialectical Theology's contribution to Luther studies, but he countered that Wolff's own critique of Holl and others was heavily indebted to that theological school. Although he agreed with Wolff that Barth, Gogarten, and others in the Dialectical Theology had not achieved a usable understanding of Luther, he suggested that they had laid the foundations for current Luther studies: "The impulses that they contributed have had a great resonance, and they are unmistakably present in any contemporary interpretation of Luther."[2] In effect, the Dialectical Theology served as a powerful catalyst for the course of development of Luther studies. Loewenich admitted his own debt to Emil Brunner's *Mysticism and the Word of God* (1924) in the composition of his own first book, *Luther's Theology of the Cross* (1929).

This appraisal receives a kind of backhanded confirmation from Paul Althaus, a theologian of confessional Lutheranism, basically unsympathetic to the Dialectical Theology. For Althaus one of the bizarre, distorting factors in the theological polemics between the Luther Renaissance and the Dialectical Theology was that neither side could conceive that there might be a difference between Luther's ideas about justification and the theologically correct doctrine of justification.[3] As a corollary to that, both parties insisted on the identity of Luther's and Paul's doctrines of justification, not as a historical finding, but as a theological axiom. The result, said Althaus, was that their interpretation of the Reformer was *derived* from their systematic theology. (One might pursue this idea further and call the Luther Renaissance a theological system at least ostensibly based on Reformation studies, while the Dialectical Theology produced a notion of the Reformation derived from its theological assertions.) Both the Dialecticians and the Holl school were disinclined to accept criticism from confessional Lutherans at Erlangen University such as Althaus and Werner Elert. Behind the Luther Renaissance stood the Union Protestantism of Prussia, and among the Dialecticians were a considerable number of Swiss Reformed (Barth, Brunner, Eduard Thurneysen); both of these groups tended to dismiss confessional Lutheranism as a faulty, "Melanchthonian" reception of Luther. Perhaps more fundamental, the Holl people and the Barth people were joined in sophisticated scorn for the orthodox – even when they turned against theological liberalism, they sustained their modernist scorn for the old-fashioned counterplayers of the liberals.

Unlike the Luther Renaissance people, the Dialectical Theologians were not a succession of professors and their students; nor were they compatible colleagues joined by a shared tradition like the confessional Lutheran theologian-historians at Erlangen University. They were theologians of various origins drawn together – for a while – by mutual admiration of each other's writings. They contributed to the periodical *Zwischen den Zeiten* (Between the Ages) in the years from 1923 until the group broke up and the journal ceased publication in 1933. The leading figures were Karl Barth, Rudolf Bultmann, Emil Brunner, and Friedrich Gogarten.[4] Barth and Bultmann were two of the most important Protestant theologians of the twentieth century, but Bultmann never quite fit into the group, and his impact was primarily on New Testament studies. Barth and Brunner were Reformed, but Bultmann and Gogarten were Lutheran. Brunner and Barth's friend Thurneysen remained Swiss figures at a remove from the German Reich, while Barth, who had received most of his theological education in Germany, played a major role in German Protestant theology and church life during the years 1921 to 1935, in which he taught in German universities. Gogarten, a pastor for most of the Weimar years who became a part-time academic in 1925 and a theology professor at the beginning of the 1930s, was like Barth in conceiving of the Dialectical Theology as a restoration of the theology of the

Reformers. Indeed his opinions about the Reformation played a bigger, more explicit part in his writings than was the case with Barth. This chapter will deal only with Barth and Gogarten.

Karl Barth, despite his Swiss Reformed background and allegiance, which brought with it a great respect for Calvin, pretty obviously identified with Martin Luther. The self-description of how, groping for support on a winding staircase in an old tower, he grabbed a rope and was astonished to hear the ringing of a bell which adorns Bainton's much-loved Luther biography was so much cut to the measure of contemporary notions of Luther's tower experience that Barth must have been suggesting when he used the image that he was the Martin Luther of his day.[5] Barth began as a liberal theologian, a student of Adolf von Harnack and Wilhelm Herrmann – to put the matter in his terms, just as Luther began as a medieval monk or Paul a Pharisee.

Indeed, we have a Karl Barth autobiographical fragment of 1957 that, in unconscious parody of Luther's Autobiographical Fragment of 1545, poses severe interpretive problems. Analyzing the decline of nineteenth-century Protestant liberal theology, Barth declared:

The actual end of the nineteenth century as the "good old days" falls for evangelical theology, as for other things, in the fateful year 1914. Fortuitously or not fortuitously, at any rate symptomatically, it happened just in that year that the recognized leading systematic theologian of the then most modern school, Ernst Troeltsch, finally crossed over from the theological to the philosophical faculty. For me personally one day at the beginning of August that year stamped itself as *dies ater* ("dark day"). It was that on which 93 German intellectuals came out with a manifesto supporting the war policy of Kaiser Wilhelm II and his counsellors, and among them I found to my horror the names of nearly all my theological teachers, whom up to then I had religiously honoured. Disillusioned by their conduct, I perceived that I should not be able any longer to accept their ethics and dogmatics, their biblical exegesis, their interpretation of history, that at least for me the theology of the nineteenth century had no future.[6]

Were this statement to be taken seriously, Karl Barth and Karl Holl both experienced very political conversions from theological liberalism. Just as Barth's eyes were opened to the deficient theology of Harnack and Troeltsch by their support of Germany's entry into the war in 1914, so Holl gained similar insight in 1917 from their failure to endorse unrestricted submarine warfare and expansionist German war aims. Fortunately, one is inclined to say, for the integrity of Luther studies, this is only a very small part of the truth in the one case as in the other.

Perhaps like Luther in 1545, Barth's memory was confused in his autobiographical reminiscence. He could not have been disillusioned by the petition of the ninety-three intellectuals *in August 1914*, because it was not issued until the beginning of October. Of his teachers, only Herrmann and Harnack – far from "nearly all," although Herrmann was certainly the most important of Barth's early teachers – were co-signers.[7] Truly, as a Swiss Religious Socialist, Barth was disgusted by what went on in Germany in August 1914 – the endorsement of the war by both Protestant liberals and Social Democrats. He wrote Herrmann an open letter in November 1914 denouncing the use of the professor's fundamental category of religious experience to sanctify the war: "In your school it became clear to us what it means to 'experience' God in Jesus. Now however ... an 'experience' which is completely new to us is held out to us by German Christians, an allegedly religious war 'experience,' i.e. the fact that German Christians 'experience' their war as a holy war."[8]

The point about Troeltsch perhaps gets closer to Barth's real concerns. Troeltsch was moving in the direction of putting Christianity on a common basis with other major world religions.[9] In their different ways, the Luther Renaissance, the Dialectical Theology, and the Erlangen Lutheran theologians all sensed that the absolute claims of Christianity were now being called into question, and each group in its own manner reasserted Christian exclusivity. Given both the Western and the German cultural hubris around 1914, the reaction against Troeltsch was perhaps bound to occur. But this ethnocentrism was a bad omen for the future. Many years later, after the Second World War and the Holocaust, Barth admitted to a younger colleague that he had an "allergic reaction" to Jews, even to *Judenchristen* (Jewish Christians), and he wondered whether this attitude might have "retarded" his theology.[10] This, of course, is very conscientious introspection on the part of the leader of the struggle to protect the rights of Jewish Christians in the Nazi Germany of the 1930s.

Moreover, Barth and Gogarten represented a classic generational revolt in a much purer way than did Holl, an old man surrounded by young disciples. There was certainly something incongruous about identifying Protestantism so closely with an academic method, making it a kind of knowledge, as had been done in the Ritschl-Harnack-Troeltsch succession. For most, religious knowledge was cold comfort in the hour of death – and in the years 1914–18, death was an especially prominent part of life. Those, like Barth, who saw much to correct in the self-satisfied bourgeois culture of the turn of the century slowly came to regard as blasphemous the notion of older scholars that they had arrived at a benevolent synthesis of Christianity and culture.[11] Modernism produced its self-critique; Nietzsche's image of reason biting its own tail, his assault on late-nineteenth-century morality and historicism, reached Barth partly directly, partly mediated by Nietzsche's friend Franz Overbeck. Barth always insisted that he thought well of historical criticism, also in the sphere of religious history, and that he would never dream of trying to suppress it.[12] Yet he also insisted that he had been thrown into his pastorate totally unprepared to preach the gospel, "because at the university I had never been brought beyond that well known 'Awe in the presence of History.'"[13] His generation and his time needed a stronger tonic – as the contemporary liberal theologian Gustav Krüger observed, it was a time of "hunger for revelation."[14]

The cross-currents of Barth's own background prepared him for his historic role. His father, Fritz Barth, a conservative theology professor at Bern, tried to steer his son towards the "right" influences in the German university scene. But at Berlin, Karl avoided the conservative Reinhold Seeberg and attached himself to Harnack, and then in 1908 went to Herrmann in Marburg, the location of *Die Christliche Welt* (the *Christian World*) – the very citadel of modernism. But by 1919, when he published his first commentary on Romans, Barth looked back on the memory of his father, who had died in 1912, "with reverence and gratitude." According to the son, his father had never enjoyed the respect of the theological luminaries of his day. He had been "overlooked and to a degree despised. And I will not conceal that for a moment the thought passed through my mind that I should and would in a sense pay back those persons who had so overshadowed my father, although he knew as much as they (only it was knowledge of a different sort)."[15] Barth asserted at the time that, if he had to choose between the historical-critical approach to the Bible of the liberals and the conservative doctrine of inspiration, he would choose the latter. But he always thought that he could go through the horns of that particular dilemma.[16]

In fact, the rejection of the historicism of the Ritschl-Harnack-Troeltsch tradition was not a posthumous act of filial piety by Barth. It was rooted in the kind of liberal theology that he had learned at Marburg from Herrmann. Herrmann to a degree preceded Barth in rejecting historical-critical approaches to the Bible as humankind's search for God, which must be abandoned in order to focus on God's revelation to humanity. He stood in the tradition of Schleiermacher, basing religion in one sense on the human experience of faith but more fundamentally on the miraculous self-revelation of God. This self-revelation was founded on the "inner life" of Jesus of Nazareth and transmitted by the effect that it has had on the inner life of

Christian people. For Herrmann, unlike Harnack, a Christ of faith had made the historical Jesus entirely irrelevant.[17] Hence Barth's liberal antecedents were of a different variety from Holl's. His act of rebellion against Herrmann was to deny the worth of human faith or human religious experience as a sort of coupling point between God and humankind. This view created a dramatically austere theocentric theology of revelation, stripped of divine immanence; hence in Barth's independent theology from 1915 to 1924, Christology was a problem. However, he exaggerated the extent of his rupture with Herrmann, just as he exaggerated the breaks between the several phases in his independent theological development. His account of his theological development was distorted by a tendency to self-dramatization and by the desire to break decisively with former teachers and erstwhile allies.[18]

Recent scholarship has pointed to parallels in the movement away from pre-war liberal theology in the Dialectical Theology and the Luther Renaissance.[19] As early as his sermons of 1913, Barth had taken the same path as Holl in allowing God's wrath to stand in dialectical contradiction to his love, abandoning the one-sided stress on the love of God of the whole Ritschlian tradition (which in this respect included Herrmann).[20] Even more striking is the eclipse of the "Christocentrism" which had been associated with Ritschl, Harnack, and Herrmann – and the vogue of "theocentrism," which brought with it the inevitable consequence of a weak Christology.[21] From 1924 on, Barth repaired the deficit in his Christology himself, while in the Holl school Christological focus was restored after Holl's death in 1926 by Erich Vogelsang. On the eve of the First World War both Barth and Holl were crafting ideals of community to counter the traditional Protestant individualism of pre-war liberal theology. Dialectical Theology and Luther Renaissance had more in common in the 1920s than either was prepared to admit.

But having returned from Marburg to Switzerland as pastor at Safenwil (1911–21), Barth developed a politics that coloured his religious ideal of community and distinguished him from all the other theologians discussed in this book. He became a man of the left, and although he came to realize that leftist ideals, too, fell infinitely short of the Kingdom of God, he insisted that in the penultimate reality of this world, leftist programs and policies were simply "more Christian" than those of the right. His experience as pastor of a working-class congregation certainly contributed to his questioning of the theology of Herrmann, which seemed too comfortably compatible with bourgeois individualism and the unjust society before the First World War. Religious Socialism was further developed in Switzerland than in Germany, and Barth participated in the movement. However, he soon realized the folly of identifying socialism with the Kingdom of God as just another historicist heresy. Nevertheless, without illusions about the religious worth of socialism, Barth remained an active member of the Swiss Social Democratic Party as long as he remained in Switzerland. His political ideal was a radical democratic socialism that rejected both the authoritarian revolutionary violence of Lenin and the German SPD's revisionist accommodation with bourgeois society. From across the border he watched the emergence of the Weimar Republic with reserved detachment. Certainly, he had no truck with Wilsonian democratic messianism, another worldly perversion of the Kingdom of God. But he nevertheless regarded the new German republic, with its diluted socialism, as worthier of the allegiance of its Christian citizens than its imperial predecessor.[22] Even this degree of political involvement ceased in 1921 when Barth was called to be associate professor in Göttingen as a resident alien. It was made clear to him that in Germany he would have to forego leftist political advocacy. He became a German citizen with his appointment as full professor in Münster in autumn 1925, but until the last years of the Weimar Republic he remained silent on matters of politics. Nevertheless, his leftist orientation continued to distinguish him from his nationalist peers. He declared that as a Christian theologian he was equally unimpressed with Marxist and nationalist ideology, but that as a Christian citizen he preferred socialist to right-wing policies.[23]

The beginning of the First World War was surely the moment of crisis and disillusionment for Barth, unlike all our other protagonists, for whom the German surrender, the collapse of the German, Austrian, and Russian empires, the wave of communist revolutions, and the "dictated" Versailles peace settlement marked the end of the world in which they had grown up. Barth seems never to have accepted the Leninist theory of capitalism and the inevitability of wars. In the years leading up to August 1914 he saw things in terms of arms races and nationalism, and he hoped that the international brotherhood of working men might yet avert catastrophe. He was crushed to see both the German theologians and the German socialist leaders revelling in the euphoria of national solidarity during the first war year. He was inspired by this shock to "return to the theological ABC's"[24] and to deliver a commentary on the Epistle to the Romans, that central text of Protestantism. By the time that he had something ready to give the world, the general crisis of 1918–19 was washing over central and eastern Europe.

By 1918 he had a manuscript, and the next year, after three rejections, the Berner publisher G.A. Bäschlin produced an edition of one thousand copies.[25] This work, from which Barth distanced himself quickly enough, was a revolutionary eschatological pronouncement, described by the Catholic theologian Hans Urs von Balthasar as conceptually grounded "not primarily in Scripture, not even in Luther and Calvin, but in Plato, theological Right Hegelianism, and Religious Socialism."[26] Certainly, its dominant theme, that the old world was destined to pass away and be overcome by the Kingdom of God, contained echoes of the revolutionary euphoria of 1918–19. When Barth long afterward reissued it with a brief foreword, he observed that the main justification for its republication was that Harnack's deflating prophecy of forty years earlier had indeed been fulfilled: "colleague Barth is probably better to be regarded as an *object* than as a subject of academic theology." It was no doubt necessary to have this work accessible if one wanted to study Barth, but the *second*, 1922 edition of *Romans*, not this book, was the work that he stood by. But he unduly minimized the impact of this first, 1919 Romans commentary. It won him wide attention among theological students and cemented the theological alliance between him and Gogarten. Moreover, it was not so totally unlike the 1922 edition as he claimed. Possibly the greatest importance of the 1919 commentary was that to it he owed his call to the special professorship in Reformed theology at Göttingen, set up with the help of American Presbyterian donations.[27] By the time that he left Safenwil for Göttingen in 1921, the manuscript of a revised Romans commentary was ready.[28] As he said, in what appears to modern scholars as hyperbole, the restructuring of the text was so drastic that, in comparison with the earlier edition, "hardly one stone remained upon the other."[29] With the publication of the 1922 edition, Barth's interpretation of Romans attained celebrity throughout the Protestant world, and, most important for our purposes, what Karl Barth wrote about the Word of God and about Paul began to play back into German Protestant interpretations of Luther.

Barth was not taken altogether seriously as an exegete of Paul. Although Bultmann was so impressed with his *Romans* as a theological statement that he worked with him in *Zwischen den Zeiten* in the immediately following years, he felt obliged to record at the start that Barth's "'*Kommentar*' violates [*vergewaltigt*] the individual life of the Epistle to Romans and the richness of Paul."[30] Adolf Schlatter, who gave the Romans commentary what Barth described as a "friendly rejection" from an orthodox standpoint, complained that Barth presented his readers with a letter to Romans that lacked any concern at all with the "Romans" (first-century Greeks and first-century Jews) to whom it was addressed.[31] Katherine Sonderegger, writing in 1992, points out that this assessment – that Barth was doing something other than biblical exegesis – although practically the unanimous consensus of his admirers and detractors, was tenaciously resisted by Barth himself.[32] In his preface to the English translation, he insisted: "In writing this book, I set out neither to compose a free fantasia upon the theme of religion, nor to evolve a philosophy of it. My sole aim was to interpret Scripture. I beg my readers not to assume from the outset – as many in Germany have assumed – that I am not interpreting Scripture at all, or rather, that I am interpreting it 'spiritually' ... I felt myself bound to the actual words of the text, and did not in any way propose to engage myself in free theologizing ... My book deals with one issue, and with one issue only. Did Paul think and speak in general and in detail in the manner in which I have interpreted him as thinking and speaking?"[33] But all this must be taken together with his complaint that liberal "awe in the presence of history" smothered the pastor's attempt to interpret Scripture and preach the gospel.[34] What he seems to have meant is that the historian's care to avoid anachronism interfered with his capacity to render classical texts relevant to the present. (Holl, although he would certainly never have expressed himself in this way, acted out such a notion in the difference of his Luther scholarship from his earlier method of studying Greek patristics.)

The importance of Barth's *Romans* is that he made "Paul" speak to Weimar Protestants about issues of deep concern to them. In a broad sense his was a Lutheran Paul (although at the time his reading of Luther was remarkably thin) whose God reveals and justifies himself by electing sinners, apart from the law. In Barth's *Romans* the law opposes the gospel, in that it demands a level of moral purity that is absolutely unattainable. It does so in order to convict human beings of sin and to proclaim to them that they may be accounted righteous by grace alone. This grace is bestowed by God through faith alone.[35]

The very epitome of religion is the notion of the Pharisee that people like him are better than others. The Pharisee, the do-gooder, the religious reformer, the man of higher sensibility, is the perverse antitype of the prophet, the one who speaks the Word of the Lord: "The prophets see what men in fact are: they see them, confronted with the ambiguity of the world, bringing forth the possibility of religion; they see them arrogantly and illegitimately daring the impossible and raising themselves to equality with God ... In light of the prophetic condemnation of this final achievement we perceive the condemnation also of all previous and lesser achievements. If God encounters and confronts men in religion, he encounters and confronts them everywhere."[36] Religion is the ultimate human hubris, reaching back through the Tower of Babel to the madness of the tempting devil in the Garden of Eden – *eritis sicut deus* (you will be just like God).[37] *Romans* is a thundering against the devilish presumption of the religious that they are somehow better. "Nothing must be retained of that illusion which permits a supposed religious or moral or intellectual experience to remove the only sure ground of salvation, which is the mercy of God. The illusion that some men have an advantage over others must be completely discarded. The words, *there is no distinction* need to be repeated and listened to again and again."[38]

Religion has the mark of death upon it: "Death is the meaning of religion: for when we are pressed to the boundary of religion, death pronounces the inner calm of simple and harmless relativity to be at an end. Religion is not at all to be 'in tune with the infinite' or to be 'at peace with oneself.' It has no place for refined sensibility or mature humanity ... Religion is an abyss; it is terror."[39] But the cross of Christ reveals the divine election to death, and life, in its tones of death, hell, and God-forsakenness. Predestination "conceals itself in the antimony of Adam and Christ, so as to reveal itself in their unity." Here Barth's later teaching of universal election is pointed to: "There is no fall from God in Adam, no sentence of death, that does not have its origin at the point where the human person reconciled with God in Christ is promised life." Interpreters of Barth have spoken of an odd joining of Plato and Paul, a joining of the beginning and the end of human history in a teaching of anamnesis.[40]

Concerned to drum upon the unbridgeable chasm between God and man, the total otherness of God, Barth's *Romans* leaves the Incarnation of Christ as paradox and mystery. In the Resurrection of Christ, God touches the world only "as a tangent touches a circle, that is, without touching it."[41] Or, in another thrust against religious historicism: "In so far as our world is touched in Jesus by the other world, it ceases to be capable of direct observation as history, time, or thing."[42] So the ultimate revelation of God is of his incomprehensibility:

The revelation which is in Jesus, because it is the revelation of the righteousness of God, must be the most complete veiling of his incomprehensibility. In Jesus, God becomes veritably a secret: He is made known as the Unknown, speaking in eternal silence: He protects himself from every intimate companionship and from all the impertinence of religion. He becomes a scandal to the Jews and to the Greeks foolishness. In Jesus the communication of God begins with a rebuff, with the exposure of a vast chasm, with the clear revelation of a great stumbling-block. "Remove from the Christian religion, as Christendom has done, its ability to shock, and Christianity, by becoming a direct communication, is altogether destroyed. It then becomes a tiny, superficial thing, capable neither of inflicting deep wounds nor of healing them; by discovering an unreal and merely human compassion, it forgets the qualitative distinction between God and man." (Kierkegaard) Faith in Jesus, like its theme, the righteousness of God, is the radical "Nevertheless."[43]

Kierkegaard, whom Barth cites here, was powerfully present in *Romans*, above all in its style.[44] The interpretation of Paul as an enemy of "religion" and moralism went back to him. Prominent also was Nietzsche's friend Franz Overbeck, whose attack on Christendom paralleled Kierkegaard's and added critical and epistemological substance to it.[45] Barth's Marburg teacher, Wilhelm Herrmann, had declared religious experience to be independent of knowledge and morality.[46] Overbeck trumped this assertion by insisting that people like Herrmann were simply moving religion from a historical to a psychological foundation, and that the second was no more compelling than the first. In a gesture of breathtaking audacity, Barth reversed Overbeck's skepticism into an affirmation of faith. *No* human foundation validated religion. Instead of pursuing further humankind's search for God, which had turned out to be a blind alley, let preachers proclaim the Word of God. "Let God be God" has often been emphasized as the theme of *Romans*;[47] in another sense it was "Let dogmaticians be dogmatic." *Romans* was the Magna Charta of dogmatic theology among Protestant modernists.

In the despair of the end of the First World War and the "lost generation" of the 1920s, Barth made a powerful assertion of the absolute claim of Christianity. Religion was humankind seeking God. It had failed, and it was bound to fail because there was no common ground between Creator and creature. *True* Christianity was not just another religion; it was God seeking humanity, proclaiming his Word to humanity. The professors, the reformers, the elevated minds, had failed to provide Europe with decent leadership, even decent examples. They were the Pharisees of their day: "All reformers are Pharisees. They have no sense of humour. Deprive a Total Abstainer, a really religious Socialist, a Churchman, or a Pacifist, of the *pathos* of moral indignation, and you have broken his backbone."[48] They forgot that in Adam's fall, we sinned all. They thought that they were better than other people, and for that very reason they were worse. Barth insisted that there was absolutely no resource in human nature that enabled God to connect with humankind. Hence he was allergic to Holl's interpretation of Luther as teaching a "religion of conscience." In his 1919 Romans commentary he viewed Paul and Luther as combining themes of God's declaring the justified sinner to be righteous and of God's cleansing him of sinfulness. By the 1922 edition all the regenerative soteriology (which contemporary New Testament and Reformation scholars think to be sound) was effaced from the commentary.[49] It gave too much glory to the human creature.

Those of us lacking revelation about the meaning of the Epistle to Romans have to rely on the best scholarship, with all the lack of absolute certainty that that implies. I have ventured a half-educated guess that such scholarship points off somewhere in the directions taken by Albert Schweitzer and Krister Stendhal. Barth produced a *Romans* in the Lutheran tradition of interpretation, but a Lutheran tradition "reinforced" by Kierkegaard and Overbeck and significantly modified by the Christian philosophic Idealism of his brother Heinrich Barth.[50] Urs von Balthasar insists that the spirit of Nietzsche's devastating epistemological critique of nineteenth-century knowledge brooded over these troubled waters. He reminds us that this was the age of expressionism, and he labels Barth's *Romans* "theological expressionism."[51] At any rate the Lutheranism of Barth's *Romans* was a "reinforced Lutheranism," a Lutheranism reinforced by the powerful self-critique of modernity.

Barth was self-conscious about this intellectual pedigree. He conscientiously acknowledged forebears in whom he was for the most part thinly read. He and those who saw things his way, he wrote in 1922, were "descendants of an ancestral line which runs back through Kierkegaard to Luther and Calvin, and so to Paul and Jeremiah." He identified with "The negation and loneliness of the life of Jeremiah in contrast to that of the kings, princes, priests and prophets of Judah, the keen unremitting opposition of Paul to *religion* as it was exemplified in Judaism, Luther's break, not with the impiety, but with the *piety* of the Middle Ages, Kierkegaard's attack on *Christianity*."[52] He was also very explicit about who did not belong in his line: Harnack and Ritschl did not need mentioning, but Schleiermacher, Melanchthon, and Erasmus were singled out for exclusion.[53] Barth's attitude to Augustine, as we shall see presently, was more complex than a simple rejection in the manner of the Holl school.

The dialectical element of *Romans* was present but muted (the faith of Abraham: "he heard the 'No' of God and understood it as his 'Yes.'")[54] It has been the intention here to avoid exaggerating it,[55] but undoubtedly the disposition to interpret Luther's theology as the faith in God's gracious Yes concealed under his wrathful No owes something to the vogue of the Dialectical Theology.

That Barth did not produce academic knowledge, as a professor should, but was on his way to becoming himself an object of study, as Harnack remarked, was not taken kindly by academic theologians. Holl wrote to Schlatter after the 1919 edition, expressing himself about Barth in terms that he saw no reason to revise later:

You select what fits with your own "experience," your "feeling," sometimes being quite free with the text, at other times slavishly literal. Then you polish it up in Nietzsche-style – I see Nietzsche everywhere in our contemporary theology from the conception of the Old Testament prophets to the idea of the Holy. Then you can posture as at the same time a man of the future and a conservative theologian. And you scorn academic method, logic, etc. in the name of the "irrational." I'm sufficiently patristic that intellectual rigour and seriousness are for me still part of the seriousness of faith.[56]

However that may be, Barth forced himself and his followers into German Protestant theology with a combination of his special vitality and brilliance and the resonance of his theology with the special needs of the Weimar era. Given the dogmatic resistance of the Dialectical Theologians to making historical distinctions among their heroes of faith, their image of Luther tended to merge with those of Paul, Kierkegaard, and even Jeremiah – and not only Barth but Luther, too, was "polished up in Nietzsche-style."

A peculiar source of information about this process in Barth's own thinking comes from the beginning of his lectures on Calvin, which were given in Göttingen in 1922, the year that the spectacular second edition of *Romans* appeared. The Calvin lectures were first published in 1993,[57] and it is necessary to receive this work with some of the caution that should have, but did not, accompany the publication of Luther's Romans lecture of 1515–16 in 1908. In both cases these were semi-private documents addressed to a small audience of students. They inform us of the state of mind of the lecturer but not of his public impact. Moreover, without losing sight of Barth's intelligence or his outstanding powers of expression, we should note that he was something of an amateur in this area – he was not drenched in Reformation source material as were Holl and Hirsch. He was working out his understanding of Luther, Calvin, and the Reformation, certainly not least under the influence of his own emerging theology, which had been advertised as a renewal of the theology of the Reformers. When we take all these reservations into account, what astonishes is how often Barth correctly anticipated future developments in Luther and Reformation studies.

His dialectics preserved him from the excessive glorification of the Reformers, their "mythologizing," that he recognized as the vogue of his day. Because God was wholly other than humankind, the Reformation could not be wholly other than the Middle Ages. This theological circumspection, he argued, corresponded with the sober self-assessment of the Reformers themselves. They felt that they had brought it about that the Word was proclaimed with special purity in their time; but they were not historicists, nor did they have notions of historical progress.[58] Hence they would never deny that the Word had been proclaimed, and proclaimed well, at other times. Indeed, the struggle between the Word and the world was unremitting.[59] "Whoever permits himself to be taught by the study of the Reformation what is truly old and what is truly new cannot set up a rigid, essentially mythological opposition between two ages, two historical groups ... As far as I can see, *the Reformers themselves* thought much more reservedly about the epoch-making character of their work than might have been expected, and than did later church historians."[60]

Nevertheless, Barth was convinced that for a metahistorical moment, and before their work was institutionalized and betrayed, the Reformers at least aspired to proclaim God's Word.[61] Since this was his own self-understanding, he described their mission in terms that made the Reformers, and Luther in particular, disappear behind Karl Barth.

They made the discovery that theology had to do with *God*. They made the great, shattering discovery of the *object* of all theology. Their secret was simply that they took the character of this object *seriously*. They called God *God*; they let God be *God*, the object that could not possibly through human handling, curiosity, or encroachment be made to become one object among others.[62]

Certainty about God is to be expected here, but of such a sort that it is the cause of the highest uncertainty about life. This makes our life a problem, a question, a task, a distress. It makes the Christian life a struggle for existence in which we are constantly confronted with the impossible and unbearable (which the scholastics knew how to evade so delicately, at least in their teaching), in which really God alone is willing and able to be our help.[63]

[In the Reformation] all the evil spirits of disharmony seemed to be aroused. All possibilities of quiet, academic exchange between one view and the other seemed out of the question. Everything became a matter of principle, so fearfully intense, so angry ... Delicate spirits such as Erasmus, who did not like this, withdrew as far as possible from the turmoil for this reason alone.[64]

Just as in *Romans*, Barth had rediscovered his whipping boys, the liberal theologians, in the Pharisees, so this time he was Luther, and Harnack and Troeltsch were spokesmen of the scholastic "theology of glory." He described the opposition between Reformation and scholastic theology as one that confronted a "theology of the cross" and a "theology of glory." In the conflict so described, he was squarely on the side of the Reformers.

This antimony was to have a solid future, particularly in contrasting Luther's theology with that of his scholastic predecessors. It was structured chiefly from Luther's Wittenberg "Theses against Scholastic Theology" (1517) and, even more importantly, from his theses at the Heidelberg Disputation (1518).[65] In short form in 1922 Barth foreshadowed the emphases of Walter von Loewenich's book *Luther's Theology of the Cross* of seven years later, the first independent contribution to Reformation studies by one of his students (although Loewenich was also subject to other theological influences).

The theology of glory was the medieval synthesis, the ladder from reason to revelation, leading upwards to the beatific vision of God, "the completion of reason through revelation and the comprehension of revelation through reason."[66] This medieval soteriology took everything into account, "nature and grace, man and God, freedom and dependence, proper human self-respect and humility in the sight of God, activity and receptivity, human merits and God's gifts, time and eternity. You will find hardly an element in later Reformation soteriology that is not also given its due in scholasticism, at some point powerfully emphasized and underscored."[67]

In opposition to this wonderful theological structure, the genuine, first-generation Reformation was a work of destruction, a "conscious, angry casting off" of the medieval theological style, "a totally wild, elemental event."[68] In blunt one-sidedness, Reformation theology expounded the idea that in all circumstances the human being stood under God's judgment. At the same time it stressed the mercy of God as revealed in the cross of Christ. Barth drummed on the 19th, 20th, and 21st theses of Luther's Heidelberg Disputation, sometimes translating, sometimes paraphrasing, as the core of his presentation of Reformation theology:

A proper theology sets its eyes upon the visible God, whose back is turned to us (*visibilia et posteriora Dei*) in suffering and the cross, and does not try to gaze upon his majesty and glory directly – those invisible things of God (*invisibilia Dei*) allegedly accessible to us through spiritual depth. For, as Luther grounded this sentence, it does not help anyone to know God in his glory and majesty if he does not know him in the abasement and disgrace of the cross ... The theologian of glory called bad good and good bad; the theologian of the cross calls things by their *proper* names. For, Luther declares, the theologian of glory fails to recognize God hidden in suffering (*Deus absconditus in passionibus*), therefore he prefers work to suffering, glory to the cross, power to weakness, wisdom to folly, and generally the bad to the good ... "God hidden in suffering" *is* the living God who loves us, the sinners, the bad, the foolish, the weak, in order to make us just, good, wise, and strong.[69]

In this way, Barth stressed divine election of the ungodly, the inaccessibility and mystery of God to human morality and knowledge, the *Deus absconditus in passionibus* revealed by the despairing Christ on the cross.

He identified fully with this dialectical, paradoxical, Kierkegaardian Luther:

Whoever clearly understands that the Middle Ages indeed knew the vertical too, but lived totally in the horizontal, while Luther knew the horizontal too, but lived totally in the vertical – or to put it more precisely, lived in the breakthrough of the vertical through the horizontal – such a person no longer is surprised by the sharp Either-Or that had to take place, by the shattering of the security of life which came to pass as a result of the Reformation, by the fragmentary and incomplete character of its theological writings, by the meagreness of its metaphysics, by the atmosphere of wrath that lay over the whole first half of the sixteenth century and only went away when the spirit of the Reformation, too, had vanished.[70]

Certainly, Luther sometimes suggested that the Reformation of his day had not come, that he was only a pre-Reformer like Hus or Wycliffe, who were "sons of a transition period, just as we today are possibly once again." These pre-Reformers, although they lacked glory, nevertheless maintained their dignity: "And dignity is probably the only thing that we can strive for before the forum of history. The other is neither goal nor task, but grace."[71] Truly, glory was owing to God alone; but it is impossible not to suspect Barth in 1922 of assessing himself as a world-historical figure – by the grace of God, to be sure.

As previously remarked, Barth made a theological principle of denying the essential historical discontinuity between the Middle Ages and the Reformation. On the subject of medieval traditions that continued into the Reformation, he offered a bundle of intuitions that strike us at a later stage of Reformation research as impressively perceptive. On Augustine and the medieval Augustinian tradition, Barth parted from the Luther Renaissance's disparagement of the church father (which, as we have seen, had distinct foundations in theological liberalism). "Where Augustine had an influence, even a strongly diluted one, there glowed under the ashes a remembrance of the vertical."[72] The late-medieval Augustinian tradition of Thomas Bradwardine and Gregory of Rimini was a starting point for Luther. Oddly, unaware of the late-medieval efforts to de-Platonize the Augustinian tradition, Barth affirmed both the Platonic and the Pauline elements in Augustine's writings, just as Plato had an incongruous presence in Barth's Romans commentary.[73] Even more striking was his insistence that the late-medieval theology of Duns Scotus and William of Ockham, with its pronounced theocentrism and "its critical questioning of the ladder from reason to revelation" so typical of the theology of glory, was a legitimate part of Luther's and Calvin's pedigree. Ockham raised some of the same issues as Calvin, if in an unserious "playful and speculative" manner. Nevertheless, even the speculations about the *potentia absoluta* of God had as their underlying purpose the strengthening of the *potentia ordinata*, the actual, historical revelation of God.[74] Reading the Barth of 1922, one sees anticipations of an interpretation that gained credit only with Heiko Oberman.

In his brief comments on Luther and mysticism, Barth did not fall prey to the disposition of his time and subsequent generations of Luther scholarship to turn late-medieval mysticism into an anthropocentric theology, a full-blown anti-Lutheran heresy. Truly, the mystical disciplines, as a method to make contact with God in his immediacy, were the highest and most dangerous sort of works righteousness. But the younger Luther's favourable comments about Johannes Tauler and the anonymous author of *German Theology* could not simply be brushed aside.[75] The exaggerated and rapturous language of these spokesmen of German mysticism came about, as Luther was half-aware, "because they found themselves in the dilemma of wanting to say something that cannot be said even in the strongest words and that nevertheless they felt compelled to express in some way: the presence, the occurrence, the intrusion, the being, of the connection between human beings and God."[76] They wanted to speak out the Word of God. Barth's caution about an undialectical opposition (or an undialectical linkage) between Luther and those mystics whom he liked and continued to speak well of throughout his life could very well serve as a maxim for continuing scholarship into this as yet unresolved issue.

The humanists of the Renaissance were according to Barth in no sense forerunners of Luther.[77] Here he expressed a perhaps incorrect perception that was shared by everyone in his day – Harnack, Troeltsch, Holl, Althaus. However, he surmounted this universal error (if such it be) dialectically. Zwingli and Calvin were Renaissance men who, whether or not they got it from Luther, shared his concept of the saving Word of God come down from above.[78] The fact that Luther was a monk and they were Renaissance men, however, brought it about that they, not he, worked out the necessary business of applying the Reformation insight to life in the world.

Here, as in the whole focus of the lectures on Calvin, Barth expressed himself as a Swiss Reformed among the German Lutherans: "We are different among other things from the Lutherans in that we, as the disciples of Luther's most loyal disciples, are as unwilling as they to detract from Luther, while they in support of the reputation of their man are never quite able to avoid open or secret polemic against our men."[79] There follows some sophistry about how, unlike mere sycophants such as Melanchthon, Zwingli and Calvin were able to further develop the teaching of their master, Luther, and thus were his "most loyal disciples."[80] The opposition of Luther and Calvin-Zwingli was presented in dialectical form.

The tragedy of Lutheranism is that, despite its *greater* closeness to the Kingdom of heaven, it has *no* force in the *world* and in this way the *Kingdom of heaven*, however close it may be, becomes a *questionable* presence ... The tragedy of the Reformed is that in their case something great *happens* in the world but that in this way the Kingdom of heaven is moved *further away*, and in this way even the *greatest* events in the world become a *questionable* presence. Lutherans and Reformed really have no cause to set upon each other with instructions and reproaches. Normally they can only bear together what in various ways is their common dilemma and common promise.[81]

Barth took the side of Holl against Troeltsch on the issue of whether Luther had an unresolved conflict in his ethics between the Sermon on the Mount and natural law.[82] Nevertheless, whatever fine things Luther wrote about ethics, they were a secondary matter for him, a necessary corollary of his experience of justification by faith, but only that.[83] Conversely, "Calvin's total Christianity is built on the necessity that *for the honour of God something must happen.*"[84] This is what is primary for him, and the fact that he insists so rigidly on double predestination betrays the fact that individual soteriology was the "threatened point" of his theology, the area that needed buttressing.[85] Luther took God's grace and mercy for granted; Calvin had to drum on predestination essentially because it was for him secondary to work in the world for the glory of God. " 'The just person lives by *faith!*' says Luther. Yes, Calvin answers and uses the same words, only he changes the emphasis and says, 'The just person *lives* by faith!' The third possibility, the one statement that says both, seems to be for all times the theological squaring of the circle, the impossible possibility, which in the strictest sense it is reserved to God alone to proclaim."[86] Although in 1922 Barth used this dialectical contrast between Reformed and Lutheran primarily to make the broad theocentric point that all historical theologies of the Reformation fell short of the Word of God, later it became for him an explanation of the insufficiencies of German Protestants in the politics of the thirties and forties. He had no doubt that the Third Reich was a judgment on Lutheranism.

On the Holl-Troeltsch controversy about the modernity of the Reformation, Barth's position was a very dialectical plague on both the contending spirits. The Middle Ages had more in common with modernity than either period with the Reformation. Goethe was closer in spirit to Dante than to Luther.[87] "Modernity is only the Middle Ages become clever and tired"; the theology of Harnack and Troeltsch is an inferior copy of the theology of glory of Thomas Aquinas. "The Reformation, and the medieval and modern elements that belong to it, is both anti-medieval and anti-modern. Its front cuts right across the opposing fronts of these two adversaries."[88]

In Barth himself, revealed in these unpublished lectures, the theology of his *Romans* produced a mixture of polemic, insight, and confusion about Luther and the Reformation. The polemic is least important perhaps. Since Barth's theology evolved, the dogmatic assertion that Luther and the Reformation stood "between the ages"[89] faded in importance even for him. Doubtless, the most problematic consequence of his polemics was that he sold his generation on the notion that shrill polemics were the very essence of the Reformation. The contrast of "theology of the cross" and "theology of glory" was adapted from Luther himself, but the question became one of whether 1518 was really a good vantage point from which to assess his theology – whether, for instance, he meant the same thing by the *Deus absconditus* in 1518 as he did in 1525 in *De Servo Arbitrio*. Here Barth advanced a genuinely fruitful series of problems for Luther studies. His mainly theological insight that there was something spurious about the notion of an almost absolute discontinuity between Reformation and Middle Ages led him to make remarkably sensible suggestions about Luther's relation to Augustine, late scholasticism, and German mysticism. In this area, Barth was way ahead of the field, but his was a brilliant intuition lost on Weimar Reformation studies. At this distance his insistence on putting Plato together with Paul and Augustine can only be described as strange – a mischief-making flaw in his perspective glasses going back to the influence of his philosopher brother, Heinrich, on his Romans commentary. Fixated on Lutherans and Reformed and their *Unierten* enemy brotherhood in German churchmanship, Barth was limited in his perception of the Reformation. Although self-consciously Reformed, he shared the Union church's prejudices against Melanchthon, not to speak of Melanchthon's older friend Erasmus. Those whom Luther called "Schwärmer" were even further outside the circle of Barth's attention than was the case for Holl.[90] Troeltsch's peripheral vision on the Reformation was much better than that of Barth or Holl. Still, Barth did not bring such zeal to the project of shunning and excommunicating whole areas previously thought to belong to the province of Reformation studies as did his contemporary Dialectical Theologian Friedrich Gogarten.

Gogarten was above all a polemicist. It is a commonplace that in the 1920s the Dialectical Theology was more negative than positive, more concerned with anti-liberal theological critique than constructive dogmatics.[91] Barth admitted as much. Gogarten held it against him that he changed; so in the 1930s Barth too became a target of Gogarten's polemics. Gogarten polemicized against a wide assortment of theologians – Troeltsch, Elert, Holl, and Hirsch – as well as profane historian Gerhard Ritter,[92] when he ventured to write a Luther biography. Barth's theology ultimately affected Luther scholarship as a provocative stimulus to wrestle with his ideas, some wayward but most fruitful. Gogarten's impact consisted more in attacks from without that Reformation studies had to absorb. We are just now putting behind us various ideas of what Reformation studies should *not* do to which Gogarten was a major contributor.

He shared many of the background influences that shaped Barth, but there were important differences, and the two were uneasy allies from the start. Gogarten was a student of Troeltsch and a careful reader of his writings on historicism. Since history was a finite human project, the young Gogarten, who had a strong mystical orientation, early concluded that religious truth was not to be found in history.[93] His attraction to the Swiss Religious Social movement, going back to the pre-war years, first brought Barth to his attention. In fact, the rhetorical attack on "religion," as opposed to faith in the living God, which was very important in the usage of both Barth and Gogarten, went back to the social resentment against upper-class organized religion of the Swiss Religious Socialist Hermann Kutter.[94]

However, unlike Barth, Gogarten experienced no religious crisis with the outbreak of the First World War. He thought it proper to cultivate a distinctively German Christianity in the war years and hoped that wartime suffering would deepen the inner piety of the nation. Such suffering, like the suffering of Christ on the cross, might be a moment of revelation of the eternal God in the human condition.[95] Hence, their common Religious Socialism notwithstanding, during the war years Gogarten cultivated a piety that Barth would have abhorred. But contrary to his hopes, in the final war years and in the collapse of 1918, Gogarten, like Holl, saw nothing but the disolution of true religion. In late 1919 he came to the conclusion that there was nothing of the divine either in human history or in the human person's inner self. God was "totally other" than humankind. He revealed himself only as the negation of all human history, knowledge, and inwardness.[96]

The slogan that, at the beginning of the 1920s, one age had played itself out and another had not yet begun, that the Germany of the new Weimar constitution was "between the ages," was articulated by Gogarten in a famous article published in 1920 in the *Christian World*.[97] This perceived eschatological moment was to be one of revelation: "The space is open for questions about God. The ages fell apart and now time stands still. For a moment? For an eternity? Must we not now be able to hear God's Word? Must we not now be able to see his hand at his work?"[98] Above all, "Zwischen den Zeiten" embroidered the theme of a theological generation unwilling to continue the work of its predecessors because it no longer believed in what they had done. The establishment liberal theology had taught the young that everything was a product of the flux of history: "Now we draw the conclusion. Everything that is in any way a human work not only originates; it also passes away." The alienation of the young from their teachers was so great, declared Gogarten, that Nietzsche, Kierkegaard, Meister Eckhard, and Lao-Tse became their real teachers.[99] With this pronouncement, he first attracted Barth's approving attention as a Lutheran common spirit across the confessional divide.

Gogarten's totem, if not his teacher, was Martin Luther. This idea is expressed most generously by Jürgen Moltmann, who says that Luther was "the basic source of Gogarten's theology." Friedrich Duensing, in a book on Gogarten and Werner Elert, provides a necessary elaboration:

Gogarten's relation to [Luther] forcibly confirms the fact that understanding of Luther is always more or less "system oriented," that is, relative to a standpoint in theology or church history. To be sure, this applies to Gogarten in a particularly pronounced manner, because after the early controversy with Holl he did not really bother with the continuing academic Luther research, and because his more existential, communicative access to Luther was virtually unrestrained by a personal historical-philological methodology – as is perhaps the prerogative of a systematic theologian.[100]

In short, although Luther was very important to Gogarten, Gogarten's approach to him was sovereignly dogmatic.

From Gogarten's standpoint the different ways in which he used Luther at various stages of his theological development were evidence of his growing understanding of the Reformer. In the pre-war years he looked at Luther in the manner of Ritschl and Harnack, as divided within himself between the traditional Christianity of the ancient creeds and a "new piety that is not turned away from the world but wills to rule and shape the world."[101] In the early 1920s he picked up a sneering comment by Holl's friend Adolf Jülicher about his "holy egoism" and turned it into a slogan, the "holy egoism of the Christian." Here he used a text from Luther's *Commentary on the Magnificat* (1521) to make his point: the Christian should be self-absorbed, "as if he and God were alone in heaven and on earth, and God occupied himself with no one but him."[102]

The transcendent God of the early Dialectical Theology was somewhat difficult to relate to the fundamental Christian doctrine of the Incarnation. In 1923 and 1924 first Gogarten and then Barth elaborated their theologies with traditionally orthodox Christologies. Gogarten did so in a very Lutheran way, concentrating on Luther's distinction between the law and the gospel in his *Commentary on Galatians* of 1535.[103] Because in the Incarnation, Jesus Christ redeemed the finite world, he freed human persons from the law's demand for an unattainable holiness. The good news that in Jesus God became human freed the human being from the essence of sinfulness, the aspiration to be like God. Holl's emphasis on Luther's as a religion of ethical obligation, according to Gogarten, stood Luther on his head. It made his religion focus on the law instead of the gospel.

Although Holl was the target of Gogarten's polemics, they were joined by a systematic polemical opposition to Troeltsch's ideas about the connection of Protestantism to the modern world. Troeltsch's celebration of Protestantism and modernity as the religion and culture of freedom was a red flag to Gogarten's bull. In 1924 he published an edition of Luther's *De Servo Arbitrio* (On the Bondage of the Will) with a long concluding essay, "Protestantismus und Wirklichkeit" (Protestantism and Reality).[104] Here he opposed *Bindung* (connectedness) to Troeltsch's modern freedom. By 1932, just before Gogarten greeted Hitler's accession to power, the appeal to *The Bondage of the Will* had become stronger. Now *Hörigkeit* (servile bondage) replaced *Bindung* in his usage.[105]

In his polemics against Troeltsch, Gogarten introduced the particularly wilful notion of the *unreformatorisch* in the Reformation era. Whatever Troeltsch valued was not really part of the Reformation: continuities to modernity were to be found, when one looked closely, "not with genuine Protestantism but with the Anabaptists, sectarians, mystics, and humanists of the Reformation era." Since Troeltsch viewed Erasmus as an ancestor of neo-Protestantism, Gogarten used Luther's attack on Erasmus to establish "that a theology of historical-critical thought and sensibility going back to Erasmus cannot have any connection with the Protestantism of the Reformation."[106] Gogarten's influence tended towards establishing a doctrinal test to distinguish a "theologically correct" "genuine Protestantism" as the only proper subject matter of Reformation studies.

What offended Gogarten most of all, however, was Troeltsch's belief that neo-Protestantism was, with all necessary qualifications, the heir to the Reformation. What Troeltsch viewed as historical continuity, Gogarten declared to be apostasy. Neo-Protestantism "has nothing to do with the Reformers."[107] The "modern spirit," according to Gogarten, is in no sense "the legitimate continuation and development of Protestantism."[108] On the other hand, by destroying the unified ecclesiastical culture of Europe, the Reformation "broke a breach in the bronze wall with which the medieval Catholic church enclosed the world."[109] The consequence was not that the secular world accepted its connectedness or bondage to God's higher reality, as Luther wanted, but that "modern culture and its ideal of inner-worldliness and freedom"[110] were set loose. Modernity lacked the Reformers' sense of sin; but at the present hour, inwardly shaken, it might at last be ready to face what they really had to say.[111]

The point that most aroused Gogarten about Troeltsch's celebration of modernity was not the doings of the Western master peoples, the British and the Americans, or humanism and the sectarians – all that he could simply exclude – but Troeltsch's description of the German *Sonderweg* itself as "Lutheran idealism," a living synthesis of Lutheranism and the modern German philosophic tradition. That that, in Troeltsch's terms, was "the translation of Protestant Christianity into general truths of reason"[112] – the notion that such a translation could occur – was what goaded Gogarten into reissuing *The Bondage of the Will*. As a philosophic tradition, Idealism denied the knowability of the object and thus made all knowledge subjective. Consequently, God can only be known as immanent, "in us." This, said Gogarten, was no less than the rebellion of the creature against its Creator described in Genesis 3.[113] As he went on to analyze Kantian ethics, his point was that a morality based on human freedom, the person following a law which he gave himself in his own freedom, made the modern relevance of *The Bondage of the Will* doubly clear.[114] As Luther wrote against Erasmus, freedom of the will was an exclusively divine attribute, and there could be no greater blasphemy than for human beings to claim it for themselves.

Following this statement came polemics against the human penchant to assign nobility to human love – eros. This love was a self-intoxication of the ego: "In eros the ego seeks itself, and again and again only itself." Expressions by Luther about the Christian's identity as a bubbling spring of selfless love, passing on to friend and foe the self-giving love of Christ, are brought in here to make the distinction between selfish pagan eros and generous divine agape. The love of Corinthians 13 that "seeketh not its own" is contrasted to the ultimately wicked (and usually *obviously* wicked) erotic mania of modern times.[115] Thus the rake's progress of modern man is shown as a movement from breaking the barriers of ecclesiastical culture to seeking God within one's soul, into the depths of solipsism and narcissism. Toward the end of this diatribe, Gogarten made it explicit that he opposed political freedom as well as personal freedom: "This freedom applies not only to the person's inner self but also to the social and governmental structuring of human life. The notion that freedom is the special characteristic of Protestantism must be rejected in both cases."[116] It is a mark of the differences between Barth and Gogarten that the events of the early 1930s made Barth see that there was something wrong with this holy frenzy against freedom, but that they had no such effect on Gogarten.

Troeltsch did not live to read this assault against him by Gogarten, but he was aware of the younger scholar and wrote a brief comment observing the similarities between him and Kierkegaard, "An Apple from Kierkegaard's Tree":

The encounter with the Absolute, its radical opposition to the world, the self-condemnation of the individual person in this absolute situation and the disdain of all mediation between God and the world [which, according to Kierkegaard, is the essential interest and work of all churches] – that is the Christendom of the Absolute or of the Either-Or, of authenticity and depth of soul, of historical reality and of the ideal. Absolutely nothing else can be brought into connection with it. While Kierkegaard was above all opposed to the churches, Gogarten turned against culture and its social demands and learned concepts, which are all either historical or intellectual ... This is substantially concealed by appeals to Jesus or to Luther ... [Kierkegaard] struggled for a purely individual and abstract, purely personal and absolutely radical Christendom. His early death, his total loneliness and peculiarity, which seemed to go together with a psychopathic disposition, spared him the necessity to work out the positive, affirmative side of his religion or to relate it to the world in some constructive way ... Ultimately he produced only polemic after polemic and nothing positive; in relation to himself he had only the self-condemnation that arose out of the "absolute situation" vis-à-vis God ... Gogarten experienced ... the loss of the radical Either-Or, the radical Christian dualism – for that is what he meant by "the Absolute." I can very well understand that feeling and I suspect that his psychological disposition is somewhat similar to Kierkegaard's.[117]

Another observer made the point that, while Luther taught the radical sinfulness of individual persons, the Gogarten polemics asserted the sinfulness of "whole intellectual traditions and cultural programs."[118] (This distinction may be overdrawn; one needs only to think of Luther's condemnation of the Papacy, the *Schwärmer*, the Jews, or even the legal profession.) Certainly, the attack on German philosophic Idealism as the denial of Gogarten's transcendent God was very close to his heart.[119]

His sharp sensitivity to the taint of neo-Kantianism in the German Protestant theology of his time led Gogarten from attacking Troeltsch to attacking Troeltsch's enemies in the Luther Renaissance. In the previous chapter we have cited Gogarten's witness to Karl Holl's idiosyncratic beliefs about Luther, Jesus, and God.[120] It is characteristic of him that, while Walter Bodenstein presented this view of Holl's as a private religious insight guarded from public view by the man's characteristic reticence and Erich Seeberg regarded it as a debt to Harnack's theological tradition, Gogarten announced that he had discovered a Christological heresy in Holl. That Holl, who had at that time had made his full peace with his church, limited himself to rebuffing the insult seems only appropriate.

Gogarten's polemical attention extended from Holl to Hirsch. At issue was the Luther Renaissance's rebuttal to Denifle, that Luther's teaching on justification was not a teaching about God's "self-deception" because in it God not only *declared* the sinner righteous; he *made* him righteous. This view, which Luther scholars justified easily enough with citations from his lecture on Romans of 1515–16, was not countered at that time by the retort that these were the views of the early, "Catholic Luther." Gogarten did not bother with merely historical issues of that sort. Instead, he talked down to the scholars from the eminence of Luther's theology of law and gospel. Unwilling that Luther should be measured by the belittling standard of Kantian ethics, he trumpeted a Luther whose faith was "beyond good and evil." (As Holl said, "I see Nietzsche everywhere in our theology!")[121] "For God revealed himself to the Reformers in the forgiveness of sins. Forgiveness of sins, however, is not an ethical principle, but rather the break with the reality of the ethical. It is beyond good and evil."[122]

Gogarten's theological concern, which for a long time "solved" the question of whether Luther could have had a "real" connection with mysticism (overshadowing Barth's more empirical intuitions, discussed earlier in this chapter), was the denial of any positive anthropological resource which might have been a coupling point for an immanent God. The rigorous transcendent religion of the Dialectical

Theology was dogmatically assigned to Luther because it was true religion. "And therefore we oppose religion, culture, and morality, because we oppose this pretension and this striving for a direct, unmediated contact – that means a contact based on works – between the man and his most noble part and God. And we think that in this struggle against 'the teaching about the best piece of the man, through which a person is raised above the kingdom of Christ and the kingdom of Satan, so that he is a God over God and a Lord of Lords' (Luther, *De Servo Arbitrio*), we act in personal agreement with the Reformation."[123] As always, Gogarten got personal. He accused Emanuel Hirsch of the ultimate sin of wanting to be like God[124] because he made the classic mistake of theological method – confusing law and gospel. The gospel, Gogarten wrote: "is no law and no command, rather a gift, a promise; and because it is a gift and a promise, it is not something attained or fallen short of, also not the unreachable goal that human activity aspires to; but rather, it cuts sharply through and across each deed in the same manner, whether what is done is moral or immoral."[125]

In 1935, two years into the new political order, Gogarten had the chance to prepare a biography of Martin Luther for *Die großen Deutschen: Neue deutsche Biographie*. It was an odd biography, almost an attack on the genre. Only a page and a half of the fifteen-page article gave a terse summary of Luther's life; the rest was all theology and theological psychology.[126] Barth had been reserved about the superlatives that Luther assigned himself;[127] Gogarten seemed to want to surpass them in hyperbole: "No one since the days of the apostles had a deeper understanding, a sharper perception, a more devouring experience of the transcendence of God than Luther."[128] "Deeper and more radically than anyone of his day – indeed, than anyone since the days of primitive Christianity – he knew about the uncanniness of the world, which threatened to destroy the person who was aware of it in the innermost ground of his being."[129] Gogarten wrote of this sense of the uncanniness of the world, which was the expression of divine wrath, and of course about Luther's *Anfechtungen*, which were a continuing aspect of his experience of grace: "not only at the beginning but always when someone experiences mercy, there comes the bitterness, the fear, the accompanying suffering under which the old man sighs, because in this experience he must subject himself to bitter death."[130] Luther's secret, according to Gogarten, was that he shunned the peaceful conscience offered by Catholic penance. He persevered in "that abyss of despair, which is so full of salvific power and so near to grace."[131] One thinks of the Kierkegaard of Troeltsch's description, who "had only the self-condemnation that arose out of the 'absolute situation,' "[132] the despair which he insisted was dialectically adjacent to faith. But Gogarten said that Luther persisted in the abyss of despair because he found the crucified Christ there.

When Luther speaks of the Christ who died on the cross for the sins of the world and through his death redeemed human beings from their "tyrants" – death, sin, and the devil – he speaks of the Christ who stood before God in his most naked self in a way no other person did. When the Scripture says of Christ that he was placed under the law and became a curse, Luther understands that to mean not only that Christ has to obey the commands of the law and that as the Crucified he was accused in the eyes of men, but that he tasted death and hell, and that in his conscience he knew himself to be accursed of God, so that he was terrified and in flight from the face of God. He wants that taken as the full truth and does not want it watered down. In this way Christ is absolutely human … , standing in the most extreme forsakenness before God, finding all creatures "nothing but God and the wrath of God."[133]

This powerful theme of the theology of the cross, important also to Barth as the distinction between medieval and Reformation theology, is given psychological depth by Gogarten. Certainly, it has a basis in Luther, but one is inclined to see this theological psychology as bearing the special trademark of the intense early twentieth century. For English readers the ties that connect it to Gordon Rupp's *The Righteousness of God* are unmistakable. After his brush with Holl, Gogarten did not bother himself with the academic approach to the Reformation, but his theology built up around it a field of force into which later academic studies ordered themselves as if by inertia. Whoever has read Anders Nygren's *Agape and Eros* or Philip Watson's *Let God Be God* should ponder how much of Gogarten they contain. And his exclusionary principle about what should be left out in the study of "genuine Protestants" is still around to the present day, although perhaps reduced to a rearguard action. Stephen Ozment's *The Protestants* gives a reductionist view of the German Reformation, concentrating on Lutheran and Reformed and ignoring Erasmus and the Peasants' War, Anabaptists, and Spiritualists.

The rupture of the bond between Barth and Gogarten was in part a result of a growing belief on both sides that the confessional differences between Reformed and Lutheran were, after all, important. When Barth was offered the special professorship in Reformed theology at Göttingen, his Reformed identity was weak. At the time he described himself as "moving rapidly towards Lutheranism."[134] But just as Gogarten drew heavily on Luther in developing his Christology in 1923, when Barth began working out a dogmatic Christology in the following year, his inherited Reformed standpoint became of increasing importance.

As a prototype for his lectures on dogmatics at Göttingen, he employed Heinrich Heppe's orthodox book of Reformed dogmatics.[135] The principle that had been so important to Zwingli in polemics against the Lutherans – *finitum non capax infiniti* (the finite is not capable of the infinite) – guided Barth in constructing a genuinely Reformed Christology.[136] God as the eternal Son in the Incarnation assumed a human nature without any alteration of his divine nature, which maintained its independent being.[137] The Lutheran conception of the *communio naturarum* (the community of natures), which allowed the human nature of Christ to share some of the qualities of the divine nature, such as ubiquity, and which supported Luther's distinctive ideas about the real presence of the body of Christ in the Lord's Supper, violated Barth's Reformed Christology.[138] For him there could be no salvation from the creature and only God could reveal God. Jesus in his human nature is the veil of God's revelation. In the same Reformed sense all canonical Scriptures, not a particular theological line within the Scriptures, are the veil of God's revelation. Contrary to Luther's view of God in *On the Bondage of the Will*, according to which an uncanny hidden God *(Deus absconditus)* lurks behind and beyond the revealed God *(Deus revelatus)* of the cross of Christ, for Barth there is no God other than the revealed God of the Incarnation.[139]

In his lectures Barth said that these points of controversy among the Reformers arose from different aspects of the New Testament, and that, although they were matters which people should decide about, they were no cause for divisions in the church.[140] Still, in the judgment of contemporary theologian Gerhard Ebeling, in a sense the quarrels of the sixteenth century were returning as Barth gradually turned his Reformed dogmatics against Luther.[141] Gogarten based his theology, at least ostensibly, from 1923 onward on Luther's distinction between law and gospel. But there was much else about Gogarten's style and his ideas that rankled with Barth. The common journal of the Dialectical Theology, *Zwischen den Zeiten*, in 1923 began, adopting the title of Gogarten's famous essay. He had wanted to call it *Das Wort*,[142] which struck Barth as blasphemy, because only God could speak the Word of God. In the pages of the journal, Gogarten praised Oswald Spengler's *Decline of the West*, which put him in the company of right-wing theologians such as Werner Elert. For his part, Barth disliked the book and complained that Spengler had given theological respectability to the notion of fate.[143]

Barth was unlike Gogarten (and Bultmann and Brunner) in that he never fully accepted Kierkegaard's theological subjectivism.[144] Like

Holl, after an early period of fascination with the Danish thinker, he gradually wearied of him. For Gogarten, however, the Kierkegaardian style of polemical encounter was the essence of theology, and he consciously wedded it to existentialist philosophy. This idea of an encounter with God as a kind of predisposition for faith seemed to Barth too much a return to the renounced preoccupation with human subjectivity that he had learned as a student from Wilhelm Herrmann.[145]

From the standpoint of Gogarten in 1929–30, in leaving behind existential polemics for rational dogmatics, Barth had abandoned his prophetic persona. But Barth responded by assuming a "dialectical," and somewhat ironic, attitude to his old self:

I was and am a regular theologian at whose disposal stands not the Word of God but at best a "doctrine of the Word of God." I feel myself neither justified nor obligated to persist in the demeanour of the prophet, in the attitude of the breakthrough, in which some clearly perceived me for a moment and in which they now want to perceive me again and again, to their joy and comfort … I am not conscious of having ever done anything else than – old? new theology? – in any case, theology, whereas the Word of God spoke for Himself or did not speak when and where it pleased God.[146]

Is it reading too much into this statement to suggest an inference that the Word of God was (perhaps?), by the grace of God, spoken in the Romans commentary of 1922? In any case, here Barth insists that there is no formulaic method for setting up shop as a prophet and launching into the prophetic discourse: "Thus saith the Lord."

Although he wearied of his erstwhile Lutheran ally Gogarten, for a long time Barth avoided criticizing the great "Dr Martin." In the first publication of *Church Dogmatics* in 1932, he cited Luther often and always with approval and veneration – indeed, in terms of the frequency and weight of his citations, this marked the high point of Barth's reception of Luther. Moved to Bonn University in 1930 and become a theological celebrity in the German Evangelical Church, he began his *Church Dogmatics* in an effort to reach out to the Evangelical Union.[147] In terms that he had once used in the Calvin lecture of 1922, he reconciled Calvin and Luther according to the principle "To understand Luther – to be sure also against Luther! … as if in Calvin he particularly renewed and continued himself."[148] Ironically, this is just exactly the approach that Karl Holl had taken with Luther on the topics of predestination and divine monergism – to the horror of the confessional Lutherans. Then without warning in 1935, in a famous address on "the gospel and the law," Barth responded to Gogarten's drumming on Luther's teaching of law and gospel by implicitly criticizing the Reformer himself.[149] Adolf Hitler had in the meantime come between Barth and Luther, and Barth had been expelled from Germany for refusing to take an oath to the Führer. In a statement from the first months of the Second World War, he attacked "the error of Martin Luther about the relation of law and gospel ... through which [the German people's] heathen nature ... has been ideologically transfigured, confirmed, and strengthened," as well as the baleful influence on modern theology of Luther's teaching about the humanity of the Redeemer, which called into question the ancient Christian doctrine that humankind's redemption comes from God alone.[150] More soberly, in 1938 Barth gave another dialectical twist to his exegetical wrestling with Luther and Calvin: "Calvin is a teacher of the church in a purer sense [than Luther], since it was his gift more than Luther's to lead the church to Holy Scripture with his distinctive teaching, to connect it to the substance of things, and only in seeking the substance of things to connect the church to himself."[151] But Barth himself was, after all, much more a theologian of Luther's style than of Calvin's.

Karl Barth's critique of Martin Luther belongs to the years after he left Germany and is out of the purview of our study.[152] Undoubtedly, however, it had its roots in his turn to Reformed dogmatics, his rejection of any existential philosophical grounding for theology, and the disintegration of the Dialectical Theology, all of which occurred in the Weimar years. It is more than possible that, just as Friedrich Gogarten could never distinguish between Luther's theology and his own, construing all of his twists and turns as a better understanding of Luther, so Karl Barth eventually saw too much of Gogarten when he tried to understand Luther.

Barth and Gogarten confronted the historicist theology of cultural Protestantism more directly than Holl and his students. Like the Luther Renaissance, they invoked a theocentric dogmatics against the historical approach of the older generation and claimed it to be the word of Luther as well as the Word of God. The Dialectical Theology, however, provoked scholarly discourse on Luther's theology of the Word and his theology of the cross. Its polemical manner created antagonism between it and all the other theological schools of its time, including the Luther Renaissance. Its relation to Luther and German nationalism could be either critical in the manner of Barth or simply dogmatically affirmative in the manner of Gogarten. It related dialectically to Reformation studies, stimulating them in new directions in Barth's manner or narrowing them according to Gogarten's prescriptions. In the Luther Renaissance and the Dialectical Theology, dogmatics shaped church history – covertly, in Holl's manner, or overtly, as with Barth and Gogarten. Among the confessional Lutheran theologians at Erlangen University, to whom we now turn, dogmatics was more firmly anchored in the traditional Lutheran confessions and paradoxically *less* likely to infringe upon an independent historical study of Martin Luther. But the confessional Lutheran theologians were, like the Luther Renaissance, greatly concerned to be relevant to the cause of post-war German nationalism.

4 The Confessional Lutherans at Erlangen

Werner Elert and Paul Althaus, both professors at Erlangen University in the Weimar years, are the most conservative of our protagonists. Both politically and theologically conservative, they appeared to Holl students such as the young Robert Stupperich as "old fashioned."[1] From their own point of view, however, they were determined to participate in adapting Lutheranism to the needs of their time. A stand-pat orthodoxy taught in the traditional manner of Melanchthon and the *loci communes* was not a satisfactory theology for the twentieth century.[2] The authoritative confessions of Lutheranism had not lost their authority, but they could not be merely repeated; they had to be applied. The New Testament was the preeminent witness to the faith of the Christian community; but the biblical writings and the creeds did not in themselves possess authority, nor did any theological interpreter – not even such a great one as Luther.[3] Christian dogma was inherently problematic because "it is entangled in the contingency of history."

The basic assumption of all dogmatics, that dogma nevertheless contains universally valid truth, gives the dogmatic theologian the special task, on the one hand, to regard traditional dogma as given on account of the axiomatic assumption of its universal validity; however, on the other hand, to subject it to critical examination because of the historical contingency of its emergence. If this second task is seriously undertaken, he must as a matter of principle consider the possibility that traditional dogma rests on false premises, or for some other reason contains not truth but error. If this should in fact turn out to be the inescapable conclusion which he arrives at, then he must draw the same consequences that Luther did in the case of medieval dogma.[4]

That the vehicle of divine revelation was human, historical, and contingent was acknowledged unabashedly by these theological conservatives; they should not be misunderstood as Lutheran fundamentalists who believed in the verbal inspiration of the whole Bible. (North America, of course, has its Lutheran fundamentalists.)

Elert's critique of the Ritschlian tradition as it ripened in Troeltsch was that it substituted for the faith of a community (the Lutheran community) the fragile speculative intelligence of a succession of detached theological intellectuals. The theology of Luther and Lutheranism was that of real life in the real world, "in contrast to certain currents in modern dogmatics, in which the purely spiritual character of the church is twisted into something purely intellectual." "In this way, spiritualism is made the essence of the church community, and this has the practical, if not the theoretical outcome, of turning the theologians into the pre-eminent representatives of the church. It is not the 'socio-ethical' barrenness of Protestant theology but its spiritualism, far removed from the real world, that accounts for the fact that it has so little influence on the concrete course of current history."[5] Elert saw his task as one of recovering the relevance and immediacy of Protestant theology in the face of a tendency for it to take on increasingly sublime and intellectualized forms.

These confessional Lutherans did not share the Dialectical Theology's aspiration to construct a theological dogmatics wholly other than philosophy, history, or worldly culture. Elert, however, was an almost perfect counter-Troeltsch. The modernity that Troeltsch naively celebrated Elert quixotically deplored. It was not so much that Christianity had nothing in common with culture as that he did not want to compromise it by an affiliation with a disintegrating, decadent culture in the manner of the more prestigious and fashionable theologians of the liberal establishment.[6] This was the burden of what was perhaps Elert's most ambitious and interesting book, *The Struggle for Christendom*, which appeared in 1921.[7] Its topic was the fascinating and undeniable interaction and intermingling of German Protestantism and German high culture from Kant, Hegel, and Schleiermacher until his own time. The thesis was not so much that such an intermingling was inadmissible as that the classical culture of German Idealism was decadent, declining, and doomed, and that Evangelical Christianity should separate itself from this culture so as not to perish with it. Elert illustrated this decadence in the poet Heinrich Heine, whose lyrical personae could shift from ancient

Greek to Protestant to biblical Christian, but never with proper seriousness and respect, as when he ended his poetic treatment of "A Mighty Fortress is Our God" with the comment "Luther shook Germany to its depths, but Francis Drake calmed us again when he gave us the potato." This technique of desublimation, of "diffusion" as he called it, impressed Elert as the theme of the declining nineteenth century, a "disorganization of the forms of life" (*Desorganisation der Lebensgestaltung*) that was only to be expected in a culture which handed over its holiest treasures to outsiders such as Heine, the emancipated Jew.[8]

Elert and Althaus were both chaplains (*Feldprediger*) in the First World War. They were uplifted by military comradeship, accepted German conservative war aims, and absorbed a good deal of the *völkisch* romantic nationalist outlook.[9] Adding these attitudes to Lutheranism was much of what they meant by making German Protestantism relevant to the modern situation. In Elert's case, his own cultural pessimism was enriched with the ideas of Oswald Spengler's *Decline of the West* of 1919 (of which Ernst Troeltsch commented that "it was itself an active contributor to the decline of the West").[10] He was himself, of course, no believer, but he was grist for Elert's mill, the pagan of insight who provided the naturalistic, rational complement to Elert's Lutheran theology. He was to be the Aristotle to Elert's Thomas, and like Thomas, Elert thought that the philosophical prolegomena had no effect on the integrity of the theological substance. Again, like Thomas, he was probably wrong.

The way in which these elements worked themselves out in the Weimar understanding of Martin Luther first became evident in Elert's short *Draft of Lutheran Teaching* (*Die Lehre des Luthertums im Abriß*), published in 1924, which a perceptive interpreter described as "an original and astonishing work in the unity and density of its articulation," only seventy-five pages in length.[11] A second edition in 1926 was lengthened by an apparatus of Luther citations and by appendices that explained Elert's objectives and responded to such interesting critics as Friedrich Gogarten and Emanuel Hirsch. Elert wrote that he had originally intended to accompany his second edition with an apparatus of citations from major Lutheran theologians and confessions, as well as cultural and political figures from the Lutheran community of faith, but had drawn back from such an undertaking because he did not want to turn his *Draft* into an anthology in which its message was obscured.[12] The two-volume *Morphology of Lutheranism* (*Morphologie des Luthertums*) of 1931–32 subsequently elaborated the themes of the *Draft* in such a way as to identify them with mainstream Lutheranism over four centuries. In fact, as we shall see, the insistence on interpreting Luther in terms of a classical Lutheran tradition did in some ways help to preserve his integrity as a historical figure at points where it was in danger of being overwhelmed by the revisionist historical "discoveries" of the Luther Renaissance or the new theological insights of Barth and Gogarten. But the attempt of these confessional Lutherans to produce an "up-to-date" theology compatible with *völkisch* politics led them not only explicitly to "improve" Luther but sometimes unintentionally to distort him.[13]

Elert was influenced by the irrationalist, vitalist ideas most impressively articulated by Henri Bergson. His *Draft* began with the conception of a universal aspiration to freedom shared by all living things, and by human beings particularly as the highest earthly creatures: "To be alive and to want to be free is the same thing for us."[14] This universal aspiration was, according to Elert, to unbounded freedom, a more-than-Promethean striving, essentially a Nietzschean will to power. However, it was checked, thwarted at every turn, by surrounding and opposing forces, which Elert collectively called "fate" (*Schicksal*): "The product of all the factors which, apart from our aspiration to freedom, shape our life is our fate."[15] This fate (the Spenglerian echo is clear) is described as a unified force that dominates human lives, its dominance best illustrated in the irretrievability of the past and its freedom in the unknowability of the future. For Elert, fate is no inanimate entity; rather, it is the vital being that dominates all other vital beings.[16] "There would be no fundamental distortion if, already at this point, we were to speak of the power of God instead of the power of fate ... Thus we find ourselves in harmony with Luther's teaching of the hidden God, of whose majesty we have a presentiment but who is unknowable for us outside of Christ the mediator (*secluso mediatore Christo*), even in his relation to created things."[17] But this inscrutable, hidden God is in a sense revealed as the God of wrath through the revelation of the law; it stands in dialectical opposition to the gospel of Christ, which fulfills, abolishes, and transforms the revelation of the law. We are in the territory here of Luther's polemic against Erasmus's affirmation of free will, where he declares that for human beings to claim free will is the ultimate blasphemy since free will is a predicate of God alone.

Elert's description of fate is of a hostile vitality that enslaves human beings, and, with death, ultimately destroys them. Yet at the same time, their fate bestows on them their own will to power, which in life is endlessly frustrated and in death destroyed. Fate first taunts human beings and then kills them.[18] "If by ourselves we can arrive at no perception beyond the enmity of God, the Bible deepens that impression through statements about God's motives. It speaks of his will to destroy (Genesis 6:6f.; Acts 3:23), his retribution (Romans 12:19), his vengeance (Michah 5:14); it says he laughs at people, mocks them (Psalms 59:9), and hates them (Psalms 11:5). His wrath appears as the dominant theme of his enmity."[19] God's wrath, then, is the basic answer to Job 7:20: "Why do you make me the object of your attack?"[20]

Of course, this revelation of God to Spengler and Bergson, and in carefully assembled parts of the Bible, is not the full revelation of God in Christ that Elert presents in his *Draft* and his *Morphology*. It is the revelation of God to natural humanity in our time, and like any revelation of the law, its object is to bring human beings to repentance and faith.

Elert goes on to claim this insight about the enmity of fate (by which he means the enmity of God) as the original experience (*Urerlebnis*) of Lutheranism. It is "the original dread of the human being confronted by God" (*Urgrauen des Menschen vor Gott*).[21] Here he makes no speculations about Luther's biographical road to Reformation, in the manner of the contemporary Luther Renaissance unriddling of the Experience in the Tower, but obviously Luther had to have something important to do with an *Urerlebnis* of Lutheranism. Elert thought that he found evidence of a similar dread of a predatory God in Luther's *Enarratio Psalmi 40* (1534) and of course in expressions from *De Servo Arbitrio*. Generally his arguments have been rejected as extremely one-sided interpretations of particular Luther texts.[22] When Luther answered Erasmus's charge that he was constructing a hostile God whom humans would more appropriately hate than love, his point was not that he did indeed bow down to such a God but rather that the *Deus absconditus* was beyond human comprehension, and that Erasmus, of all people, as the enemy of inappropriate scholastic theological speculations, ought simply to revere the unsearchable mercy of God in Christ. The post–Second World War West Germans who renounced *völkisch* "improvements" and extensions of Luther's theology were equally allergic to a Luther with Spenglerian traits.

Elert, like Althaus but less ambitiously than he, expressed his political and cultural values in connection with Luther's theology of the two realms. The realm of grace (*Gnadenordnung*) aspired to extend itself over all of human life, but was thwarted by the kingdom of Satan.[23] Therefore God placed a realm of creation (*Schöpfungsordnung*) beside the realm of grace. Each was guided by different rules, the former committed to preserving the world of nature for the time being, the latter to realization of the eternal Kingdom of God. Mortal Christians, at the same time justified and sinners, had duties both to the realm of grace and to the *Schöpfungsordnung*. In the realm of creation they "struggled against evil with natural means," in order to preserve human community embodied in families, kinship groups, clans, nations, races, and humanity as a whole.[24] But the smaller units, starting with the family, were the most basic, and "it is only possible to speak of the genuine vitality of humanity as a whole if the particular vitality of races and of the nations that they contain is not infringed in the process."[25] So there is an explicit place in God's realm of creation for "the soldier who uses weapons in defence of national freedom."[26] The church should keep its distance from decadent cultures, and one's individual vitality is heightened by expressions of hate and contempt for decadent art.[27] Through Elert in the Weimar years, the national conservative mindset found Luther's teaching on political ethics a congenial mode of expression. The result was to obscure rather than to sharpen historical understanding of Luther's writings on temporal authority, first by making them into a fixed theological topic and secondly by melding them with the political objectives of Weimar conservatives.

The appendix of 1926, in which Elert responded to the critique of Gogarten and Hirsch, amounted to a controversy over the meaning of *De Servo Arbitrio* (The Bondage of the Will), which from then on became a major issue in Luther studies. Against Gogarten's assumption that *Bondage* established Luther's theocentrism, his confession to the "timeless" revelation of a transcendent God, Elert reminded Gogarten that in the same period Luther had written *On the Heavenly Prophets* and preached sermons on the Lord's Supper which put great emphasis on divine immanence. Luther's doctrine of the Lord's Supper was intended above all to do justice to the central dogma of the Incarnation. The one-sided stress on the "wholly other" in the Dialectical Theology was better suited to a tendency in their "church father" Kierkegaard towards an "ontological-platonic concept of revelation" than it was to John 1:14.[28] In the *Draft* Elert argued that the fact that Christ was "without sin" in his life was the ultimate revelation of the Incarnation, and that a gospel which focused exclusively on Christ's passion, death, and resurrection was dangerously off balance. The life without sin testified to the faith of the Christian community that Christ's vitality shared the vitality of God.[29] That was the central affirmation of Christian faith. Against the one-sided insistence on divine transcendence in the Dialectical Theology, Elert asserted a more conventionally orthodox balance of transcendence and immanence. Luther's faith, as opposed to the Dialectical Theologians, was not in the transcendence of God in itself but in "the immanence of the Transcendent."[30] "It would be better if they had left Luther out of this. For Luther opposed the God of judgment to the Incarnate God in a way that is anything but dialectical. The concept of the Incarnate God is a clear reference to John 1:14, and it is in absolute opposition to all transcendentalism. For Luther the Incarnation, and thus revelation, lies not in the first place in the death on the cross but in the assumption of human nature and consequently also in the historical life of Christ. Revelation is to him the entry of God into history, not the negation of history."[31]

Elert's response to Hirsch got, if anything, even closer to the core of his dispute with the Luther Renaissance and the Dialectical Theology over the meaning of *The Bondage of the Will*. Holl had often been accused of Calvinizing Luther with his high theocentrism, and Barth, who termed Calvin "Luther's most loyal disciple," was, after all, Swiss Reformed.[32] The confessional Lutherans at Erlangen were concerned above all to protect the integrity of Lutheranism. Elert insisted that the theology of Calvin was in "irreconcilable contradiction" to Lutheranism. He made this point above all by a sharp opposition between law and gospel – illustrated by his contrast of the realm of creation and the realm of grace, discussed above. Reformed theology, from Zwingli on, insisted on the compatibility of law and gospel. It posited a "third use of the law," as a code of conduct for redeemed Christians in civil society. One of Elert's concerns as a Luther interpreter was to prove that the Reformer, in his authentic writings never accepted this "third use of the law," which would in a Calvinist manner associate the law with Christian conduct.[33]

The Bondage of the Will, in which Luther seemed to assert double predestination against Erasmus, brought him very close to the theology of Zwingli and Calvin. Elert, the vitalist, needed some sort of human freedom in his theology. Essentially, he took the Augustinian position that redemption in Christ gave freedom to the blessed.[34] Also in the *Draft* he reasserted the traditional Christian paradox that, although election comes through God's grace independent of the human will, damnation results from wilful human rejection of God's mercy when it is offered.[35] To Emanuel Hirsch this view sounded much more like the soteriology of the Council of Trent than Luther's *Bondage of the Will*. Elert countered that Luther in *Bondage* always affirmed human freedom in earthly matters (that is, in things not pertaining to salvation), that he blamed the damned for their rejection of God's mercy, and that he sometimes went so far as to refer to faith as a work.[36] Elert insisted that his "distinction between freedom and unfreedom is precisely that of the Augsburg Confession (Article 18) and the subsequent theology of Lutheranism that is based upon it."[37] He was giving short shrift to attempts to drive a wedge between Luther's theology and Melanchthon's Augsburg Confession.

Elert's answer to Hirsch reaffirmed confessional Lutheranism's investment in Luther's later years, as opposed to the insight of revisionist theologians and historians about the years up to 1525: "Anyone who knows Luther after 1525, and does not assume that from then on he no longer understood his own theology, knows that the warning against a 'one-sided emphasis on the idea of election' was virtually a dominating theme of his whole theology. Anyone who is blind to this point in his reading of Luther will always fail to see one of the most basic grounds for the differentiation of the types of Western Christianity that was then beginning."[38] Contemporary Luther studies have doubled back from the discoveries of the Weimar years to a renewed interest in Luther's amply documented last two decades. Not the least irony of Elert's career in Luther scholarship was that his influence tended to be positive when he stood pat on tradition and negative when he cut his own path to modern relevance.

Paul Althaus joined Werner Elert in 1925 as a member of the theological faculty at Erlangen, where he held the post of professor of systematic theology. Like Elert, he was a confessional Lutheran, and like him, he tried to make a place for *völkisch* impulses in a modern Lutheran theology. Yet despite his confessional affiliation, he sought a less abrasively partisan stance than that of Elert, with whom he maintained a subtle rivalry.[39] Robert P. Ericksen in *Theologians under Hitler* describes Althaus's role in the Third Reich as that of a "mediator."[40] In the debates of the 1920s, too, he instinctively moved toward a commonsensical middle ground that could mediate between contending extremes. After the brief unpleasantness of de-Nazification in the late 1940s, Althaus went on to more than a decade of further productivity as a leader of the West German theological establishment. At the end of his career, following his formal retirement in 1956, he rounded out and developed positions in Luther scholarship that he had first set forth in the Weimar years.

Theologically, ethically, and politically, Althaus was closer to the Luther Renaissance than to the Dialectical Theology, although at least in his later years he recognized that Barth, Holl, and he himself had participated in the common rejection of theological liberalism and *Kulturprotestantismus* that separated the innovating theologians of the 1920s from the previous generation. Althaus was a student of the conservative theologian Carl Stange. When Stange set up the *Zeitschrift für systematische Theologie* in May 1923 as an explicitly anti-liberal journal, Althaus joined Holl's favourite student, Emanuel Hirsch, as a junior editor.[41] Holl's declaration to Stange that for him "the *Zeitschrift für systematische Theologie* is *the* theological journal" showed how far he had moved at the end of his life from his liberal beginnings to theological conservatism. The *Zeitschrift für systematische Theologie* was set up to oppose *Die Christliche Welt*, but with characteristic hypersensitivity, Barth assumed that it was directed against his *Zwischen den Zeiten*, which was, of course, begun the same year.[42] Althaus criticized both Holl and Barth, but his polemic against Barth was far harsher. Nevertheless, he hit the nub of the matter when he observed, "Both Holl and some of his critics [he was probably referring to Gogarten], when they search for Luther's ideas about justification, are at the same time seeking the correct teaching on justification. Their own systematic insights get insinuated into their interpretations of Luther."[43] Unlike Holl, Althaus at least made the effort to distinguish his own theology from Luther's, and to distinguish Luther's theology from Paul's. Quite early in his publications he took his mentor Carl Stange to task for reading into Luther's writings his own theological distinction between the Greek belief in the immortality of the soul and the Christian belief in eternal life. In substance, he said, Stange's distinction was theologically valid, but it was a *historical* fact that Luther did not distinguish between the two concepts.[44] Althaus's carefully maintained separate identity from the Holl school, however, did not prevent his being chosen president of the Luther Society when Holl died in 1926, a post that he held until 1964,[45] through the vicissitudes of the collapse of Weimar, the Third Reich, and the early years of the Bundesrepublik.

Althaus's early biography pointed toward his later allegiances in politics and theology. His father, Paul Althaus senior, was a professor of systematic theology at Göttingen and Leipzig. Stange was his father's successor at Göttingen, and the younger Althaus was much influenced by Martin Kähler's assertion of the pointlessness of the quest for the historical Jesus. Just as he was finishing his theological studies in 1914, the First World War began. The young theologian now served in a military hospital in Poland.[46] During the war he identified with the concern of eastern Germans to resist the westward spread of the Polish linguistic area (which the nationally assertive Poles of course regarded as an undoing of the Germanization that had succeeded the eighteenth-century partitions of Poland).[47] Like other conservative nationalist Germans, Althaus attached a religious significance to the apparent spiritual elevation and solidarity of all Germans at the beginning of the war in August 1914. Looking back from the vantage of 1934, he described himself as "disgusted by the shameless voluntary surrender of the Germans, the impeachment of the leader, and the undignified confession of German guilt for the war."[48] In 1921 he wrote a pamphlet critical of Religious Socialism in which he singled out the young Karl Barth for more respectful and friendlier treatment than he gave to other Religious Socialists.[49]

Barth responded in 1922 with the publication of "Grundfragen der christlichen Sozialethik: Auseinandersetzung mit Paul Althaus" (Basic Issues of Christian Social Ethics: Controversy with Paul Althaus),[50] in which, he explained to Althaus, he wanted to clarify that his break with his former friends in the Religious Socialist movement did not make him an ally of Lutheran conservatives. This writing of Barth has since been noted as the beginning of the theological discussion of Luther's doctrine of the two kingdoms.[51] He refers to Althaus's own – "that means the Lutheran solution, the paradoxical teaching of the two kingdoms" – which served to reject the moral-religious self-righteousness of the Anabaptists and similar nonconformists, only to substitute for it "a new 'Christian' self-righteousness with a conservative stamp."[52] Barth's polemic unfolded:

[According to Althaus] the vocation of a nation is supposed to be an "issue of transcendent depth" because here the "irrational" and the "creative act" are involved, and politics suddenly becomes "in its depth a religious matter" ... now everything is possible. Now war can no longer be called murder but a "mighty encounter of the nations about leadership and the future" ... How is it that the notion of "Prussia" or "Bavaria" is said to possess higher dignity than that of a "League of Nations"? ... How is it that in his enthusiasm for nation, state, war, etc., Althaus entirely forgets the idea of *original sin* and does not develop his ethics from that starting point?[53]

The discussion of Luther's two kingdoms theology began with this first encounter of Barth and Althaus. Earlier, the categories of scholarly analysis were Luther's theological conceptions of the state, the church, and the household.[54] Althaus developed the conception of ordinances of creation (*Schöpfungsordnungen*) in a pamphlet of 1934, defining them as "the forms of social life of people, which are the indispensable conditions for the historical life of humanity."[55] These ordinances were part of an original revelation of the law that could only be properly understood in terms of the revelation of the gospel through Jesus Christ. The original revelation was ongoing and progressive, and it unfolded new ordinances unknown to Luther and the Reformation – above all, that of the nation, *das Volk*.

If Barth was unwilling to confuse the projections of liberal or socialist humanitarianism with the Kingdom of God, he was at least equally on guard against those of romantic nationalism, with their claims to be "organic." Althaus responded in an essay of 1923, "Theologie und Geschichte: Zur Auseinandersetzung mit der dialektischen Theologie" (Theology and History: Controversy with the Dialectical Theology), with the assertion that Barth's dialectical theology by its absolute dichotomy between God and history was, in effect, rejecting the historical religion of the Bible and the Reformation.[56]

It is true, wrote Althaus, that anyone who has taken *The Bondage of the Will* to heart realizes that there is an uncanny, incomprehensible quality in God, the negation of everything human.[57] (He said that Barth's was "a theology of the unknown God.")[58] But this perception oversimplifies Luther's message: "Barth's theology lacks a substantive idea of the love of God."[59] Luther's sermon on the Canaanite woman insists, on the contrary, that "under and over the No there is a deep secret Yes, with its firm belief in God's Word."[60]

Althaus identified Luther with his own affirmation that "ethical norms themselves are a revelation of God."[61] True, Luther excluded ethical achievement from the salvation process, but in other respects he "dignified the moral command as a direct revelation of God, hence as the foundation of faith."[62] Luther recognized that Jesus preached the highest expression of God's law, the command of love.[63] Althaus differed from his colleague Elert, who, in his concern to draw clear lines between Lutheranism and Calvinism, denied that Luther had ever, like Calvin, affirmed a "third use of the law" – the law as a guide for the Christian life.[64] Against Barth, Althaus insisted in Luther's name on the inextricable connection of justification with moral renewal: "Justification does not only sanctify human beings religiously, but also morally." The notion of a forgiving act of God that did not creatively renew people would have been blasphemous for Luther.[65] So Althaus insisted that Barth (and Gogarten), in radically separating God from human morality, misrepresented Luther and his justification theology: "It is completely impossible to claim Luther one-sidedly for the forensic conception of justification."[66]

For Althaus the great weakness of the Dialectical Theologians was that "their conception of God remains under the elevation of the New Testament and Luther."[67] It is basically "empty" because of its theoretical aridity. Here the poverty of theocentrism came into focus. For all of Barth's use of the idea of a resurrected Christ outside of history, if a distinctly Christian idea of God was to have substance, it had to go back to the Jesus of the New Testament. (In the following years Barth did move to a more substantive, New Testament Christology.) To Barth, wrote Althaus, "Jesus is no more a direct revelation of God than any other fact of history."[68]

Barth's estimate of the story and of the death of Jesus, as well as of the Resurrection, dissolves the meaning of the New Testament faith in Christ ... Surely, Golgatha means the crisis of Jesus' "religious" relationship to God, but not only the crisis – at the same time its highest confirmation. The God to whom Jesus as the God-forsaken confessed in prayer is the God of Psalm 22, the God of the "religious" history of Israel and of Jesus himself with all his substantive traits. He is no other. It is true that Jesus on the cross knew himself forsaken by this God, but it is equally important that he confessed to this God. Therefore the cross is a religious act ... Two things are missing in Barth's picture of the cross: the first is the one that Luther expressed so incomparably in his sermon on preparation for death of 1519: that Jesus overcame the temptation [*Anfechtung*] (!) of God-forsakenness with his powerful love of God; the next is Jesus' trait of suffering, forgiving love of sinners.[69]

In the 1960s Bernd Moeller would warn that Luther research had become "one of the battlefields where contemporary theological schools air their differences."[70] Althaus was one of the Weimar-era theologians most aware of this danger both to theology and to history. Nevertheless, it is hard to escape the impression that his controversy with Barth had a formative influence on his interpretation of Luther's theology, with respect to the relation of church and state, justification and sanctification, and particularly God and Christ. Because Barth ("superficially") seemed so close to the Luther of *The Bondage of the Will* and also to the theology of the cross set out in Luther's Heidelberg Disputation theses of 1518, Althaus devoted himself especially to these subjects, not only as a systematic theologian but also as an interpreter of Luther.

Defying Barth's dictum that human religiosity fell under God's No, Althaus wrote of Luther, "Because in faith he experienced the meaning of God's love, he could say with the strongest words of mysticism that under God's love the human person becomes one with God."[71] But mysticism was foreign not only to the Dialectical Theology but also to the Luther discovered by Karl Holl. The article on Althaus in *Theologische Realenzyklopädie* declares that his interpretation of Luther was most indebted to Holl.[72] Certainly, he did not engage Holl in the way that he did Barth, but it is necessary to be cautious about identifying Althaus too closely with Holl. In 1955, at Werner Elert's death, he wrote a long eulogy. He said of Elert, "He discovered and transcended the errors and limits in Karl Holl's conception of Luther without explicit critique, above all the distortion of the theology of justification and the failure to recognize the *propter Christum*."[73] These are by no means incidental or secondary issues in any interpretation of Luther's theology. One suspects that Althaus was speaking not only for Elert but also for himself, and it is arresting that a distorted theology of justification and an inadequate Christology were precisely the theological charges that Althaus levelled at Barth.

In 1929 Althaus published an essay, "Zum Verständnis der Recht-fertigung" (Understanding Justification), in which he seemed to make exactly the same sort of correction of Holl (who had died three years earlier) that he was later to attribute to Elert. Clearly, he had no objection to Holl's insistence that Luther's justification theology connected justification with moral regeneration. Further, he put aside the issue of whether Holl correctly interpreted Luther.[74] His concern was to outline an adequate theology of justification, whether Luther held it or not, and he did not find the theology that Holl presented as Luther's to be entirely adequate. He disliked the idea that renewal was the "sufficient foundation" for justification which rendered it "morally possible and authentic."[75] God's forgiveness of sin needed no rational or moral foundation; it was freely given. Humankind's guilt was real and serious, even if, once justified, a human being was in a process of moral renewal. In this sense, justification remained inexplicable in rational or moral categories: "to the Greeks foolishness, to the Jews a stumbling block."[76] Nor did Holl's ideas of predestination and divine monergism satisfy Althaus. He insisted on the freedom of the human decision for or against faith, "and we have no right to treat it as anthropomorphic thinking that the Bible presents God as wrestling with people over this decision, as awaiting the decision of human beings. It is not acceptable to abolish this basic antimony of our life in the sight of God by doing away with the human standpoint, by supposedly subordinating it to the standpoint of God. That leads in the end to making God into the effector of evil."[77] Holl, with his preference for Calvin's solution of these issues over Luther's, was surely the object of Althaus's critique.

There was something else – when Althaus wrote about the cross of Christ as the highest experience of God accessible to human beings, he warned: "Theologians have often tried to find the essence of Christianity simply in the fulfillment of the prophetic witness to God through Jesus' preaching of God and the soul. But such attempts render us defenceless against the recommendation of any kind of monotheistic rendering of non-Christian religion as of equal standing with Christianity."[78] Harnack was an obvious case in point here, but did not the comment apply equally to Holl? When Althaus wrote about the "Jewish question" in 1929, it was as a theologian, not as a nationalist, although he acknowledged that a political problem had been created by "the living of the Jewish nation among us."[79] He was again concerned to maintain the uniqueness and primacy of the Christian religion: "The [modern Jews] who curse Jesus stand nearer to the seriousness of the decisive question than Martin Buber and the others today who think that they can without difficulties assimilate

Jesus into the tradition of prophetic Judaism."[80] Whether the issue was theological or political, Althaus's concern was to preserve Christianity and Germanness from creeping liberal-humanitarian assimilation. It is important to underscore that neither Althaus's Christianity nor his nationalism was shrill. As opposed to Barth's declaration that all religion was bankrupt in the sight of God, he credited all religion with a partial awareness of God.[81] One loved one's nation, not "because it is grander than others," but "because it is my nation."[82]

Althaus's Luther interpretation arose from political and theological discourse with the Luther Renaissance and the Dialectical Theology in ways that should be obvious. He was a shaper of interpretations of Luther's theology of the cross and of his doctrine of the two kingdoms which served to correct the theological and political inadequacies of the opposing schools. In his essay "Die Bedeutung des Kreuzes im Denken Luthers" (The Significance of the Cross in Luther's Thought; 1926), Althaus identified beliefs about the cross experience as central to the Reformer's theology of justification.[83] He again cited the words of Luther which he had used against Barth about how "under and over [God's] No" there was a "deep secret Yes."[84] Love masked under wrath had no more meaningful archetype than the cross of Jesus. It was true that in Luther's early expressions the statements about the cross were vehicles for a monastic piety of humility, but "this basic conception of Luther's runs through his entire theology."[85] For instance, in his exegesis of Psalm 117 in 1530, "Grace appears externally as though it were pure wrath."[86]

The central content of the cross theology was a universal identity in death through the Christian's identification with the suffering Christ on the cross: "Luther places beside one another the suffering of God in Christ and the suffering of the Christians. God is known only in suffering – that has a double sense or, rather, it signifies the deep correlation: the suffering Christ in whom God is known corresponds to the suffering human being who alone knows God ... The cross of Christ means that God meets us in death."[87] Or, as Erik Erikson paraphrased this same idea in 1958, "The Passion is all that man can know of God: his conflicts, duly faced, are all that he can know of himself."[88]

The cross of Christ was also explicitly the negation of the reason of the Greeks and the morality of the Jews. Not only is the *theologia crucis* the opposite of the *theologia gloriae* that knows God by reasoning from his works in nature; as death in disgrace, it is the antipode of the good conscience, of moral self-esteem[89]: "The cross is the concealment of God and thus the end of grasping God in our thought by means of self-conscious reason; the cross is the sign of judgment and thus the end of grasping community with God for self-consciously good people."[90] Not only is the individual Christian like his Christ in suffering and disgrace, but the same applies to the community of Christians. Luther pronounced that "the holy Christian people must suffer all misfortune and persecution, all kinds of *Anfechtung* and evil from the world, the flesh, and the devil; [they must experience] inward sorrow; they must be frightened, externally poor, despised, sick and weak, so as to be like their head, Christ."[91] Just as only faith can see God in the crucified Jesus, the church, too, is visible only to faith.

Against Barth, Althaus contended "that Luther's theology of the cross is not a dialectical intellectual principle of a theoretical character. The 'dialectic' in question here is bitter reality, God's concealment in his opposite, therefore the battle of faith between death and life, real *Anfechtung* and danger of death, in which the miracle of faith makes itself at home."[92] But Holl, too, with his linkage of justification and sanctification, could be accused of making the Christian faith morally presentable; with his missing Christology, his concepts of divine monergism and predestination, he could be charged with making it rationally comprehensible. Althaus was closer to the tradition of *credo quia absurdum*, or, as Luther wrote in *The Bondage of the Will*, "the impossibility of understanding makes room for the exercise of faith when these things are preached and published."[93]

When in 1925 Althaus published "Luther's Position in the Peasants' War: A Contribution to Lutheran Social Ethics,"[94] he revealed a good deal about his own political ethic, particularly with reference to revolution. Luther's various statements on the Peasants' War were all analyzed with care and impressively contextualized. The essay was equally strong in its mastery of the Luther texts and of the political and social events to which they responded. What distinguishes it from virtually the whole scholarly literature on the Peasants' War that has appeared since 1975 is its strong partisanship against the rebels. Rather than being a semi-violent series of boycotts against landlords and political authorities that was transformed into a badly conducted defensive war through the bad faith of the lords, particularly the Swabian League, Althaus's Peasants' War was something else entirely. It presented the rebels as the ones who negotiated in bad faith in order to gain time. "The Twelve Articles, the official program of the peasants' movement, was only a tame list of minimum demands, far exceeded by the claims of the peasants."[95] Thomas Müntzer, generally assessed now as a minor, peripheral figure in the rebellion, was presented as a leader of decisive influence, at least regionally: "The uncanny dark glow of Taborite-theocratic ideas connected itself with the embitterment of the peasants."[96] Truly, Althaus interpreted the events of the Peasants' War in Luther's own terms.

As for Luther, Althaus pointed out correctly that his harshest pamphlet against the rebels was written at a time when they seemed on the way to total victory. Rather than the Reformer being a lapdog of the princes, his was the sole voice calling for principled resistance at a time when the political classes (foremost, his own Frederick the Wise) had been paralyzed into inaction.[97] Knowing Althaus's political affiliations, we can easily perceive that he thought that someone like Luther had been just what Germany lacked in the last months of 1918: "The Luther who risked everything, his position before the people, even his own life, for the sake of conscience is of no lesser greatness than the Luther at Worms before emperor and estates."[98]

It was important for Althaus that, in Luther's writings against the peasants, he was maintaining a consistent theological standpoint based on his *Von weltlicher Obrigkeit* (On Temporal Authority; 1523).[99] Using the language of his controversy with Barth of a few years earlier, Althaus referred to Luther's "often preached and proclaimed basic ethical idea of the two kingdoms, the kingdom of God and the worldly kingdom."[100] The idea, parallel to that of the theology of the cross, was that God's wrath masked his love: "Luther saw the service of the state as a work of love, the serious, responsible exercise of force against wickedness as a deed of mercy, war as a service to peace."[101] That everything fitted together so well was for Althaus "a testimony to the systematic power and wholeness of [Luther's] theology."[102] The theme of Luther's unique consistency and integrity could be overworked. Althaus commented on how offended the Reformer was at the hypocrisy of the victors in the Peasants' War, who denounced the rebellion of the commoners even as they plotted their own rebellions – nobles against princes, princes against the emperor.[103] Yet when the Schmalkald League was organized in 1531, Luther accommodated himself to the resistance of the princes against the emperor.

Althaus remarked on the limitations of Luther's conceptions of history and the state. He thought of wars and political struggles as pitting justice against injustice; but in the fluid process of history, matters were not so simple: "History often permits right to clash against right, and justice must always be sought anew." This concept applied even to the upward struggle of oppressed classes and estates.[104] But "it is a misfortune for the state when its social situation is determined simply by the temporary balance of struggling estates and powers. The state has to impose its own strong will to justice and health above the contending powers ... A will is needed that is responsible for the whole nation, beyond the play of interests and powers." That this statement expressed a conservative critique of parliamentarianism was clear when Althaus named Bismarck as a statesman who expressed Lutheran political ideals in the modern situation.[105]

Even more interesting as an insight into Althaus's politics was the hypothetical question he posed about what would have been called for had the peasants won in 1525. Were resistance pointless, assuming that the peasants had stopped their murdering and plundering and established a kind of order, "Then that must be accepted, and one must bow to the new order as to the devil. It would have just as much legitimacy as the devil. Woe, however, to anyone who lets himself be inwardly won over by the success of the rebels. It is not acceptable to submit to the revolution except with protest against it, since it rules not by the grace of God but by the devil."[106] It need hardly be added that the object of this denunciation was not so much Thomas Müntzer, imagined as victorious in 1525 in spite of everything, or even the Bolshevik revolution. The target was much closer to home; it was the Weimar Republic!

Elert and Althaus, despite their association with the Luther Renaissance in the same journals and learned societies, represented a distinct voice in Weimar-era theologians' debate about Luther. They were limited in their theological independence in that they did not regard themselves as free dogmaticians. They spoke for the community of faith that held to the historic Lutheran confessions; hence they could not assert that Luther had been misunderstood in the Augsburg Confession or the Book of Concord, and they could not be "original" in Luther's name. They invoked the later Luther against the theocentrists' inferences from *The Bondage of the Will*. In their way, Elert and Althaus spoke up for the religious relevance of ethics, human freedom, and history, for the immanence of God, and for the life of Christ, as well as his death and resurrection, against the one-sided dogmatics of the Luther Renaissance and the Dialectical Theology. Their critique pushed the two opposing schools from extreme transcendence and theocentrism towards renewed attention to Christology, and their contribution to the interpretation of Luther's theology of the cross helped this Christological focus. Althaus, in rejoinder to Barth, began the discussion of Luther's theology of the two kingdoms. Knowing that they could not make Luther a German nationalist, Elert and Althaus tried to be theologically relevant to the Germany of the 1920s by means of inventions such as Althaus's progressive revelation through creation or Elert's attempt to reinforce traditional Lutheranism with Spenglerian vitalism and fatalism. Unlike these two men, Holl's successors in the Luther Renaissance tried to find a saving message for Germany as they deepened themselves in the Weimar Edition of Luther's works.

5 The Luther Renaissance in Transition: Emanuel Hirsch and Erich Vogelsang

Emanuel Hirsch was one of the most brilliant theologians of his time, a scholar of vast learning and productivity. He wrote in all the divisions of theology, with the characteristic exception of Old Testament,[1] since he had a distaste for Jewish religiosity and legalism. His philosophical work was significant in its own right, and it also influenced the character of his theology. Although Hirsch repeatedly endorsed the post-war Protestant awakening with its assault on cultural Protestantism, he was, much more than Althaus, Elert, Gogarten, Barth, or even Holl, the heir of the intellectual, historicist theologians of the pre-war era. For him rejection of Enlightenment rationalism in theology, or placing theology outside the sphere of rigorous academic investigation, was unthinkable.[2] It was not the religious beliefs but the political beliefs of the pre-war generation that put them outside the pale for him. Hirsch's nationalism and his anti-Marxism made him an enemy of the Weimar Republic, which was in his eyes imposed by the victorious Entente with the collaboration of the Social Democrats. As he himself said, the division between black-white-red and black-red-gold, not the pre-war differences between theological conservatives and liberals, set the tone for the writing of theology and church history in the 1920s.[3]

Like so many German intellectuals, Hirsch was son of a Protestant pastor. Like Barth and Harnack, he moved away from the conservative theology of his father but continued to owe it a strong religious and emotional debt. Studying theology in Berlin, Göttingen, and Bonn, Hirsch was most strongly influenced by Karl Holl, who came to

Berlin in 1906, the same year that Hirsch began his university studies. Told by his teachers that German Idealism was passé, Hirsch and his student friend Paul Tillich decided to investigate the matter for themselves. Tillich encouraged Hirsch to study Johann Gottlieb Fichte in order to wrestle with the epistemological issues so central to a reflective Christian faith. Tillich soon moved on to the study of another Idealist, Friedrich Schelling, but Hirsch stayed with Fichte, writing his Göttingen dissertation in 1914 on "Fichtes Religionsphilosophie" (Fichte's Philosophy of Religion) and then in the next year at Bonn making "Christentum und Geschichte in Fichtes Philosophie" (Christianity and History in Fichte's Philosophy) the subject of his *Habilitationsschrift*, the second dissertation required of German students intending to enter the professorate.[4] Fichte was a fateful choice for Hirsch; his subjective epistemology coloured Hirsch's Christian faith. Above all, Fichte was the philosopher of dawning German nationalism after Prussia's disastrous defeat by Napoleon in 1807. Hirsch, who volunteered for military service in 1914 but was rejected for medical reasons, carried on his study of Fichte amid the early enthusiasm and apparent unity of Germans of all classes at the beginning of the First World War. He later attributed his belief "that God meets me through volk and fatherland" to inspiration received from Fichte, Kleist, and Treitschke. Like his mentor, Holl, Hirsch regarded his studies as wartime service to Germany, "fighting the battle by other means."[5]

In 1921, at the youthful age of thirty-three, Hirsch was called to a professorate in Göttingen, where he remained throughout his career until 1945. During the Weimar years his appointment was in church history. Later, in 1936, he moved into the chair of systematic theology and history of theology. Just after the Second World War his years of research on church history culminated in his most highly regarded publication, a five-volume history of modern Protestant theology, which placed it in the context of the general movements of European thought.[6] At the beginning of the 1920s he began the other scholarly project for which he is best known, the study of Søren Kierkegaard. For this task he learned Danish. Karl Barth, who came to Göttingen the same year as Hirsch and was for a time on cordial terms with him, shared his fascination with Kierkegaard. Barth commented at the time to a Danish Kierkegaard scholar: "I am unfortunately not as industrious and clever as my neighbour, Hirsch, who learned Danish in an instant."[7] Hirsch's writings on Kierkegaard and his initiation after the Second World War of the twenty-six-volume annotated German translation of Kierkegaard can be said to have marked the breakthrough to worldwide accessibility for the Danish theologian, whose study had hitherto for linguistic reasons been restricted primarily to Scandinavia.

Hirsch was, of course, equally fascinated with Karl Holl's Martin Luther. Holl had introduced him to Kierkegaard when he was a student at Berlin in 1908, and Hirsch participated in the next year in seminar study of Luther's recently rediscovered lecture on Romans (1515–16): "The reading of Luther's early lecture on Romans in Karl Holl's church history seminar in 1909 marked my awakening to independent theological struggle [*Ringen*]."[8] Hirsch's independence in treatment of Luther was, however, a qualified independence. As he wrote on the occasion of reviewing Holl's Luther volume of 1921, at that time (1909–10) "the way that Holl presented the theology of justification opened up for me the path to the understanding of Luther."[9]

By the appearance of Holl's Luther book the teacher was in certain respects learning from the student. Holl's conceptions of Luther's great significance for subsequent German culture were, for instance, reinforced by Hirsch's publication about the Reformer's influence on Nietzsche. Hirsch's was a more fluid, synthesizing mind than his teacher's. As he wrote later in life, Holl "had little grasp of specifically philosophical questions."[10] Perhaps for that reason he was not on guard against the danger that Hirsch's preoccupation with modern philosophers such as Kierkegaard, Nietzsche, and Fichte might colour his conception of Luther. This perception, certainly, appears among current interpreters of Hirsch. Heinrich Assel writes of "the dialectical educational process in which Fichte is interpreted in terms of Holl's Luther and Luther is interpreted in terms of Fichte."[11] John Stroup makes the same point more sweepingly and less convincingly: "Hirsch's political theology ended by assimilating so much from Nietzsche, Spengler, and Idealism that he parted company with Christianity without realizing it."[12] (Probably, theologians should not claim the right to determine who is a Christian.)

Hirsch declared that Holl was his only real teacher.[13] At the time of his mentor's death, when the Berlin theological faculty drew up a list of possible successors to his chair, Hirsch was described as "the disciple of Holl who penetrated most deeply into the spirit of his master."[14] Looking back from the vantage of the 1950s, Hirsch saw the matter somewhat differently. He paid tribute to Holl for maintaining a warm personal friendship with him, although "I went beyond him and researched against him; although I sought a form of Christian reflection in which the mindset of Luther was abandoned more radically than by Holl [the notion that he himself had abandoned Luther's mindset at all would probably have shocked Holl] but in which the relation to Jesus on his way into death was grasped more deeply and essentially."[15]

One area where Hirsch influenced Holl, as remarked above, was in adding substance to Holl's assumption of Luther's pervasion of later German thought. In his essay "Nietzsche and Luther," for instance, Hirsch began with a forceful argument that Nietzsche's negative comments about Luther were based on an uncritical acceptance of Johannes Janssen's *History of the German People since the End of the Middle Ages*, untempered by the reading of any serious Luther scholarship, not to mention anything beyond a cursory skimming of Luther's own writings.[16] However, Nietzsche seemed too important for Hirsch simply to dismiss; his anti-liberalism was congenial and his anti-Prussianism could in the circumstances of the 1920s be given an anti-Weimar application.[17] There were things about Nietzsche's personal style that reminded Hirsch of Luther: "his courage in search of truth, the independence of his spirit from the judgments of others, lack of concern for his own person, and total commitment to his causes."[18] Beyond that, some of Nietzsche's most fundamental beliefs were unconscious imitations of Lutheran piety. Dionysius, like the God of *The Bondage of the Will*, is a combination of opposed characteristics: "destruction and creation, cruelty and the highest benevolent kindness."[19] Presumably this was a translation of the Hegelian dialectic into Nietzschean language, but the Hegelian dialectic arose from a culture drenched in Lutheranism. Without knowing it, Nietzsche sided with Luther against Catholicism in rejecting the worth of any virtue based upon reward.[20] Zarathustra's love is nothing less than Christian agape: "divine love, which despises and loves and transforms the loved one."[21] Ultimately, notwithstanding all Hirsch's sharp criticism of the insufficiencies of Nietzsche's atheism and naturalism, a figure who had rightly grasped so much must be regarded as a Christian in spite of himself: "In the deepest abyss of his soul Nietzsche was unable to suppress the Christian image of pure, self-sacrificing love as the highest expression of human personality. Secretly – indeed, without admitting it and certainly against his will – he believed."[22] Retrieving Nietzsche for the faith in this way was surely connected with Hirsch's Christian apologetics aimed at the rebellious youth of his day. Later it would make it easier for him to conceive the Nazi movement as Christian, despite the disconcerting things that some of its leaders said.

What Hirsch owed to Holl was nowhere clearer than in his little booklet *Luthers Gottesanschauung* (Luther's Idea of God), published in 1918.[23] At the same time the piece had Hirsch's own mark on it, the disposition to be radically systematic, whereas Holl made his presentation of Luther credible by a more expository manner. In the introduction Hirsch singled out *The Bondage of the Will* and Luther's second lecture on Psalms as his major sources.[24] He read *The Bondage of the Will* as a quintessentially theocentric statement, presenting a dialectic of a revealed merciful, loving God and a hidden, wrathful, angry God. There, more than in his other writings, the hard truths of the election of the few and the rejection of the many were starkly presented by Luther. Writing before the appearance of Holl's Luther book, Hirsch referred his readers to Theodosius Harnack, who presented Luther's theology with a stress on the divine wrath, as well as Holl's essay on Luther's Romans lecture of 1515–16.[25] In Hirsch even more than Holl there appeared the Luther Renaissance disposition to justify God from God's own point of view, which was unacceptable to a confessional Lutheran such as Althaus. Hirsch had none of the reservations about *The Bondage of the Will* of Elert or of Althaus, who, particularly with reference to Luther's later writings, believed that to present the Reformer too exclusively in his polemical mode against Erasmus was to subtly distort him. Hirsch valued *The Bondage of the Will* for its systematic power. Rather than an occasional polemic against Erasmus, it was a systematic statement about God.[26] "The view of God is the vital centre of Luther's faith. That he based each of his studies on it gives his thought its systematic consistency."[27]

Hirsch affirmed the basic ideas of Holl's theocentric theology, presenting them of course as Luther's: rejection of the pursuit of happiness in whatever form, affirmation that God's justifying act is at the same time a morally regenerating act and therefore ethically justified, and above all, divine monergism with its corollary, rejection of human free will as a blasphemous idea. "God confronts us as angry judgment and merciful forgiveness."[28] "God's anger is nothing other than the holiness of his mercy."[29] "God leads us through fear to joy, through death to life. He multiplies sin in order to overcome it."[30] "Monergism is the backbone of the Lutheran conception of God. If the creature would be able to want something without its being determined by the divine omnipotence, God would be a mockery, he would no longer be God."[31] And at the same time came the demand that "we honour God by believing his word,"[32] as though such an imperative cohered unproblematically with the principle of divine monergism.

The last third of Hirsch's booklet was devoted to the mysteries of predestination, which he insisted were stringently related to everything else in Luther's conception of God. "The dual outcome of world history – that is, the pardon of only a portion of humanity – was taken for granted as a presupposition of his thought. It said so in the Bible, and on this matter as on others he could not ignore the clear words of Scripture. He had no reason to do so, moreover, as experience seemed to confirm Scripture. The number of those who receive the gospel is indeed only a limited one."[33] Hirsch moved back and forth from insisting that predestination was a mystery too deep for human beings to speculate about, and that attempts to explain it were impious, to broadly suggesting just such explanations. God's ways are not ours, and we must humbly accept his ways of doing things, just as a child submits respectfully to the incomprehensible decisions of his parents. "Otherwise our Father would be diminished and become a mere playmate."[34] Nevertheless, Hirsch could not resist suggesting that God's grace came into proper focus only when set against the background of the damnation of the many: "He makes us aware of the richness of his mercy to the pardoned through his judgment of the doomed. If God's mercy were general and taken for granted, we would not be able to be aware of it and grasp its significance."[35] "Perhaps it was necessary to create many in order to perfect a few."[36] In any case, Luther demanded no certainty of election from the faithful. In the Romans lecture he had pointed out that it was a special blessing to submit to God's will unreservedly, even if that entailed one's own damnation.[37] In this section Hirsch developed Holl's assumptions to particularly abrasive conclusions.

On the matter of where Christ fitted into this theocentric framework, Hirsch was again recognizably Holl's student. The main point, never baldly stated but certainly clearly implied, was that God's relation to humankind was revealed with full adequacy by the *Rechtfertigungslehre*, and that Jesus Christ "merely" proclaimed and confirmed this revelation. "In Christ and his gospel we are confronted with the eternal will of God as the most exquisite mercy, *dulcissima misericordia*, which demands our self-surrender."[38] Human seeking and pondering by itself, without Christ, would never have grasped "God's essence and manner." Empirically, therefore, divine forgiveness of humankind could not have occurred without or outside of Christ. However, to say that justification occurs because of Christ, *propter Christus*, does not add a new or additional quality to the description of divine mercy: "Therefore we can completely exposit Luther's conception of the justifying God in its general substance without thinking about justification occurring because of Christ."[39] The curious concern to make Christ theologically irrelevant to divine justification, while conceding that historically or "concretely" he revealed this justification, reflected Holl's own squeamishness about Christology in the name of fully monotheistic theocentrism. The Hirsch of 1918 might have added that *The Bondage of the Will* gave a more balanced revelation of God than the gospel of Christ, because Jesus, like Ritschl, concentrated one-sidedly on God's mercy.

In a publication of 1920, "Zu Luthers Persönlichkeit und Lehre: Initium theologiae Lutheri" (On Luther's Personality and Teaching. The Beginning of Luther's Theology), Hirsch took some major independent steps in Luther scholarship. The Autobiographical Fragment of 1545, to which Denifle had devoted malevolent attention, would be treated with considerable reserve by Holl in his Luther book of 1921, but other Luther scholars – Friedrich Loofs, Otto Scheel, Heinrich Boehmer – were drawn to it with a powerful fascination. Was Luther really claiming that he worked out his *Rechtfertigungslehre* in 1518–19 as he prepared the *Operationes in Psalmos*, which seemed to be what he said in 1545? Had his memory slipped so badly that he confused the *Operationes* with the *Dictata* of 1513–15?

Hirsch, too, was drawn to explore the Autobiographical Fragment, which was so important to his generation of Luther scholars. He did not believe that Luther's intention was to date his theological discovery, but rather to discuss its content.[40] Nevertheless, a skilful exegesis of the Autobiographical Fragment, projected onto Luther's early lectures, might go far towards fixing the date of the Reformer's theological discovery. Hirsch, like the other Protestant interpreters of the early twentieth century, was not about to argue with Denifle on one essential point: the Romans lecture of 1515–16 presented Luther's *Rechtfertigungslehre*. So attention shifted to the *Dictata* and whether it and the Autobiographical Fragment could be used to make sense of each other. The Autobiographical Fragment did clearly indicate, said Hirsch, that Luther's theological grasp of Paul and Romans 1: 17 had greatly advanced when he was preparing the *Operationes*, compared to where it had been when he began the *Dictata*.[41] Differing from Holl, Hirsch found in the early parts of the *Dictata*, not Luther's justification teaching, but a variant of late-medieval Catholic soteriology: "In the first lecture on Psalms, Luther was still of the opinion that the saving power of the gospel was dependent upon human beings' freely opening up their wills. Christ is both justification and judgment, in each case depending on the disposition of the individual human being. These opposing dispositions could hardly be anything else than humility and pride."[42]

It was true that in 1509 Luther had made the first step toward his characteristic theology of justification. He declared that the meaning of the Incarnation was that God wanted to reveal human sinfulness in the mirror of Christ's sinlessness. In this way *propter Christum* people could achieve the required humble disposition, self-condemnation. Luther "learned to see it as his task to remain in the enormous psychological tension of knowing himself guilty in the eyes of God without relaxing the pressure and also without despair. It was this tension from which he had [earlier] wanted to be free through wiping out his sins."[43] Of course, this theology of 1509 was an insufficient soteriology because it made superhuman demands on an already highly sensitive conscience.

When Hirsch analyzed the Autobiographical Fragment, with its description of the substitution of a "passive" theology of justification, by which God justifies us, for an "active" theology of justification, by which God judges us, a further difficulty arose. The linguistic distinction between "active" and "passive" was nowhere to be found in the *Dictata* – nor in the Romans lecture or even in the *Operationes*, for that matter – it first emerged in *The Bondage of the Will*. Hirsch explained that in Luther's usage any genitive that is not a "genitive of possession [*Eigentumsgenitiv*]" is classed as passive rather than active. In the case of the "righteousness of God (*iustitia dei*)," the subject of discussion in the Autobiographical Fragment, if the sense were "God's own righteousness" (the standard that he applies in punishing unjust sinners), the term would be a genitive of possession, or, in Luther's terminology, it would have an active meaning. If, however, *iustitia dei* were taken to be a "genitive of authorship" and its meaning "the righteousness which God gives to us," then Luther would refer to it as having a passive meaning. This was a perfectly satisfactory explanation of the Autobiographical Fragment; the trouble was that the first time that Luther made this distinction between active and passive usage and applied it to the righteousness of God was in 1525, and only from 1531 did it become the fixed meaning of the term. "In the well-known preface of 1545 Luther was not saying that at the time of his discovery he labelled the righteousness of God as having a passive sense; rather, in referring to it as 'passive,' he was simply using the terminology of his later years."[44] In other words, he was discussing the substance of his discovery using terminology developed much later.

In this way Hirsch defined Luther's "breakthrough" or "discovery" as the moment when he stopped focusing on the disposition of the sinner/believer required to satisfy the righteousness of God and instead looked upon the righteousness of God as something freely given by him to the sinner/believer. Hirsch found the first soteriology at the beginning of the *Dictata* and thought that he saw it replaced by the latter soteriology, which first properly "Let God be God," at a further point in the *Dictata*. According to Luther's Autobiographical Fragment, this discovery took the form of a new understanding of Romans 1:17: "For therein is the righteousness of God revealed from faith to faith; as it is written, The just shall live by faith."

According to Hirsch, Luther's scholiae (theological notes) to Psalm 31 (32):1 "are his first, timid attempt to transmit as teaching to others his hard-won personal exegesis of Romans 1:17."[45] Hence, by some time in 1513 Luther had arrived at his theology of justification and begun to teach it publicly. His exegesis of the Psalms and his conception of justification were in this case clearly his own, independent of St Augustine, the revered founder of his order.[46] The identification of the *iustitia dei* with the *iustitia fidei*, the righteousness of God with the righteousness of faith, was facilitated by the Quadriga, the medieval exegetical method according to which Scripture had four senses: literal, allegorical, anagogical, and tropological.

Medieval exegesis had always insisted on the primacy of the literal sense of Scripture in the definition of doctrine, but it had tended to a method aimed at multiplying rather than narrowing the meanings and associations of sacred literature. Once the literal meaning of a text had been determined, the Quadriga established the framework for figurative amplification of that meaning, encouraging the search for ecclesiological (allegorical), moral (tropological), and eschatological (anagogical) ramifications of the fundamental literal sense. Furthermore, literal interpretation was not entirely straightforward. In the case of the Psalms, which Luther was interpreting in the *Dictata*, medieval Christian convention had established that each psalm was to be regarded as literally spoken by Christ or referring to Christ.[47] Building on the studies of Holl, Hirsch said that in the *Dictata* Luther privileged the Christological and tropological interpretations: "Understood literally, the Psalms speak of Christ, understood tropologically, of the believer. The believer, however, to the extent he is a believer, has the inner disposition of Christ, so the two interpretations are often hardly to be distinguished."[48]

Hirsch's Luther, accordingly, succeeded in enriching the once-forbidding notion of "the righteousness of God" to mean "the righteousness of faith" (which God bestowed on the believer) and Christ himself ("whom God gave us for our salvation and life")[49]. Hirsch went on to explain: "That Christ and faith can both be called *iustitia dei* and accordingly belong together is so easily conceivable for Luther because everywhere in the first lecture on the Psalms he describes Christ as tormented [*angefochtenen*] and conceives of this torment [*Anfechtung*] of Christ as a loving sharing of our guilt and need during his earthly life. Both for Christ and for the believer, to be tempted [*angefochten*] and to be and have the righteousness of God do not exclude one another."[50]

In this very important essay of 1920, Hirsch went significantly beyond Holl and laid some of the more important foundations of the

Luther interpretation of the early twentieth century. He, more than Holl, who thought that he was studying a Reformation theology virtually from the beginning of Luther's preserved writings, convinced himself that Luther's early lectures documented the change from a characteristically medieval soteriology to a distinctly Lutheran theology of justification. Moreover, this change was the outcome of a fundamental religious experience rather than the working out of a "scholarly, logical" theological formula: "It arose for Luther as something living and unfathomable, that was compatible with a multiplicity of theological articulations."[51] Hirsch certainly was one of the early major detectives in the investigation of Luther's Experience in the Tower.

Unlike Holl, who stated that the Autobiographical Fragment of 1545 simply reflects the older Luther's perception that his theology had reached maturity at the time of the second Psalms lecture of 1519 – and that this view of the old Luther is contradicted by the public record, especially by the excellence of his early lectures on the Psalms and Romans[52] – Hirsch contributed to the contemporary project of mining the Autobiographical Fragment, seeking to extract a fundamental understanding of Luther from its inscrutable text. Obviously, the Autobiographical Fragment could not simply mean what it said: in Hirsch's view, Luther's soteriology was mature before 1519, and he did not write about the distinction between the active and passive senses of the *iustitia dei* until 1525. Nevertheless, brilliant intellectual historian that he was, Hirsch filled Luther's dubious reminiscence of 1545 with plausible meaning. Not only was the righteousness of God the righteousness of faith, but Christ was the righteousness of God. Here Christ is no longer the sun at out backs, as he was said to be in Holl's theocentric theology of justification – the sun begins to emerge from behind the cloud of monotheistic transcendence. And joining the spirit of Kierkegaard with the inheritance of Harnack and Holl, something human – psychological torment, or *Anfechtung* – joins the suffering and passion of Christ to the individual Christian's struggle for faith.

It is a distinctive quality of the Holl school that, although Holl begat Hirsch and Hirsch begat Vogelsang, there was no party line on the beginnings of Luther's theology of justification. Without any disturbance of personal amity in each case, the disciple differed with his master and the master declined to change his mind.[53] This characteristic is particularly striking in the case of Hirsch and his "student and later dear friend Erich Vogelsang," since Hirsch for the time being withdrew in Vogelsang's favour from Luther studies, so that their work would not overlap and he could concentrate on his many other scholarly projects.

What seems to have tied academic father, son, and grandson together was something apparently even closer to their hearts than their Luther studies, the *Anfechtungen* of the German volk caught between black-white-red and black-red-gold. As a conservative editorialist wrote in March 1919,

Black-red-gold, these will be the colours of the Reich from now on. That is what it says in the new draft of the definitive constitution of the Reich currently being discussed in Weimar. Thus the black-red-gold International will raise its future banner. From the moment that they established their control of the majority in the Reichstag, our national disaster in the war began. It was sealed in the revolution. It came to expression in the armistice. It will be completed in the peace treaty. The black-white-red banner that preceded the German people in the days of its ascendancy in glorious victories and decisive successes has been trampled in the dirt. Germany's great past is carried to the grave. The International has triumphed over the national.[54]

Hirsch was deeply indebted to the theology of community that Holl thought he had derived from Luther's *Rechtfertigungslehre*.[55] He elaborated it in *Deutschlands Schicksal: Staat, Volk und Menschheit im Lichte einer ethischen Geschichtsansicht* (Germany's Destiny: State, Volk, and Humanity as Illuminated by an Ethical Idea of History), a book that he first published in 1920 and continued to bring up to date in new editions until 1925.[56] Holl wrote enthusiastically that *Deutschlands Schicksal* "hit the nail on the head."[57] It brought Hirsch to the attention of an educated nationalist readership. In this work and related essays throughout the 1920s Hirsch combined Fichte's Idealist nationalism with Luther's beliefs about state and church, which from the 1930s onward would be discussed in the framework of the "doctrine of the two kingdoms," an analytical concept which, as we have seen, was first coined by Karl Barth in his polemic against Paul Althaus.[58]

In Hirsch's eyes the German Lutheran ideal of national community was a middle way between the materialist extremes of Anglo-American capitalist individualism and Bolshevik collectivism. The nation-state was not to be confused with the Kingdom of God on earth. It was transient and mortal, and since it dealt with a brutal and sinful world, it could not apply the morality of the Sermon on the Mount in its external actions. But built on family and tribe as it was, it was a natural order of God's creation. Democracy, socialism, pacifism, the League of Nations, and the Second or Third International, the embodiments of internationalism as opposed to nationalism, all assume that people are better than they are. It was one of the main points of the Holl school to believe in human depravity as an act of religious faith.

In trying to create an external Kingdom of God on earth, internation-
alists make the human situation worse than it need be. The invisible
community of Christians, on the other hand, has the potential to be a
leaven in the nationalist community. Although even the true invisible
church can not perfect the state, it can nevertheless raise it above
itself. Hirsch's aim was to distinguish the state from the Kingdom of
God without separating them absolutely, thus avoiding the mistakes
of democratic and socialist idealists, but at the same time avoiding
the Barthian error of making human history and divine revelation irrelevant to each other.[59]

Hirsch identified with Fichte. Like the earlier thinker, he was rally-
ing the Germans to resist a foreign yoke. Versailles, the League, and
the Weimar constitution were components of the anti-national international order imposed by the victorious Entente. Hirsch had a difficult time envisaging the new conservative Christian order that would
one day replace the Weimar Republic. Like Holl, he believed that the
Hohenzollern had lost their honour and their credibility in the catastrophe of late 1918. He speculated in *Deutschlands Schicksal* about a
more authoritative executive, a stronger president and civil service, to
replace the parliamentary power so at variance with German tradition: "Even more important is something spiritual: we must learn
once again to consider our state and our law sacred."[60] And then, at
variance with the disordered society of Weimar, there was the agenda
of social conservatism – monogamy, virginity before marriage, and
superiority of men over women, parents over children, and in general, superiors over subordinates.[61] The Christian religion was invoked against "the spirit of the times" on behalf of hierarchy and
authoritarianism. Lutheran moral pessimism was enrolled in the battle of nationalism against internationalism. Like Holl, Hirsch was a
supporter of Alfred Hugenberg and the German National People's
Party,[62] the main opposition to the Weimar order and Germany's
compliance with the Treaty of Versailles during the 1920s. But Holl's
commitment to partisan politics was tepid in the 1920s, while Hirsch
was the most political of all major German theologians in these years.

Erich Vogelsang is remembered above all as a Luther scholar. His efforts side by side with Hirsch on behalf of the German Christians in the
1930s are mercifully forgotten. He lost his life in Russia in 1944 when
the Red Army overran the military hospital in which he was serving.[63]
His classic monograph on the young Luther's Christology was dedi-
cated to the memory of two brothers, one of whom had fallen in 1916
on the Somme and the other the next year at Verdun.[64] But his book,
Die Anfänge von Luthers Christologie nach der ersten Psalmenvorlesung

(The Beginnings of Luther's Christology in His First Lecture on Psalms; 1929), was in no sense a political manifesto. It seemed to solve the problem of the time and content of Luther's evangelical breakthrough, the Experience in the Tower. It was cited with approval by Luther scholars throughout the world until the end of the 1950s.[65]

With his opening tributes to Karl Holl and Emanuel Hirsch, repeated many times throughout his book, Vogelsang placed himself squarely in the Luther Renaissance tradition. But he hastened to add that he would state the points at which he disagreed with his teachers.[66] To treat Luther's first lecture on the Psalms, the *Dictata* of 1513–15, as a key to understanding his theology was to follow the Holl school in its departure from previous scholarship. To focus on Luther's Christology was to strengthen Holl's interpretation of the Reformer at the point where it encountered the sharpest criticism.[67] Although Vogelsang in his preface wrote that he "had learned fundamentally from Karl Holl – also on the subject of Christology,"[68] in pushing Christ to the centre of his interpretation of Luther's *Dictata*, he engaged in some subtle revisionism. He moved away from the high monotheism that Hirsch and Holl had inherited from Adolf von Harnack and made Christ the focal point of Luther's early theology. Like Holl, Vogelsang undertook to systematize the new elements of the Reformer's thought, putting aside the traditional beliefs that Luther had not yet discarded.[69] But in his book of 1929 he made a credible case that the young Luther's new theology contained an original, anti-scholastic, biblical Christology. The supporting evidence on this point was so strong that Vogelsang's presentation of Luther's early theology thereby gained an appearance of historical authenticity. Here, it seemed, was no mere twentieth-century theology borrowing credibility by calling on the name of Martin Luther.

Like Holl, Vogelsang claimed special authority based on the presumed superiority of his source materials. The editing of Luther's *Dictata* in volumes 3 and 4 of the new, critical Weimar Edition was seriously defective, as acknowledged by the eventual re-editing of this source in volume 55 in the 1980s. Following the prescription of Heinrich Boehmer, Vogelsang worked with the three original manuscripts. Luther wrote both exegetical glosses and theological scholia on the Psalms, apparently with the glosses done in advance of the scholia, so that the publication of the glosses and scholia together in the Weimar Edition connected the parallel manuscripts more closely than was justified. Later additions were inserted, particularly in the glosses, as could be detected from different colours of ink. Many citations from patristic and scholastic commentators were there simply for Luther to expound upon in his lectures, sometimes, but far from always, with approval.[70] The use of these complicated manuscripts in one sense put Vogelsang closer to the Luther of 1513–15, but it also allowed him to lay claim to special insights – even psychological insights based on the state of the handwriting[71] – that could be verified only with great difficulty. The character of the manuscripts of the *Dictata*, for instance, seemed to Vogelsang to justify Holl's methodology: "Distinguish what is traditional from what is really Luther's; put the 'old material' aside, conceive of the new material as unified in outlook, and move from it to the fighting and praying heart of the Reformer."[72] Clearly, Vogelsang ran the risk of predetermining his conclusions with such methodological premises.

He continued Holl's project of extracting Luther's full-blown theology of justification (very much as Holl conceptualized it) from the *Dictata*, but like Hirsch and unlike Holl, he sought to prove that it emerged in the course of the preparation and composition of the *Dictata*. Like Hirsch he tried to match the *Dictata* with Luther's later reminiscences about the Experience in the Tower, particularly the Autobiographical Fragment of 1545. He differed from Hirsch on the point in the *Dictata* where Luther's evangelical discovery emerged, connecting it with the scholia on Psalm 70 (71) instead of Psalm 31 (32), almost a year later, in autumn 1514. Moreover, while Holl and Hirsch claimed only to have discovered a theological precipitate of the Experience in the Tower in the whole *Dictata* (Holl) or part of it (Hirsch), Vogelsang thought that in the scholia on Psalms 70 (71) and 71 (72) he encountered Luther writing under the full subjective impact of the Experience.[73] In a time fascinated with subjective psychology this interpretation made Vogelsang's findings particularly attractive, not only to devout Protestants but also to cultural historians and literary psychoanalysts such as Lucien Febvre[74] and Erik Erikson.

Vogelsang fully accepted Hirsch's finding that it was fruitless and unnecessary to go looking through the *Dictata* for the point when Luther talked about changing from an active to a passive sense of *iustitia dei* in his interpretation of Romans 1:17. This terminology was first used by the Reformer only in 1525, no doubt as the result of his new awareness of the grammatical peculiarities of Hebrew through his translation of the Psalms in 1524 in the course of preparing the Luther Bible.[75]

Vogelsang made repeated use of the notion of Luther gradually and progressively filling old scholastic terms with new meanings in his first lecture on the Psalms.[76] This process applied above all to the chief *terminus technicus* of justification: *iustitia dei*, "the righteousness of God." In both Psalms 30 (31) and 70 (71) the phrase reoccurs: "Deliver me in your (God's) righteousness." On the first occasion the notion of God's vengeful righteousness threw Luther into acute anxiety (reflected in the handwriting, according to Vogelsang);[77] on the second, Luther had grasped the comforting insight that human faith was the righteousness of God. What Hirsch saw as the first evidence of the Reformer's justification theology in the scholia to Psalm 31 (32), Vogelsang interpreted as the beginning of a year-long phase of intellectual wrestling and transition which was finally terminated by a moment of powerful religious insight. What Hirsch discovered in the scholia to Psalm 31 (32) was indeed a relaxing of "the deepest tension of *Anfechtung*" that Luther fell into when discussing the previous psalm, but it was no "entering through open gates into paradise" as described in the Autobiographical Fragment. "In the following glosses ... we have short testimonies of how Luther tried to wrench himself free from the old notion of the vengeful justice of God. The righteousness of God was for him primarily 'the righteousness that is acceptable in the sight of God (*coram deo*),' which means, however, the righteousness which God demands of us. In this way the old outlook is not yet overcome."[78]

For Vogelsang the scholia to Psalms 70 (71) and 71 (72) marked the completion of Luther's wrestling with *iustitia dei*. As in Holl's and Hirsch's explanations, the exegetical discovery was helped by the meeting of the Christological literal and the tropological senses of the text, as permitted by the principles of late-medieval biblical exegesis. In the Christological literal sense, Christ is the righteousness of God, and tropologically, as applied to the individual Christian, the righteousness of God is faith in Christ.[79] This interpretation seemed confirmed by Luther's reminiscence of 1540: "Praise God, then I understood the matter and realized that *iustitia dei* means the righteousness which justifies us through the gift of righteousness in Jesus Christ. Then I understood the grammar and for the first time I liked the Psalter."[80] A reference to the conversion experience in the *Confessions* of St Augustine in Luther's scholia to Psalm 70 (71) was a further proof for Vogelsang that this was a moment of conversion for Luther.[81] "The character of the handwriting, which by itself naturally cannot be taken to mean too much, taken together with the content, confirms that there Luther was struggling for resolution of the question in a very special way. I would like to take these pages of the Dresden Psalter as a direct precipitate of the much-discussed discovery about Romans 1: 17, or at least as its objectively most reliable theological expression, which of all of Luther's clear writings on the subject stands closest in time to the event."[82]

More important than the dating of the discovery was Vogelsang's forceful insistence on its Christological substance. He presented

Luther as putting aside the philosophical logos Christology that was so strongly rooted in both the patristic and the scholastic traditions,[83] and as avoiding a Christological mysticism. Supposedly Luther went back to the Christology of the New Testament, above all I Corinthians 1:23 and even more 2:2: "For I determined not to know anything among you, save Jesus Christ, and him crucified." Thus instead of being primarily the divine Word, Jesus Christ was the suffering human being on the cross[84] and at the same time God's total revelation to humankind.[85] Joined with this primitive Christian theology of the cross, Vogelsang found a second major Christological theme in the *Dictata*, the daily advent of Christ in the believer.

To touch the latter theme first, Luther found justification in his exegetical principles, which connected the Christological literal and the tropological senses of Scriptures, for the notion of a second coming of Christ in the individual Christian. This second advent stood between the first advent, when he was born of the Virgin Mary, and a third, eschatological advent when he returned to earth in glory.[86] Before the historic Incarnation, under the Old Testament law, God's revelation was "provisional, figurative, shadowy, veiled," but his spiritual advent in the Christian believer was said to have all the clarity and fullness of his revelation as God incarnate.[87] Although, as a matter of historic fact, Vogelsang acknowledges that at the time of the composition of the *Dictata*, Luther knew and approved of the mystical writings of Jean Gerson and St Bernard,[88] he denies emphatically that the Reformer's ideas of a daily spiritual advent of Christ in the Christian are in any respect mystical. He will not even say with Holl that Luther had a Christ-mysticism but not a God-mysticism.[89] "This 'unification' is not a woolly, mystical, saccharine, ecstatic union but consists in the clear element of the word, the faith, and the conscience. The essence of mysticism, the *unio mystica*, is really alien to Luther."[90] Such a comment is an affirmation of the Luther Renaissance's resolute hostility to mysticism, which it took to be the peculiarity of Catholics and Schwärmer. In general, late-medieval mysticism tended to focus on the modest first stage of purgation, to the virtual exclusion of speculations about union. In any case, it was strictly orthodox, and whatever it meant by union, it did not entail surrendering the distinction between Creator and creature.

Justification in the later parts of the *Dictata*, wrote Vogelsang, meant "Christ in us" or, the same thing, "faith in Christ": *fides Christi, qua iustificamur, pacificamur, per quam in nobis regnat*.[91] He continued, "Luther did not know any faith that was not faith in Christ."[92] The sanctifying process in each justified individual is the work of Christ the good shepherd who searches out the lost sheep or Christ the good

Samaritan who comes to the aid of the man who has fallen among thieves.[93] So in Holl's manner, justification is no mere change of the sinner's relation to God but a change of the sinner himself. Nevertheless, the justified person is always at the same time a sinner, so that the regeneration process is always starting anew. There is no once-and-for-all-time conversion, as for Augustine. In this sense the daily advent of Christ in the soul of the justified continues throughout life. Vogelsang wrote, "The [sinner's] progress is a constant new beginning, and yet, although the person is unconscious of it, progress."[94] So the contours of Holl's justification theology – unacceptable to the Dialectical Theology or the confessional Lutherans – are maintained, with the all-important insertion of Christ.

Even weightier, and absorbing the theme of the daily advent of Christ in the soul, was the focus of Luther's Christology, as interpreted by Vogelsang, on the cross. For him the cross of Christ brought together, in the manner of Holl's theology, the seemingly opposing themes of the wrath and the love of God.[95] But in a note he remarked in passing that, "oddly," Holl had missed "the Christological foundation of the teaching about the *opus alienum*" (God's wrath).[96] Had Vogelsang been engaged in polemics against Holl, which he was not, this aside could have been enlarged into a devastating critique – both of the specifically Christian character of Holl's theology and of the accuracy of its perception of Luther.

As Vogelsang saw it, Luther first (Psalm 30 [31]) was terrified by Christ as divine judge and eventually (Psalms 70/71 [71/72]) felt pacified and justified by concentrating on the human anguish of the crucified. The points of contact between the Psalms and the New Testament lent themselves to Luther's exegesis. Psalm 21 (22), especially, seemed a prayer of the crucified. It begins: "My God, my God, why has thou forsaken me? Why art thou so far from helping me, and from the words of my roaring?" It continues: "All they that see me laugh me to scorn: they shoot out the lip, they shake the head, saying: He trusted on the Lord that he would deliver him: let him deliver him, seeing he delighted in him"; and "the assembly of the wicked have inclosed me: they pierced my hands and my feet. I may tell all my bones: they look and stare upon me. They part my garments among them, and cast lots upon my vesture."[97] Luther came to see the Christological literal sense of the Psalms as revealing the crucified Christ's real fear of being rejected by God because of the burden of humanity's sins which he bore.[98] With this crucified Jesus' anguish, and with his "descent into hell" between the Crucifixion and the Resurrection, Luther in his *Anfechtungen* could fully identify.[99] Literally, the Psalms are the words of Christ, and tropologically-morally they are the Christian's faith in Christ. In Holl's theology, human faith is in the first place faith in our utterly debased and sinful character, even if it is not always evident to us. We are thus placed under the wrath of God – where we belong. In a theology of the cross the human person, fully conscious of being in sin and under God's judgment, can identify with the Christ who cries out: "My God, my God, why hast thou forsaken me?"

Vogelsang commented: "This inward participation of Luther in the exegetical and theological subject with which he was occupied cannot be better exemplified than in the way that Albrecht Dürer put his own self-portrait into the countenance of the crucified Christ as he struggled in sketch after sketch for the right understanding of the Passion."[100] When Erik Erikson translated Vogelsang into the language of revisionist psychoanalysis, he borrowed the Dürer image.[101]

The cross perfectly joined Holl's twin stresses on the wrath and the love of God. Externally, and in a very real sense, it expressed God's wrath, but this wrath was a necessary way of working out his merciful purpose – it was an *ira misericordiae*. "In Christ, the pattern and source of all his works, God revealed his wrath as his 'alien work' and the sanctifying goodness enclosed within it as his 'genuine work.'"[102] The experience of God-forsakenness and condemnation of the crucified reappears in the soul of each Christian through the second, or daily, advent of Christ in the believer.[103] As the crucifixion of Christ heals the sins of the world, the spiritual torment of the believer under the judgment of God is a necessary first step in his moral regeneration. According to Vogelsang, this perception amounted to Luther's rupture with the Anselmian satisfactionary-atonement doctrine, according to which the sacrifice of Christ propitiates the wrath of God.[104] Such a division of Christ and God was totally uncalled for. "The wrath of God is removed only in the sense that it is fulfilled as serious punishment, as pain of conscience, as *ira misericordiae* ... , as love which is not squeamish about causing pain in order to heal."[105] "God forgives sin in the persons reborn in Christ in that in his ungrounded mercy he does not hold it against them. He excuses our sins by really driving them out through Christ in our hearts by means of disciplining, punishment, and pain of conscience."[106] This was Luther Renaissance, not confessional Lutheranism – Althaus would argue that it detracted from the reality of unmotivated divine forgiveness.

Also characteristic of the Luther Renaissance was Vogelsang's determination to find in the *Dictata* a real Lutheran theology of justification (although not its Melanchthonian distortion, as he continually stipulated).[107] Previously, Lutheran scholarship had echoed Luther in

1545 in regarding the early lectures as very imperfect journeyman exercises on the way to his mature theology of the 1520s and 1530s.[108] Then Denifle had invited himself into the discussion, labelling them as late-medieval Catholic theology, far beneath the Thomist *niveau*. In 1921 a Scandinavian scholar, Arvid Runestam, studied the Romans lecture of 1515–16, which followed the *Dictata*, and discovered that human humility was still for Luther at that time a necessary disposition for the reception of divine grace.[109] Since the Holl school insisted that divine monergism, in which God did everything to the exclusion of any human initiative whatever, was the central characteristic of Luther's theology, such a finding would have consigned both the *Dictata* and the Romans lecture to the uninteresting status of pre-Reformation writings.

With the eye that most good scholars have for the deadly counter-argument which could invalidate their conclusions, Vogelsang assaulted the interpretations that found a disposition for grace in the *Dictata*: "There are innumerable passages in the *Dictata* which speak of self-condemnation as the indispensable presupposition for the reception of grace. In previous research they are as a rule interpreted in the sense of a scholastic theological *dispositio ad gratiam*, a *facere quod in se est* (a doing of one's very best), a *meritum de congruo* (an approximation of merit). In this way the repentance and self-condemnation of the person created the possibility for God to declare the sinner justified. The person would merit grace (*de congruo*) through his self-condemnation."[110]

Vogelsang argued, basically, that had Luther really held such views, it would have been bad theology: "After Luther had learned to understand the tropological meaning of judgment and righteousness from the literal meaning of the cross of Christ, it would have been exactly as nonsensical for him to call human self-condemnation a 'disposition for grace' in the scholastic sense as, for instance, to see Christ's death on the cross as a 'disposition' for the Resurrection. Judgment as *opus alienum* is God's work, exactly as is justification as *opus proprium*."[111]

Apparently, Luther had come to similar conclusions to Vogelsang's: according to some credible interpretations, as early as the lecture on Romans;[112] according to others, only in preparing the *Operationes* (1519), the second lecture on the Psalms.[113] Present scholarly consensus, however, is that in the *Dictata* Luther's soteriology operated precisely in those medieval terms – *pactum* (covenant), *dispositio ad gratiam*, *facere quod in se est*, and *meritum de congruo* – that Vogelsang wanted to hurry him away from. Furthermore, even after divine predestination completely overshadowed human response in

Luther's theology, by no means was this soteriology necessarily out-side the bounds of Catholic orthodoxy as then defined. The Augus-tinian tradition in the Catholic world was far too broad and strong for that. Vogelsang and the Luther Renaissance generally adopted Deni-fle's deadly error of not subjecting late-medieval Catholic scholastic theology to serious and respectful study.

It breaches the time frame of this study (and anticipates the epi-logue) to conclude our discussion of Vogelsang with his little essay *Luther's Struggle against the Jews* (1933).[114] This work does, however, help to identify who Vogelsang was: an active member of the German Christians, with all that that implies. Above all, it is an extreme exam-ple of the disposition of the Luther Renaissance to raise *all* Luther's writings to a near-canonical status. The confessional Lutherans made it a matter of principle not to do that. Accordingly, there is a charac-teristically different tone in Vogelsang's and Althaus's writing on the "Jewish question" – one that is not adequately accounted for by the slightly earlier appearance of Althaus's writing and the temperamen-tal differences between the two men.

Vogelsang starts by commenting that pre-war Protestant scholars found Luther's anti-Jewish writings embarrassing.[115] Now, of course, nationalist and Nazi politics have made a vogue of them, but it will not do simply to make a racist out of the Reformer.[116] On the other hand, Luther's analysis of the issue was not narrowly theological; he drew the "national-political consequences" (*volkspolitischen Folgerungen*) of his religious insights.[117]

A rabbi named Reinhold Lewin had written a study of Luther and the Jews in 1911 that was broadly accepted, praised by Catholic and Lutheran alike, and used in the apparatus of the Weimar Edition. Ac-cording to Lewin, after an initial period of indifference to the Jews, Luther was led to think, following a visit of two Jews, that the new gospel would greatly ease the conversion of Jews to Christianity. Ac-cordingly he wrote "Daß Jesus Christus ein geborner Jude sei" (That Jesus Christ Was Born a Jew; 1523). But the-hoped for conversions did not occur; – instead, in the 1530s the emergence of Anabaptist Sabba-tarians led Luther to fear that Jews were effectively proselytizing for their religion among Christians. Finally in 1542 and 1543 the aging Luther wrote two fanatically anti-Jewish pamphlets. Vogelsang com-mented that "it was hardly surprising that Lewin as a rabbi was not able to grasp Luther's real concerns, despite his efforts at objectivity and scholarly methodology."[118] In substance, Vogelsang tried to make Luther much more consistent in his attitude to the Jews from begin-ning to end of his career – seeking to find system and consistency in Luther's writings as much as he possibly could. But the optimism of

the 1523 tract was so clear that Vogelsang ended by quibbling with
Lewin more than revising his findings.[119] The attack on Lewin was
not surprising in the climate of 1933, but it exposed the weakness of
the Luther Renaissance's commitment to presenting the Reformer's
writings as systematic theology yet claiming historical veracity for
their scholarship.

Vogelsang's main point was that the Jews were the epitome of the
rejection of Christ, of stubborn refusal to accept God's forgiveness
mediated through the cross of Christ. They were the archetype of the
damned, hence their disastrous history was a perpetual object lesson
to humankind. Had they not said, when Pilate did not wish to condemn Christ to the cross, "Let his blood be upon us and our children"? God's curse upon the Jews took the historical shape of the
destruction of the Temple in 70 CE and their subsequent dispersion
throughout the world. The "wandering Jew" of their external history
symbolized their internal state of bad conscience. As a people, they
were the rightful successors of Judas, the betrayer of Christ.[120]

Not only were they a volk without a country; they recognized no
solidarity, no moral obligations, to the peoples among whom they
lived.[121] Luther mingled his German ethos with his Christianity in
upholding the dignity of honest work. The Jews hated real work and
lived by usury, by exploiting and cheating their host peoples. Nineteenth-century liberals thought that Luther's denunciations of usury
were economically primitive, but by the 1930s the evils of capitalism
were manifest and it was clear how far-sighted Luther had been.[122]
His solution in his tracts of the 1540s – that the Jews should be expelled from Germany, following the example of other Christian countries, sent back to Palestine, and forced to live by honest labour – was
wise and far-sighted.[123] Vogelsang paraphrased Luther in such a
manner that the difference between them almost disappeared. It was
clear that for him everything that Luther said and wrote was wise
and far-sighted.

Even on such a matter as Romans 11, where Vogelsang acknowledged that the dominant scholarly interpretation was that Paul proph-
esied the conversion of the Jews at the end of days, Luther was
permitted the last word in rejecting any such exegesis.[124] The Reformer's scorn of the narrow literal and grammatical biblical exegesis
of the rabbis in the Talmud and the Kabbala was duly registered.[125]
And despite Vogelsang's eschewing a merely racist analysis, Luther
was granted the honour of being a forerunner of the racist standpoint:
"The German national [volksdeutsche] point of view in [Luther's]
struggle against the Jews can no longer be overlooked. He remarked
that the Jews speak 'pig Latin' [Rotwelsch] and compared them repeat-

edly to the Tartars and gypsies in their foreignness. He said that their degeneration was caused to a significant degree by racial mixture, because of their proselytizing among their host peoples, with the result that 'the Israelite blood has become mixed, impure, watery, and wild.'"[126] Above all, Vogelsang repeatedly gloried in the superiority of his national German viewpoint, as compared to the philo-Semitic cosmopolitan, liberal perspective:

> Whoever, like all nineteenth-century liberals, proclaims "the duty to recognize in Judaism a divinely willed path to the solution of life's deepest questions (Lamparter)," or, as in Lessing's Parable of the Three Rings and the whole Enlightenment, regards Christ and Judaism as only variants of a "religion of reason" that is basically everywhere the same, will never come close to agreeing with Luther and the New Testament that the fate of the Jewish people can only be described in the categories of curse and blindness, the wrath and anger of God, and can never be explained in the superficial categories of human rationality and causality. The liberal will consign to the sphere of legend the invisible complex of power and money and blood and fate that is the reality of world Judaism and will refuse to recognize that with the German revolution of 1933 the Jewish question, a world-historical issue that has been covered up for a century and a half, is once more visible.[127]

Vogelsang has usually escaped the conservative theological guild's condemnation for "turning political," an accusation that made his mentor Hirsch a convenient scapegoat after 1945; but Hirsch generally avoided crudity in his championing of the Nazi cause. The same cannot be said of Vogelsang's essay on Luther and the Jews, which its author doubtless regarded as a purely religious, historical, and theological treatment of the subject.

The theological development of the Luther Renaissance demonstrated that theocentrism alone was not enough – certainly not for dogmatic theologians of an Evangelical Christianity insistent upon its superiority to other monotheistic religions. As Hirsch and Vogelsang supplied the Christological deficit in Holl's theology, they focused increasingly upon Luther's theology of the cross. At the same time, by insisting on finding the antecedents of this cross theology in Luther's early lecture, the *Dictata*, they thoroughly confused the discussion of the Autobiographical Fragment of 1545. Their theological nationalism, which was more intense than that of any of our other protagonists, spilled out into their historical scholarship. It bore fruit only during the Third Reich in Hirsch's speculations about Jesus' ethnicity and Vogelsang's repetition of Luther's viciousness against the Jews.

Conclusion

A minimal conclusion from the present study is that Luther research was one of the battlefields where the Evangelical theological schools of the Weimar era aired their differences. Moreover, their different approaches, both to Luther scholarship and to the struggles within the German Evangelical church in 1933–34 (to be described in the epilogue), confirm that three distinct schools were in conflict: the Karl Holl school, which has subsequently been called the "Luther Renaissance," the Dialectical Theology, and the confessional Lutherans. Although there was friendly exchange between the confessional Lutherans and the Luther Renaissance and both used the *Zeitschrift für systematishe Theologie*, they had distinct approaches to theology and to Luther studies. Although the leaders of the Dialectical Theology were regarded as bumptious outsiders in the 1920s, and they were creative theologians rather than theological scholars (one of the several meanings of Harnack's telling Barth that the latter was better suited to being a topic of theological study than to being a professor of theology), there is a growing recognition that they were not as different from the other two groups of theologians as they at first seemed or as they claimed to be.

The major contemporary interpreters of the Karl Holl school, or Luther Renaissance, Johannes Wallmann and Heinrich Assel, now view it as a parallel phenomenon with similar aims to those of the Dialectical Theology – the Luther Renaissance was "the other awakening" of the 1920s in the title of Assel's book. Both groups now appear to have been attempting a new beginning for Evangelical theology, responding to the perceived bankruptcy of theological liberalism and *Kulturprotestantismus* in the aftermath of the First World War.

It is the case that the contending theological schools examined here had more in common than their sharp disagreements would have made it appear. The nineteenth-century theology of Albrecht Ritschl, which interpreted Luther's theology of justification in such a way as to stress religious individualism, the love of God, and the centrality of Christ, was regarded as saccharine and out of balance. The new watchword was "theocentrism," a transcendent monotheism equally visible in Karl Holl and Emanuel Hirsch and in Karl Barth and Friedrich Gogarten in the early 1920s. All four insisted on an uncanny, wrathful, unknown God in dialectical tension with the loving, saving, revealed God. Hirsch and Gogarten discovered in Luther's *Bondage of the Will* an eminently satisfactory statement of their personal theologies.

Pre-war liberal theology, which had adopted the goal of seeking a harmony of Christianity and culture and seemed to be a celebration of bourgeois individualism, took part of the blame for a world that had gone very much awry in the years 1914–19. Whether approaching the subject from the left, as did Karl Barth with his early ties to the Swiss Religious Socialists, or from the right, like Karl Holl with his association with the Fatherland Party, theologians were moved to supplement their individual soteriologies with a theology of community. Indeed, Holl said that Luther's theology of justification was only accessible to modern man through a theology of community.

In the anti-liberal, anti-bourgeois mood of the 1920s, Søren Kierkegaard became a sort of "church father" of both the Luther Renaissance and the Dialectical Theology (while the more authentic church father, Augustine, was temporarily expelled from the evangelical succession). But there were interesting nuances in Kierkegaard reception that cut across the partisan fronts. Both Holl and Barth developed growing reservations about the Danish theologian, while Hirsch became the great Kierkegaard scholar and exegete, and Gogarten remained throughout the interwar years what Troeltsch had called him in the early 1920s – "an apple from Kierkegaard's tree."

The confessional Lutheran theologians remained critical of many of the theological fashions that provided an unacknowledged link between Dialectical Theology and Luther Renaissance. Pledged to the Lutheran confessions and thoroughly aware of the rich ambivalence of Luther himself and the Lutheran tradition on the subject of predestination, they did not want to follow Hirsch and Gogarten in making *The Bondage of the Will* an authoritative foundation of their systematic theology. They mocked "church father" Kierkegaard almost as much as Troeltsch did. They insisted on a Christian God who was immanent as well as transcendent, along the lines of a Chalcedonian orthodoxy that made them wary of "theocentrism." On a theology of community they modernized Luther by stressing a revelation through ordinances of creation that included the nation *(das Volk)*. When this issue attained its full development, Holl was dead and the belief in a nationalist revelation through the law offered a mock-Lutheran common platform for Elert, Althaus, Hirsch, and Gogarten. Only Barth resisted this concept as a blasphemous distortion of the gospel, for which he was labelled in good Lutheran manner an antinomian.

Ultimately, it was intolerable to make Jesus so unimportant as he was in the early 1920s for the theocentric Luther Renaissance and the equally theocentric Dialectical Theology. As Paul Althaus warned, if Jesus were so unimportant, the outcome would be to raise other monotheistic religions to a status of equivalent value to Christianity, the error of Troeltsch in his final years. Hence as the 1920s proceeded, we see the universal trend of the return of Christological focus. Gogarten was first in 1923, followed by Barth with his Reformed orthodox Christology, begun in 1924 and completed in 1936. Meanwhile Erich Vogelsang returned Christological emphasis to the Luther Renaissance, focusing on the passion of the human Jesus.

Not only did the polemics of the Dialectical Theology and the Luther Renaissance unintentionally disguise their considerable affinity with each other, but they disguised their significant continuity with the much-maligned liberal theology of the pre-war era. The best recent study of Barth's theological evolution concludes: "however critical Barth may have been of modern theology, it is of the utmost importance – if we are to have a more accurate understanding of the history of theology in the last two centuries – to see that Dialectical Theology in the form in which it was taught by Barth was a thoroughly *modern* option."[1] As for Holl, although his move to the *Rechtfertigungslehre* (1905) was a conservative choice and his move to the Fatherland Party (1917) put him in almost exclusively conservative company, as did his publishing in Stapel's *Zeitschrift für systematische Theologie* after 1923, he never broke completely with the Harnack heritage. This was even more emphatically the case with Hirsch, the ultimate freethinking modernist. There is a partial truth in Barth's description of the German Christians, to whom Hirsch and Vogelsang belonged, as the "worst monstrosity of neo-Protestantism." The Dialectical Theology and the Luther Renaissance were, like the liberals, tied to no creed. As the confessional Lutherans said, to be "free theologians" tended to cut one off from the stabilizing connectedness of a community of faith. The difference between being a "free theologian" in an era when church history dominated theology and being such in an era when systematic theology reigned was, however, considerable. In the first case, one was tied to sacred history (and the prevalent assumption was that *all* history was sacred). In the second case, one dogmatized freely in the name of God – either explicitly like Barth or assuming the identity of Martin Luther like Holl.

Pre-war liberal theology was losing steam for purely internal reasons. It was generating problems for which it could not provide the answers. Martin Kähler's disparagement of the search for the historical Jesus of Adolf von Harnack and Albert Schweitzer was making an impact. Even with extensive and reliable source materials, history could only produce an impressionistic reconstruction of the past, and the Gospels were theological statements, not historical sources. So were not the theological symbols surrounding the "Christ of faith" obviously superior to the search for the "so-called historical Jesus"? Liberal theologians such as Barth's teacher Wilhelm Herrmann had already begun abandoning humanity's dubious search for God in their search for his revelation to humanity. To Troeltsch's suggestion that the asserted superiority of Christianity to other religions was an expression of Western ethnocentrism, a piece of cultural arrogance, they replied that the difference between Christianity and other religions was that in the other religions human beings sought God, while in Christianity God sought them. Thus the era of historic theology gave place to the era of dogmatic theology. Again the Lutheran confessionalists were more accommodating than the newly dogmatic "free theologians." Althaus recognized a limited, relative legitimacy for non-Christian religions; Vogelsang explained the persistence of Judaism as the work of the devil.

So the search for the truth about Luther in the period 1917–33 began under the sign of considerable pessimism about the possibility and worth of historical knowledge. Holl, in effect, moved from church history to systematic theology when he shifted his primary attention from Greek church fathers to Luther. Barth recognized history as an ancillary study to dogmatics, to be valued as long as it stayed in its proper place. Again, it was the "old-fashioned" confessional Lutherans at Erlangen who stayed closest to what we would recognize as history, acknowledging historically conditioned differences between them and Luther and between Luther and Paul. They did not have to renounce historicism because they had never been historicists, and they had the basic understanding that Christianity was a historic religion.

The dominance of systematic theology, of course, did not prevent Luther studies from flourishing. A lot of effort was devoted to the study of Martin Luther, and in the nature of things, that tends to produce new knowledge. The argument between the Luther Renaissance and the Dialectical Theology about whether Luther's justification theology was "effective," producing a moral regeneration of the sinner, or "forensic," simply changing the sinner's relation to God, was driven by the theological systems of Holl and Barth, which required one answer or the other. Again, Althaus had the last word – Holl was right to insist that Luther (*throughout his career*) connected regeneration to justification, but he was wrong to say that regeneration provided a godly rationale for justification; God's free forgiveness of sinners was the main point. The retreat from theocentrism, the return to Christological focus that we see in different ways in Gogarten, Barth, and Vogelsang, could not fail to improve understanding of Luther because he did believe in the Nicene and Chalcedonian creeds. As long as Holl looked away from this basic fact, working with the Ritschl-Harnack distinction between Luther's creative, new theology and his merely traditional beliefs, there was bound to be a serious deficit in the understanding of Luther. In some areas, such as the early theology of the cross, Barth and Vogelsang, working from their respective theological perspectives, complemented each other and prepared the way for future elaboration of the theme.

But there was much that was wayward in Weimar-era Luther studies. Nothing was more so than the determined search for the Experience in the Tower through close exegesis of the early theological lectures. It proved a blind alley for Luther scholarship. In that respect, Hirsch and Vogelsang, despite genuine discoveries on points of detail, represent a step back from Holl, who had too much scholarly common sense to distort the Autobiographical Fragment of 1545. With the debate exhausted, the ironic awareness is sinking in among Protestant scholars that Father Denifle, who first raised the issue, was, after all, right – the theology of Luther's early theological lectures was Catholic theology. (However, it was much better Catholic theology than Denifle gave it credit for being.) There was no early *Rechtfertigungslehre* that, in a singular case in point of ideal determinism, took hold of the young Luther internally and forced him step by step, unconsciously and unwillingly, to the break with Rome. Luther said as much in the Autobiographical Fragment of 1545 – before the controversy with the papacy, his theology was Romanist – and readers of his Latin works should recognize that it was a theology which he had left behind. The fixation on the tower experience is partly explainable through the early-twentieth- century fascination with introspective psychology. That this was the age of Freud and Jung affected the way that Grisar, Barth, and Vogelsang read Luther. So the Protestant theologians brought him to life for the 1920s, with his conflicts and torments, and then cried foul when the priests and the psychoanalysts found him psychologically interesting.

The idea that Luther and "his" Reformation represented the German world-historical moment in the history of Christianity went back to Ritschl and Harnack. They fancied themselves true to the forward-looking part of Luther's theology when as historians of dogma they dismissed the metaphysical speculations of the early Greek creeds and tried through historical study to recover the religion of the New Testament, to go back to Paul and Jesus. But historical study proved a deficient tool for the recovery of the original gospel. Karl Holl attempted to return to the gospel by an act of faith in the *Rechtfertigungslehre*, the traditional soteriology of Lutheranism. He declared that the true preached gospel of the ancient church was best reflected in Luther's interpretation of Paul's epistles to the Romans and the Galatians, and he asserted that this was a conscious insight on the part of the Reformer. The biblical canon as a whole was but a necessary evil, a barrier against false teaching. To the extent that the one God's message of redemption was proclaimed more clearly in the writings of Luther than in the writings of Paul or the sayings attributed to Jesus, the *Rechtfertigungslehre* was God's special revelation to the Germans, and Martin Luther was nothing less than the German saviour. And Holl proclaimed him to the Germans in the country's years of greatest need, 1917–21. Holl was echoed by the confessional Lutherans and the Dialectical Theology, to the extent that they accepted justification by faith through grace as the sum and substance of Evangelical Christianity. In this they were very different from leading Evangelical theologians of the pre-war years such as Wilhelm Herrmann, Albert Schweitzer, Adolf von Harnack, and Ernest Troeltsch. The business of German salvation was elaborated beyond Luther, of course, when Hirsch, Gogarten, Elert, and Althaus extended his theology of the law to include the volk. Barth, who had always been horrified by the Christian religious experience that the Germans thought they found in the last war, agreed with the other theologians to the extent that he wrote in December 1939 that such a theology of the law had its foundation in "the error of Martin Luther about the relation of law and gospel ... through which the German volk's heathen nature ... is ideologically transfigured, confirmed, and strengthened." It is safe to say that the controversies about ordinances of creation and *völkisch* theology as an extension of Luther's theology of the law contributed *nothing* to the historical understanding of Martin Luther.

That faith in Christ need not be faith in the *Rechtfertigungslehre* is obvious, but perhaps the obvious needs to be stated. First, this is not the faith of Roman Catholics or Orthodox Christians or the ancient Christian traditions continuing in Africa and the Near East. In Barth's later years as a dogmatic theologian in Germany, 1924–35, he expounded a theology based on the entire biblical canon in the Reformed manner. And if a New Testament canon within a canon be sought, Romans and Galatians are not the only possibility. Among my Pennsylvania German cousins I think of the Old Order Amish, whose sermons are based on Matthew and Luke and a following of the commands and examples of Jesus in a religion that, like Judaism, is founded on rule and practice rather than on theory. They would say of the matters discussed in this book that they are too deep for human beings to understand and that they had better be left to God.

Epilogue:
The German Year 1933
and Afterward

This study is about the origins of an interpretation of Martin Luther which arose in the Weimar years and dominated not only in Germany but also in the United Kingdom and North America until the 1960s, and which is still a strong minority position among scholars in these countries to the present day. It is not a study of the origins of the Third Reich. Nevertheless, there is some point in seeing how our protagonists divided when confronted with the destruction of democracy and the emergence of the totalitarian state in 1933.

Emanuel Hirsch endorsed Hitler early, an existential choice, as he explained, whose outcome remained unknown, but one which he never renounced, despite suffering severe professional and personal consequences from it, until his death in 1972. On the occasion of the presidential election of 1932, in which the sitting German president, Paul von Hindenburg, received 60 per cent of the vote and Hitler 40 per cent, Hirsch announced his support for Hitler in a letter to a local Nazi Party newspaper. He explained that he was a Nationalist, not a Nazi: "You know that I am not a National Socialist and that I have more than mild doubts about the NSDAP ... But I cannot get around the fact that a situation has developed without my assistance. And Hitler now is the only representative of a will to break with the mistakes of the twelve years from 1919 to 1931, the only candidate on 10 April to offer a new German beginning."[1] When Hitler became chancellor in January 1933 and consolidated his power in the elections of March that year, which were followed by the rapid establishment of a one-party state, Hirsch in effect joined his calling as theologian to that of Nazi propagandist. This was the case despite his becoming a member of the NSDAP only in 1937.[2]

For Protestants with a national or *völkisch* perspective, who regarded the Weimar Republic, with its pseudo-internationalist, humanitarian values, as an instrument of the victorious Entente, the coming to power of Hitler appeared as a sort of God-sent deliverance. Hirsch, of course, identified with Fichte, the prophet of German national revival against Napoleon. As he wrote in 1933, he had expected the resurrection of Germany to take a generation at least: "We all thought we were captured in the destiny of an old culture, in which public life restricts itself to ordering external things and the common spirit becomes a religiously and morally neutral characterlessness."[3] Hitler was adept at appealing to Protestants' resentment of the neutral state, which in their eyes had usurped the basically Protestant state of Bismarck and the kaiser. A few days after becoming chancellor he said in an official proclamation, "The national government will extend its firm protection to Christianity, the foundation of our entire morality."[4] Common to Protestant theologians of many schools was the notion that Hitler's coming to power enabled the churches to have a wonderful chance – perhaps the last – at becoming relevant to the life of the German people. Hanns Rückert, one of Holl's students, summed up this view with particular clarity in May 1933: "The church is confronted – not by any internal or external party, but by history itself – with the question of whether it possesses the inner strength to interpret, starting with God, a great turning point in the destiny of Germany and whether it can participate in the shaping of that turning point."[5]

From Hitler's point of view it was a great disadvantage that the Protestant church of the Weimar era was a loose confederation of twenty-eight provincial churches, confessionally divided into Lutherans, Reformed, and the Evangelical Union. He worked behind the scenes to unite German Protestants into a single state church, led according to Nazi principles of leadership by a *Reichsbischof*, which could be penetrated and dominated by party members and sympathizers. The Nazi goals involved a levelling of the historic confessional divisions in German Protestantism.

The German Christians (*Deutsche Christen*) were the group, organized in 1931, which worked for a practical union of Protestant and Nazi objectives. Inspired by an emotional union of Protestantism and German nationalism, they hoped to unify the fragmented Protestant churches "on the common and unsurrenderable foundation of the Reformation."[6] They sincerely enough opposed the neo-paganism that stood at the fringes of the Nazi movement and tended to scorn

the traditional orthodoxies defined by Lutheran and Reformed confessions, because many of them had abandoned these orthodoxies as
a result of a liberal religious education. The Holl school, with links to
the Evangelical Union of the Prussian state church and a confused but
unmistakable liberal theological pedigree, proved more compatible
with the German Christians than the other theological interpreters of
Luther. The caveat to this statement is that they associated only with
the factionalized German Christian movement's conservative wing.[7]
The Erlangen theologians, Werner Elert and Paul Althaus, for all their
German national and conservative politics, were not prepared to surrender the historic Lutheran confessions to Prussian Unionists and
theological dilettantes. Karl Barth, the sole committed anti-Nazi
among all our protagonists in 1933 and 1934, had the political genius
to recognize that, even if he lacked a consensus to defend constitu-
tional government in Germany in those years, a strong group of
churchmen could nevertheless be rallied to the traditional Christianity of the Bible and the Reformation-era confessions.

In April 1933 Hitler named Military Chaplain Ludwig Müller from
Königsberg his "plenipotentiary for the affairs of the Protestant
churches" – obviously Führer-designate for the proposed unified state
church. Hirsch became one of Müller's main supporters and advisers,
as did Erich Vogelsang, then a *Privat Dozent* (assistant professor) at
Königsberg University.[8] The German Christians were, in effect, an ecclesiastical party organized to achieve Hitler's objectives, but they
were somewhat too radical to create a Protestant consensus. The East
Prussian German Christians, advised by Müller and Vogelsang, tried
to steer a more moderate course, remaining silent on Nazi racist beliefs that were potentially offensive to people who, after all, used the
Old Testament in their worship services. Müller seemed to most established churchmen and theologians, Paul Althaus among them, to be a
figure of too little stature for the position of national leadership into
which Hitler had thrust him. His main credential was that he had
done some good political work for the Nazis among the East Prussian
officers. In late May the representatives of the provincial churches
elected the highly respected Friedrich von Bodelschwingh as bishop
of the Reich, but he was forced to resign after only a month because of
pressure from the government and the German Christians.[9]

When Protestant church elections were held throughout Germany
in late July, the German Christians were opposed chiefly by national-
conservative churchmen who tried to combine political loyalty to the
new government with insistence on the independence of the church.
In three important provinces, Bavaria, Württemberg, and Hanover,
these conservatives were able to go so far in accommodating the

German Christians that the two groups agreed upon a combined list of candidates in the church elections, which in the longer run preserved the independence of these confessionally Lutheran churches.[10] Since the theological faculty at Erlangen University was under the authority of the Bavarian church, this happenstance preserved for Elert and Althaus a formally neutral shelter from the church struggles.

As for Karl Barth in Bonn University, he was little more impressed with the national-conservative opposition than with the German Christians themselves. He wrote, "What we now need in the first instance is a centre of *spiritual* resistance that will give point and substance to resistance in church politics." Endorsed by Hitler in a radio speech the night before the election, the German Christians took 70 per cent of the vote, and Müller became "the first Evangelical bishop of the Reich," as he was named in the dedication to Vogelsang's booklet, *Luther's Struggle against the Jews.*[11]

The problem with the German Christians turned out to be their undisciplined radicalism. Müller appeared too moderate to many of them, and without their support, he was crippled in carrying out any effective unification of the Protestant churches. In November 1933 a mass meeting of the Berlin German Christians took place in the Sportpalast at which the chief speaker, Reinhold Krause, denounced Müller for his slowness and hesitations in creating a "*völkische* church." Krause went on to demand the purging of everything "un-German" from the worship service, the scrapping of the Old Testament, and the end of "the scapegoat and inferiority theology of the rabbi Paul."[12] Hirsch and Vogelsang were more conservative than the Berlin German Christians, but both of them, despite the loss of credit resulting from the Sportpalast rally, remained associated with the national movement. Vogelsang did break with Müller and signed a petition calling for his resignation, but as late as October 1935 he participated as a speaker in a theological conference at Wittenberg sponsored by the movement. There he read a paper on "Luther's Scriptural Exegesis." Also his career flourished, as a result certainly of his good political connections as well as his undoubted academic excellence. By 1937 he was full professor at Gießen University.[13]

The German Year 1933 was a bad one for Friedrich Gogarten, author of the programmatic essay "Between the Times" (1920) and Karl Barth's erstwhile ally in the Dialectical Theology. Gogarten's problem was to decide whether his aversion to the modernist decadence that he decried in the Weimar era was strong enough for him to make common cause with his former opponents, the theologian-historians of the Luther Renaissance. By 1930 he had already come to the conclusion that modern humanity had an authority problem, and that only a renewed reverence for authority could set it on the road to political and spiritual healing. Gogarten, who in 1931 was called from his pastorate to become theology professor in Breslau (and moved to the more prestigious Göttingen University four years later), not only accepted but welcomed the Nazi rise to power, a turn which horrified many who associated him with Barth's theology. In May 1933 he wrote: "The contemporary German suffered most deeply from not knowing to whom he belonged, whether God or man, as I wrote in my *Political Ethics*. Now he knows once more that he belongs to his volk, and in and through his volk to the state, in which the will of the volk has become sovereign power." One's own volk became for Gogarten the historical embodiment of the divine law. The woes of modernity justified a particularly severe version of the law to purge the German people of their erstwhile Weimar decadence: "When a volk that has lost its order as badly as our volk has, is to be brought back into order, it must first be reduced to uniformity. Whoever complains that this involves an impoverishment of life fails to grasp that now it is a question of preserving naked existence."[14]

Gogarten had difficulty deciding whether this endorsement of Hitler brought with it an endorsement of Müller and the German Christians. At first he joined the national-conservative position; then he decided that the German Christian slogan of "the union of the gospel and nationality" amounted, really, to the unity of law and gospel. In August he formally adhered to the German Christians, freshly victorious in the church elections. Now the National Socialist state seemed "a necessary precondition" for "the unrestricted proclamation of our Lord, crucified for our sins and elevated above all." But the spectacle that the German Christians made of themselves at the end of 1933 led Gogarten to resign from the movement and to lapse into silence for the duration of the Third Reich.[15] When he re-emerged after 1945, he was, unlike Hirsch, reconciled to liberal democracy, although, like Hirsch, he made no statements or apologies for his previous writing and behaviour.

When Barth read Gogarten's affirmation that the law of God is identical to the law of the German volk, he withdrew from the co-editorship of *Zwischen den Zeiten*. As far as he was concerned, Gogarten had betrayed the gospel. Barth regretted that he had paid little attention to the rise of Nazism until 1930–31. Its principles and its personalities had appeared to him so absurd that he never doubted that the German people would have the good sense to reject them.[16] Now, following the victory of the German Christians in the church elections and particularly their behaviour at the end of 1933, he was able to rally some conservatives to the idea that the official German

Evangelical Church had committed apostasy. As far as Barth was concerned, the German Christians were "the last, fullest and worst monstrosity of neo-Protestantism,"[17] the logical outcome of liberal Protestantism – a view that the case of Emanuel Hirsch seemed to support.

In any case the Lutheran bishops of Württemberg and Bavaria and other dignitaries joined Barth in an ecclesiological resistance movement which declared that when church leaders attack "their confessional foundation through erroneous teaching," then pastors and teachers are "summoned and assembled by the Word of God to address the congregations as a free synod"[18] and to lay down their confession representing the true church. Such a synod, composed of 139 representatives of the Lutheran, Reformed, and Union churches, met at Barmen on 29–31 May 1934, in the First Synod of the Confessing Church. Barth later claimed to have drafted the six articles of the Barmen Declaration, "fortified by strong coffee and one or two Brazil cigars," while his Lutheran co-workers had their afternoon naps.[19]

After a preamble that denounced "the errors of the German Christians of the present Reich church administration" and accused them of "shattering the unity of the German Evangelical Church," there followed six articles. Article 1 declared that "Jesus Christ, as he is attested to us in Holy Scripture, is the one Word of God whom we have to hear, and whom we have to trust and obey in life and in death." The notion that the church had to recognize "yet other events, powers, historic figures and truths as God's revelation" was singled out as a "false doctrine." Here the notion of a supplementary revelation of God through history and nature, an idea that connected Hirsch, Elert, Althaus, and to an extent Gogarten, was explicitly stigmatized. Article 2 rejected "the false doctrine that there could be areas of our life in which we belong not to Jesus Christ but to other lords, areas in which we would not need justification and sanctification through him." Here Barth, without explicitly saying so, was singling out "the four-hundred-year-old error" of the Lutheran doctrine of the two kingdoms. Article 3 stated, "The Christian church is the community of brethren in which, in Word and sacrament, through the Holy Spirit, Jesus Christ acts in the present as Lord." Given Christ's lordship, the church had no right to bend to "the prevailing ideological and political convictions of the day."

Article 4 of the declaration called on the Protestant teaching of the priesthood of all believers in order to reject any Führer principle in the church: "The various offices in the church do not provide a basis for some to exercise authority over others but for the ministry with which the whole community has been entrusted and charged to be carried out." Article 5 recognized that "by divine appointment the state, in this still unredeemed world in which the church is also situated, has the task of maintaining justice and peace, as far as human discernment and human ability make this possible, by means of the threat and use of force." But the state should restrict itself to its limited, divinely ordained task. It is a "false doctrine that beyond its special commission the state should and could become the sole and total order of human life." Article 6 defined the church's purpose as "in Christ's stead, and so in the service of his own Word and work, to deliver to all people, through preaching and sacrament, the message of the free grace of God." The church cannot be subordinated to any human purpose whatever. The declaration concluded by calling upon "all who can stand in solidarity with [it] to be mindful of these theological findings in all their decisions concerning church and state."[20] The unanimous acceptance of the Barmen Declaration was secured by referring it back to the several churches "for responsible exegesis on the foundation of their confessions." From the standpoint of many conservative Lutheran churchmen, this requirement subordinated the declaration to their historic confessions – the defence of which was the main point of their resistance to Bishop Müller and the German Christians.[21]

Elert and Althaus, however, despite the involvement of the Bavarian Lutheran church in the ecclesiastical resistance movement that led to Barmen, refused to be co-opted by Barth. Their theological opposition to the Dialectical Theology and their national-conservative politics led them to seek a position of their own between Barth and the German Christians. On 11 June appeared the Ansbach Memorandum, essentially written by Elert, although he secured the signatures of Althaus and six Lutheran pastors to the document. Composed less than two weeks after the Barmen Declaration and addressed to the National Socialist Evangelical Pastors' League, the document had as its object to stake out an orthodox Lutheran position that was pro-Nazi, although distinct from that of the German Christians and their Luther Renaissance advisers.

The Ansbach Memorandum began by affirming the historic Lutheran confessions as "the pure presentation of the content of the Holy Scriptures." As teaching (*Lehre*), these Reformation documents did not need to be improved upon, and as Elert wrote elsewhere, the Barmen Declaration implied an effort to improve on the Lutheran confessions by reconciling them with the Reformed and Union confessions. Point 2 of the memorandum was that "the Word of God speaks to us as law and gospel," an important Lutheran theological distinction that Elert felt was violated by the effective antinomianism of the Barmen Declaration. The Christocentric emphasis of Barmen applied properly only to the gospel. Elert undertook to testify to the law to Barth and his colleagues. In point 3 he specified that the law "binds everyone to the estate to which God has called him, and obligates us to the natural ordinances to which we are subjected, such as family, volk, race (i.e., community of blood)." Furthermore, God's law binds everyone to "the distinct moment in the history of his family, volk, or race in which he lives." Point 4 continued that for Christian believers the natural ordinances of God express "pure paternal, divine goodness and mercy." This applies to all of God's ordinances, even when they are distorted, because they maintain earthly life in accord with God's will; but "as Christians we distinguish benevolent and wayward rulers, healthy and distorted ordinances."

Point 5 brought the memorandum to its central affirmation: "As believing Christians, we thank God the Lord that he has given to our volk, in its moment of need, the Führer as a 'devout and loyal ruler,' and that he brings forth through the National Socialist state a 'good government,' a government with 'discipline and honour.' We know therefore that we are responsible before God to assist the work of the Führer in our vocation and estate." Point 6 indicated that members of the church are subjected to the natural ordinances and that, since governmental structures undergo historical changes, the church's connections to those structures must also change with time. Point 7 elaborated that the church has indeed received from the Lord unchanging obligations to proclaim the Word and administer the sacraments, but that matters such as church constitution and forms of worship can be adapted to the needs of the historic moment. When Elert wrote explicitly against the Barmen Declaration, he attacked its unstated objective "to break off any positive connection of the church to the contemporary historical experience of our volk." This, he said, contravened the wide latitude given to human law in the Augsburg Confession itself.[22]

The Ansbach Memorandum did not get a good reception because it undermined the ongoing efforts at self-protection of the Bavarian Lutheran church. As some theological critics remarked, it contained, under the cover of its attacks on Barmen's alleged antinomianism, an effort to identify the law of God that Luther had taught with Elert's theology of volk and race as "ordinances of creation" (*Schöpfungsordnungen*), which was definitely something new, not to be found in Luther's writings or the Reformation-era confessions.[23]

Althaus had required two redrafts of the memorandum before he was willing to sign, he insisted that he was not its initiator, and he was soon trying to put at least nuances between himself and what it said. He regarded Hirsch as a fanatic and was genuinely concerned with maintaining the independence of the Lutheran churches. Yet he had greeted 1933 with partisan joy and thought at first that Hitler was God's blessing upon the German people and his cure for the godless Weimar Republic.

In October 1933 Althaus published a book, *Die deutsche Stunde der Kirche* (The German Hour of the Church). Its conclusion was that 1933, like August 1914, was a moment in which God's hand was visible in German history: "So we take the turning point of this year as grace from God's hand. He has saved us from the abyss and out of hopelessness. He has given us – or so we hope – a new day of life."[24] But even in that book Althaus noted that the German Christian claim that Christian virtues were spread more effectively by the National Socialist movement than by the church was unacceptable to him as a theologian. In the summer of 1933 he had already had an encounter with provincial Nazi authorities in Bavaria because of a speech he had made declaring that all human life was worthy in the sight of God. He was instructed not to speak or write on subjects of "racial hygiene."[25] In a letter of September to the Lutheran bishop of the provincial church in Hanover, Althaus drew a clear line between himself and the German Christians ("It is totally impossible to indicate approval by joining them"). As for Hirsch, he "is subject to such an absolutism that it is no longer possible to have a true discussion with him. He sees in me a man who 'reasons against fate.' "[26]

Robert P. Ericksen has aptly summed up Althaus's persona as that of the "mediator" – acknowledging even the German Christians' opposition to Germanic neo-paganism, just as he recognized that the Barmen Declaration was right to oppose heretical doctrines of the German Christians. In an article on Barmen in July 1934 Althaus rejected the anti-Nazi subtext of the declaration. The church must respond to the aspirations of the volk, which Barmen denied. Further, Elert's stricture that Barmen stressed the gospel to the exclusion of the law was theologically correct. It is true that the revelation in Christ is primary, but it is supplemented by a general revelation that is meaningful to Christians. If the German Christians have distorted notions of this general revelation, it nevertheless exists. So Althaus reaffirmed much of the substance of the Ansbach Memorandum, if in a less polemical tone. As he looked back on its affirmation that Hitler and the Nazis had provided Germany with "good government," his comment of 1964 was "Just a few months later I would not have been able to sign."[27] (His reference was to the obvious breakdown of legal order in the Röhm putsch of June 1936.)

The response of Hirsch to Barmen, as might have been predicted, was the most radical of all our protagonists. He wrote to one of his theological colleagues, on the very day that the Barmen Declaration was accepted, that he had concluded that the 1918–34 experiment in the administrative independence of the Protestant church was a failure.[28] It had proven itself incapable of taking over the state's role of external direction, according to which the Protestant churches had been constituted from the time of the Reformation to the end of the Wilhelminian Reich. This view, of course, ran athwart Karl Holl's dictum in his Luther book of 1921 that the Reformer had after 1525 only grudgingly accepted princely authority in the Lutheran territorial churches as a provisional necessity, and that the end of the established Protestant churches in 1918 was a good thing.[29]

The issues sharpened when the Second Synod of the Confessing Church met at Berlin-Dahlem on 19–20 October 1934, disavowed the usurpation of Reich-bishop Müller, and called for the establishment of a legitimate church leadership. By late November a five-member Provisional Church Executive had been established under the chairmanship of the Lutheran bishop of Hanover, August Marahrens.[30] He was a conservative nationalist who had greeted Hitler's coming to power, but he was too orthodox a Lutheran to accept the German Christians. The theological faculty of Hirsch's university, Göttingen, supplied ministers for Marahrens's Hanoverian church. Nevertheless, Hirsch, as a German Christian and a close supporter of Bishop Müller, refused to recognize the Provisional Church Executive. His opposition led to his break even with some of the other former students of Holl, notably Hanns Rückert.[31]

Gradually the Nazi leadership lost interest in the intricacies of the Protestant church struggle, particularly since most of the prominent figures in the Confessing Church continued to give assurances of their political loyalty to the regime. Hirsch's policy, that the Ministry of Churches should take over external direction of the churches on the Wilhelminian pattern and that the churches themselves should "have full freedom and peace to deal with questions of faith and confession," became the law of the Reich from September 1935.[32] Reich-bishop Ludwig Müller remained in office, but virtually powerless and irrelevant to his former supporters, he restricted himself to spiritual functions until the end of his life and the Nazi regime in 1945.

Hirsch, dean of the theology faculty in Göttingen from 1933 to 1939, worked with the Ministry of Churches in Berlin rather than with Bishop Marahrens's Hanoverian church. The great majority of theology faculty members at Göttingen sided with him. When in December 1934 the Provisional Church Executive requested opinions from the universities on the civil service oath to Hitler required of all university professors, Hirsch correctly scented a tactic to protect Karl

Barth, and he moved to squelch the initiative.[33] Barth had declined to take the oath and was suspended from his teaching at Bonn University in November 1934. By the time that he was formally stripped of his professorate in June 1935, he had already returned to Switzerland. He received appointment to a chair in Basel within days of his dismissal.[34]

Hirsch rejected the liberal, rationalist intellectual heritage of the nineteenth century as "the all-encompassing debate about everything." The great significance of 1933, the reason that it marked the crossing over into the postmodern era, was that the Nazis had shut down debate: "The intellectual struggle is closed."[35] But Hirsch, as a "free theologian" at Göttingen, was entirely unwilling to restrict himself to Lutheran orthodoxy as defined by the historic confessions. In 1936 he published *Das Alte Testament und die Predigt des Evangeliums* (The Old Testament and the Preaching of the Gospel), in which he made statements about Old Testament religion that were deemed heretical. The Hanover church mounted a successful opposition in 1938 to his participation in theology examinations, the gateway to the pastorate.[36]

In 1939 Hirsch published his own *Das Wesen des Christentums* (The Essence of Christianity), full of ironic echoes of Adolf von Harnack's book of the same title of 1900. Like Harnack's earlier work, it contains a dismissal of the stories about Jesus' nativity. The Bethlehem story and the family trees connecting Jesus with King David in Matthew 1 were falsifications. Like Harnack, Hirsch stressed Jesus' connection with Galilee, but with a twist that would never have occurred to Harnack. At the time that Galilee was conquered by the Maccabean rulers of Jerusalem about 100 BCE, Hirsch argued, only 10 per cent of its population would have been ethnically Jewish. Thereafter mass conversions to Judaism occurred, but given the 90 per cent majority of non-Jews at the time of the conquest, "according to all the rules of scientific probability, Jesus was of non-Jewish blood." Then to make the case even stronger, Hirsch presented a plausible argument that Joseph, the father of Jesus, had a father with a Greek name, Panther.[37] Hirsch was having none of the Virgin Birth legends, but of course, for him the point of all this was that Jesus was not "racially" Jewish. Since Jesus worshipped in the Temple and proclaimed himself a fulfiller of the Jewish law, the issue of his ancestry was relevant only in the mad world of the Third Reich.

In the 1950s Hirsch republished his Luther research of the Weimar era and insisted that he, not Vogelsang, was right about the Experience in the Tower.[38] By that time Hirsch's younger fellow Holl student and fellow German Christian alumnus, Heinrich Bornkamm, stood at the summit of West German Luther scholarship. Bornkamm had, like most of the people discussed here, greeted Hitler in 1933, but he did not join the Nazi Party and he kept his professorship after 1945.[39] Like Roland Bainton, Gordon Rupp, and Erik Erikson, he supported the Vogelsang version of the Experience in the Tower throughout the 1950s. There were opposing voices, such as Uuras Saarnivaara (1951), but the consensus started to crumble only with the publication of Ernst Bizer's *Fides ex auditu* in 1958. Bornkamm devoted a long article in 1961 and 1962 to the defence of the Vogelsang thesis in *Archiv für Reformationsgeschichte*.[40] There our story ends. It was the last major defence of Karl Holl's legacy.

Notes

PREFACE

1 Moeller, "Problems of Reformation Research," 8.
2 Trillhaas, *Aufgehobene Vergangenheit*, 52.
3 See, for example, Georg Simmel, "The Metropolis and Mental Life," *Man in Contemporary Society*, ed. Columbia College Contemporary Civilization staff (New York: Columbia University Press, 1962), 327, where Nietzsche is singled out as a hater of the modern city who, for that very reason, is regarded as a saviour and prophet by the modern city dweller.
4 Grässer, "Albert Schweitzer," 314.

CHAPTER ONE

1 Trillhaas, "Die Evangelische Theologie im 20. Jahrhundert," 102: "die Neuentdeckung der Reformatoren." The notion of rediscovering Luther did not begin with the Luther Renaissance. In the year when Holl's essays on Luther appeared, Wilhelm Herrmann, Barth's teacher, wrote of Ritschl: "His was the task to rescue the work of Luther from the corruption into which it had fallen, precisely among those who thought that they were the most loyal heirs of the Reformer"(Herrmann, "Albrecht Ritschl, seine Größe und seine Schranke," 405). It would be difficult to foreshadow Holl's self-understanding more exactly.
2 Trillhaas, "Die Evangelische Theologie im 20. Jahrhundert," 89–90.
3 Krüger, "The Ideology of Crisis"; Trillhaas, "Albrecht Ritschl (1822–1889)," 116.

4 Trillhaas, "Albrecht Ritschl (1822–1889)," 120.

5 Ibid., 121.

6 Schott, "Ritschl, Albrecht"; Schott, "Ritschlianer."

7 Troeltsch, "Ein Apfel vom Baume Kierkegaards," 134: "deutsche Protestantismus, … teils eine halb-wissenschaftliche Kulturreligion."

8 Trillhaas, "Die Evangelische Theologie im 20. Jahrhundert," 97.

9 Kantzenbach, "Harnack, Adolf von," 455.

10 Kähler, *The So-Called Historical Jesus and the Historic, Biblical Christ.*

11 Weiß, *Die Predigt Jesu vom Reiche Gottes*; cf. Macquarrie, "Jesus Christus,
   vi," 30–2.

12 Macquarrie, "Jesus Christus, vi," 29–30: "beschritt Harnack, zweifellos
   einer der gelehrtesten christlichen Denker der Neuzeit, Wege in Rich-
   tung auf eine radikalere und undogmatischere Form der Theologie, als
   Ritschl und seine unmittelbaren Nachfolger es sich je vorgestellt hat-
   ten." Cf. Harnack, *Das Wesen des Christentums*; citations from *What Is
   Christianity?*

13 Harnack, *What Is Christianity?* vii–xviii.

14 Ibid., 128.

15 Ibid., 168–9.

16 Ibid., 230.

17 Ibid., 221 (emphasis in original).

18 Ibid., 252 (emphasis in original).

19 Ibid., 290.

20 Ibid., 282–3.

21 Harnack, *Lehrbuch der Dogmengeschichte*, 3: 817.

22 Ibid., 867.

23 Ibid., 826.

24 Ibid., 811.

25 Ibid., 813–14.

26 Ibid., 831.

27 Ibid., 832.

28 Ibid., 831n1.

29 Ibid., 808–9n1.

30 Ibid., 835.

31 Ibid., 820–1.

32 Ibid., 822n2.

33 Ibid., 825, 845.

34 Ibid., 839, 842.

35 Ibid., 840.

36 Ibid.

37 Ibid., 841: "eine ganz weltliche, im Tiefsten irreligiöse Schrift."

38 Ibid.

39 Ibid., 843n1.

40 Ibid., 811.

41 Grisar, *Der deutsche Luther im Weltkrieg und in der Gegenwart*, 9, 12.

42 Troeltsch, "Adolf v. Harnack und Ferd. Christ. v. Baur."

43 Denifle, *Luther und Luthertum in der ersten Entwicklung*, vol. 1.

44 Harnack, *Lehrbuch der Dogmengeschichte*, 812n1, 820n3, 839n1; Harnack, "Pater Denifle, Pater Weiß und Luther."

45 Denifle, *Luther und Luthertum in der ersten Entwicklung*, 1: 423–79.

46 Denifle and Weiß, *Luther und Luthertum in der ersten Entwicklung* , vol. 2; cf. Herte, *Das katholische Lutherbild im Bann der Lutherkommentare des Cochläus*, 2: 344.

47 Grisar, *Luther*.

48 Ibid., 1: 316–26. Professor Heiko Oberman has shown that the *cloaca*, the word that Luther used, was a scholastic metaphor commonly employed to mean feeling in the dumps or depressed (thanks to Werner Packull for this information).

49 Troeltsch, *Die Bedeutung des Protestantismus für die Entstehung der modernen Welt*.

50 Ibid., 8–24.

51 Ibid., 31–46.

52 Ibid., 57–64.

53 Ibid., 1, 66–70.

54 Ibid., 3, 85–103.

55 Bodenstein, *Die Theologie Karl Holls im Spiegel des antiken und reformatorischen Christentums*, 119–20 (emphasis in original).

CHAPTER TWO

1 Hermelink, *Das Christentum in der Menschheitsgeschichte*, 3: 502.

2 "Luther's Urteile über sich selbst" (Luther's Judgment of Himself, drawing on the *Table Talk*), in Holl, *Luther* 326–58.

3 Bodenstein, "Karl Holl (1866–1926)," 256–7, 259, 260.

4 Wallmann, "Holl, Karl," 515.

5 Cf. the view of Adolf von Harnack, in *Karl Holl*, ed. Karpp, 91–2.

6 Assel, *Der andere Aufbruch*, 159n45, 162n55.

7 Wallmann, "Holl, Karl," 514–15.

8 Holl to Schlatter, 8 Jan. 1920, in "Briefe Karl Holls an Adolf Schlatter (1897–1925)," ed. Stupperich, 228.

9 Riddoch, "The Ernst Troeltsch–Karl Holl Controversy," 267–8.

10 Wallmann, "Karl Holl und seine Schule," 13.

11 Ibid., 14; Riddoch, "The Ernst Troeltsch–Karl Holl Controversy," 266–7.

12 Rathje, *Die Welt des freien Protestantismus*, 353.

13 Wallmann, "Karl Holl und seine Schule," 13.

14 Wallmann, "Holl, Karl," 514–18.

15 Holl, *Der Westen*, 523. Riddoch, in "The Ernst Troeltsch–Karl Holl Controversy," 269–72, was the first Holl interpreter to recognize the importance of this self-revelation, which Holl published under a pseudonymn.

16 Schweitzer, *Mystik des Apostels Paulus*, 30; cf. Stendhal, "The Apostle Paul and the Introspective Conscience of the West."

17 Lotz, *Ritschl and Luther.*

18 Wallmann, "Holl, Karl, " 516; Jülicher, "Karl Holl," 433: "Er sah in sich wohl gern einen Schüler F. Chr. Bauers; aber abhängig vom ihm ist er nicht geworden."

19 Troeltsch, "Adolf v. Harnack und Ferd. Christ. v. Baur."

20 Holl to Jülicher, 9 June 1919 (unpub., transcript by Sonia Riddoch): "Sie wissen ja, daß Luther mich zwingt mich mit den N.T. sehr ernsthaft auseinanderzusetzen. Und ich kann mir nicht helfen, ich komme immer mehr auf Baur zurück. Der Gegensatz zwischen Paulus & der Urgemeinde, das Verhältnis zwischen Paulus & Petrus-Jakobus ist doch tatsächlich der Hebel der Geschichte und der Schlüssel zum Verständnis der neutest. Schriften. Wie kommt man sonst dazu, gerade den Namen des Paulus & des Jakobus über die betreffenden Schriften zu setzen? Und die 'ebionitisch' Züge im Lukasevangelium sind doch wirklich unbestreitbar. Mir kommt es jetzt so vor, als ob durch Ritschl & Harnack viel richtige Erkenntnis zugeschüttet werden wäre. Aber wird jemand Glauben finden, der sie heute wieder aufgräbt? Vielleicht – 'so Gott will & wir noch leben,' so sage ich jetzt aufrichtig – tue ich es doch noch einmal." Dr Riddoch was the first to bring this important statement to the attention of Holl scholarship; see "The Ernst Troeltsch–Karl Holl Controversy," 344.

21 Ibid., 345–6; cf. Baur, *Ausgewählte Werke in Einzelausgaben*, 1: 1–146.

22 For current scholarship on these issues, cf. Reumann, *Variety and Unity in New Testament Thought*, esp. 95–275, and the more iconoclastic, radical standpoint of Eisenman, *James the Brother of Jesus*, vol. 1.

23 Holl, "Die Rechtfertigungslehre im Licht der Geschichte des Protestantismus," 2, 10–11.

24 Ibid., 9.

25 Ibid., 19.

26 Ibid., 25.

27 Korsch, *Glaubensgewißheit und Selbstbewußtsein*, 159n55.

28 Holl, "Calvin," in *Der Westen*, 254–84.

29 Holl, "Luther und Calvin (1919)," in *Kleine Schriften*, 79.

30 Greschat, *Melanchthon neben Luther*, 230–42.

31 Greschat, *Martin Bucer.*

32 Assel, *Der andere Aufbruch*, 88n25.

33 Holl to Schlatter, 28 Dec. 1914, in Stupperich, "Briefe Karl Holls an Adolf Schlatter," 216.

34 Assel, *Der andere Aufbruch*, 101n64.

35 Wallmann, "Karl Holl und seine Schule," 30f; Assel, *Der andere Aufbruch*, 99.
36 Wallmann, "Karl Holl und seine Schule," 27.
37 Cf. chapter 1 above.
38 Holl, *Luther*, 256; Holl, *What Did Luther Understand by Religion?* 99.
39 Holl, "Die Bedeutung der großen Kriege für das religiöse und kirchliche Leben innerhalb des deutschen Protestantismus" (1917), in *Der Westen*, 302–84.
40 I Corinthians 8.
41 Assel, *Der andere Aufbruch*, 135n104.
42 Holl to Rade, 16 Jan. 1915: "Wer selbst in dieser Zeit die einfache Tatsache nicht begriffen hat, daß von den Völkern die einen wachsen, darum mehr Raum brauchen, die andern altern, darum nicht mehr auf ihre ganze Stellung ein Anrecht haben, wer nicht empfindet, daß das Gottes Schöpfungsordnung ist, andererseits die Augen demgegenüber verschließt, das kein Volk gutwillig aus dem Raum, den es einmal hat, weicht und auch nicht zu weichen braucht ... – mit dem streite ich mich überhaupt nicht mehr" (ibid., 125).
43 The idea of Reinhold Niebuhr's *Moral Man and Immoral Society.*
44 Assel, *Der andere Aufbruch*, 125.
45 Ibid., 116.
46 Hajo Holborn, *A History of Modern Germany, 1840–1945* (New York: Alfred A. Knopf 1969), 475.
47 Assel, *Der andere Aufbruch*, 19n10, 125n65.
48 Holl to Rade, 25 Oct. 1918, ibid., 125n65.
49 Riddoch, "The Ernst Troeltsch–Karl Holl Controversy," 287.
50 Wolff, *Die Haupttypen der neueren Lutherdeutung* , 322–3.
51 Assel, *Der andere Aufbruch*, 121, 124n57.
52 Trillhaas, *Aufgehobene Vergangenheit*, 52.
53 Holl, *Luther*, 437.
54 Müntzer, *The Collected Works*, 330–1.
55 Holl, *Luther*, 327.
56 Ibid., 430.
57 Ibid., 429.
58 Ibid., 420.
59 Althaus, "Zum Verständnis der Rechtfertigung," 727.
60 Holl, *Luther*, 442.
61 Ibid., 163–5.
62 Luther in the Weimar Edition (conventional abbreviation: WA), 54: 185, 1.12 – 186, 1.21; trans. as in McGrath, *Luther's Theology of the Cross*, 95–8.
63 E.g. Rupp, *The Righteousness of God*, 123.
64 Holl, *Luther*, 166.
65 Ibid.
66 Rupp, *The Righteousness of God*, 176.

67 Holl, *Luther*, 102.

68 Ibid., 151.

69 Ibid., 166–72.

70 Ibid., 133; cf. McGrath, *Luther's Theology of the Cross*, 72–92 (the chapter entitled "Luther as a Late Medieval Theologian").

71 Holl, *Luther*, 132n6.

72 Ibid., 415.

73 Ibid., 417.

74 Cf. Ozment, *The Reformation in the Cities*.

75 Holl, *Luther*, 177.

76 Ibid., 139.

77 Rupp, *The Righteousness of God*, 194.

78 Gogarten, "Theologie und Wissenschaft," cols. 34–42, 71–80; Wolff, *Die Haupttypen der neueren Lutherdeutung*, 375–7.

79 Holl, *Luther*, 181.

80 Ibid., 403.

81 Rupp, *The Righeousness of God*, esp. the chapter "The Bruised Conscience," 102–20, which subtly colours the entire interpretation; Bainton, *Here I Stand*, esp. the chapter "The Cloister," 37–51.

82 Febvre, *Un Destin*; Erikson, *Young Man Luther*.

83 Holl, *Luther*, 358.

84 Ibid., 328.

85 Ibid., 351–2.

86 Ibid., 352.

87 Ibid.

88 The critical view in Wirth, *Luther*, 26–34.

89 Holl, *Luther*, 328n1.

90 Ibid., 358.

91 Ibid., 338.

92 Nevertheless, they tried. Cf. Rupp, *The Righteousness of God*, 94–7; Bainton, "Luther: A Psychiatric Portrait."

93 Holl, *Luther*, 245–6.

94 Ibid., 278.

95 Ibid., 251.

96 Ibid., 253.

97 Ibid., 254.

98 Ibid., 255.

99 Ibid., 256.

100 Ibid., 275.

101 Ibid., 300.

102 Ibid., 291.

103 Ibid., 321.

104 Ibid., 325.

105 Holl, *What Did Luther Understand by Religion?* 14.
106 Quoted by Bense in Holl, *What Did Luther Understand by Religion?* 10.
107 Holl, *Luther,* 97n1.
108 Holl, *What Did Luther Understand by Religion?* 36.
109 Ibid., 52–3.
110 Ibid., 70.
111 Ibid., 40.
112 Ibid., 55.
113 Ibid., 45.
114 Ibid., 80.
115 Ibid., 76–8n49.
116 Ibid.
117 Ibid., 29.
118 Ibid., 76–8n49.
119 Ibid., 84: "whereas [Luther] often affirmed that the believer becomes 'one loaf' with Christ, he never used this expression for the relationship with God."
120 Ibid., appendix: "Gogarten's Understanding of Luther," 116.
121 Ibid., 62.
122 Ibid., 63.
123 Ibid., 65.
124 Ibid., 109.
125 Ibid., 106n72.
126 Seeberg, "Karl Holl in memoriam," 169.
127 Holl to Siebeck, 17 March 1922, from the correspondence collection of Prof. D. Dr Robert Stupperich, Münster. Special thanks to Dr Stupperich for use of his collection.
128 In the first edition of "Rechtfertigungslehre" (1906), 15, it was still "die sogenannten Schwärmer." Rehabilitating the term was a piece of conscious antiquarianism on Holl's part.
129 Bloch, *Thomas Münzer als Theologe der Revolution,* preceded by Friedrich Engels and Karl Kautsky.
130 Lohse, "Auf dem Wege zu einem neuen Müntzer-Bild," 121.
131 Holl, "Luther und die Schwärmer," 431–5.
132 Ibid., 451–2, 457–8.
133 Ibid., 462: "die bei den Täufern sich darstellende Verbindung zwischen einer mystisch gearteten Frömmigkeit und dem sozialen Reformgedanken nicht im inneren Wesen dieser Frömmigkeit selbst begründet ist. Alle mystische Frömmigkeit ist von Haus aus selbstisch."
134 Ibid., 435–45, 454–9.
135 Ibid., 435–45.
136 Ibid., 461.
137 Ibid., 466–7.

CHAPTER THREE

1 Wolff, *Die Haupttypen der neueren Lutherdeutung;* Loewenich, "Zehn Jahre Lutherforschung in Deutschland," in *Von Augustin zu Luther*, 357–43.
2 Loewenich, *Von Augustin zu Luther*, 342.
3 Althaus, "Zum Verständnis der Rechtfertigung," 727: "Bei ihrer Luther-Interpretation wirkte ihr eigenes systematisches Verständis der Sache mit."
4 Jüngel, "Barth, Karl," 257.
5 Barth, *Die christliche Dogmatik im Entwurf*, 1: 7; Bainton *Here I Stand*, 83: "What Karl Barth said of his own unexpected emergence as a reformer could be said equally of Luther, that he was like a man climbing in the darkness a winding staircase in the steeple of an ancient cathedral. In the blackness he reached out to steady himself, and his hand laid hold of a rope. He was startled to hear the clanging of a bell."
6 Barth, *Evangelische Theologie im 19. Jahrhundert*, 6.
7 Härle, "Die Aufruf der 93 Intellektuellen."
8 McCormack, *Karl Barth's ... Theology*, 113.
9 Troeltsch, "Adolf v. Harnack und Ferd. Christ. v. Baur," 290; where Troeltsch lays down his challenge to Harnack: "Die wirklichen Bedenken sind ganz andere: ob es richtig ist in diesem sehr partikulären europäischen Entwicklungsergebnis wirklich das Letzte und Allgemeine, allen Menschen und Völkern Einleuchtende zu sehen und ob es möglich ist, sich trotz aller historischen Kritik so naiv und unmittelbar zu dem 'Lebensbilde' Jesu zu verhalten ... Ich meinerseits könnte die beiden Fragen nicht bejahen."
10 Sonderegger, *That Jesus Christ Was Born a Jew*, 2.
11 Krüger, "The 'Theology of Crisis.'"
12 Barth, quoted in Sonderegger, *That Jesus Christ Was Born a Jew*, 17: "From the friendly reception by Bultmann I conclude to my very great satisfaction that the original outcry against the book [*The Epistle to the Romans*, 1922 ed.] as being an incitement to a Diocletian persecution of historical critical theology was not necessary."
13 Barth, *The Epistle to the Romans*, 9.
14 Krüger, "The 'Theology of Crisis,'" 140.
15 Härle, "Die Aufruf der 93 Intellektuellen," 222–4, has a very useful analysis, although before one can go all the way with his notion of Barth's posthumous obedience to his father, it is necessary to believe in the existence of "father complexes." It is possibly more helpful to examine the idea of Karl Mannheim *in Ideology and Utopia* (New York: Harcourt Brace Jovanovich, 1936), 281, that persons who have a mixture of incompatible outlooks contending with one another in their intellectual formation turn out to be unusually creative.

16 Forstman, *Christian Faith in Dark Times*, 34–5.
17 McCormack, *Karl Barth's ... Theology*, 49–68.
18 I find convincing, at least in its major outlines, McCormack's revision (ibid., 1–28) of the interpretation of Barth by Hans Urs von Balthasar. Balthasar's viewpoint is indeed strongly supported by Barth's reminiscences.
19 Wallmann, "Holl, Karl," 517.
20 McCormack, *Karl Barth's ... Theology*, 92–104.
21 Ibid., 453.
22 Ibid., 184–203.
23 The picture presented here of Karl Barth is that he always remained a man of the left, a radical socialist, "in, with, and under" his Dialectical Theology. His reservations about the Weimar Republic were that reforming governments of its type fell infinitely short of the Kingdom of God, and that it was, after all, a bourgeois democratic state which, whatever its socialist coloration, did not supply social justice for the working masses. Nevertheless, there is a good foundation for the assertion of McCormack, *Karl Barth's ... Theology*, 200–1, that in his Tambach address of 1919 Barth gave qualified approval to the Weimar Republic as a "*Vernunft Republikaner*" of the left.

But there is an entirely different view of Barth, Dialectical Theology, and Weimar politics, going back to the Religious Socialists, who felt that he had deserted them. According to Gotthilf Schenkel, pastor in Stuttgart, "This theology [the Dialectical Theology] is a luxury which has nothing to do with real life. I've heard with my own ears ... how members of this movement simply ignore the awakening of the church to a new feeling of responsibility in the social question; sometimes they scornfully reject it." And Paul Tillich: "It is to be attributed to Barth's influence that many theologians were simply blind to the religious problematic connected with the political situation in Germany after the First World War, because in Barth's theology a sharp dividing line was drawn between history and the realm of the transcendent. In this way theologians were hindered from applying their efforts on the side of social justice and political freedom" (Meier, *Der Evangelische Kirchenkampf*, 1: 26, 533–4).

Basically, such strictures are unfair. They condemn Barth for the apolitical concentration on theology and teaching that was a necessary part of his acceptance of the university appointment in Göttingen in 1921. He found it very odd when, in the German presidential election of 1925, most of his young theological supporters voted for Paul von Hindenburg, then the right-wing candidate. Obviously, Barth's theology could be construed in the right-wing German nationalist direction; his later experiences with Gogarten made this fact all too clear. But in his polemical exchanges with Paul Althaus in the early 1920s, to be discussed in the next chapter, Barth resisted exactly this misrepresentation of his theology.

Greschat, *Christentumsgeschichte*, 2: 224–5, illuminates the 1925 German presidential election as a manifestation of exactly the same kind of political Protestantism that came to the fore in 1917 and 1933. He quotes Joseph Gauger, a Protestant religious journalist: "Freuen können wir uns von ganzem Herzen darüber, daß der Nationalgedanke diesmal sich durchgesetzt hat und daß die so wichtige protestantische Staatsidee vorerst nicht weiter verloddert wird. Die Partei des erklärten Atheismus hat der Partei des Ultramontanismus vergeblich Wahlhilfe geleistet. Das jüdische Börsenkapital hat diesmal sein Geld umsonst ausgegeben." (To translate: The Catholic Centre Party's Wilhelm Marx, whose candidacy was backed by Socialists and Jews, was defeated by the noble, Protestant national hero, Paul von Hindenburg.)

24 Jüngel, "Barth, Karl," 257.
25 Barth, 1963 foreword to *Der Römerbrief (Erste Fassung), 1919*, 6.
26 Urs von Balthasar, *Karl Barth*, 71.
27 Barth, 1963 foreword to *Der Römerbrief (Erste Fassung), 1919*, 5–9.
28 Torrance, *Karl Barth*, 48.
29 Barth, 1963 foreword to *Der Romerbrief (Erste Fassung), 1919*, 6: "die Notwendigkeit aufdrängte, das Buch einer Revision zu unterziehen, in welcher von dessen ursprünglichem Bestand kaum ein Stein auf dem anderen geblieben ist." On the theology of the two Romans editions, cf. McCormack, *Karl Barth's ... Theology*, 135–82, 241–90. McCormack's argument that the 1919 edition, too, was informed by a dialectical theology, albeit a "supplementary dialectic," as opposed to the "complementary dialectic" of the 1922 edition (162–5, drawing on the ideas of Michael Beintker), may have theological worth. However, Barth was not primarily concerned with dialectics in either of his Romans commentaries and explained himself dialectically only because of the readers' response to the 1922 edition.
30 Rudolf Bultmann, "Karl Barths 'Römerbrief' in zweiter Auflage," in Moltmann, *Anfänge der dialektischen Theologie*, 1: 140.
31 Adolf Schlatter, "Karl Barths 'Römerbrief,' " ibid., 142–7.
32 Sonderegger, *That Jesus Christ Was Born a Jew*, 15–22.
33 Barth, *The Epistle to the Romans*, ix, x.
34 Ibid., 9.
35 Sonderegger, *That Jesus Christ Was Born a Jew*, 36; on the extent of Barth's knowledge of Luther at the time of the Romans commentaries, cf. Ebeling. "Karl Barths Ringen mit Luther," 436–40.
36 Barth, *The Epistle to the Romans*, 244.
37 Ibid., 60–1, 168.
38 Ibid., 100 (emphasis in original).
39 Ibid., 253.
40 Urs von Balthasar, *Karl Barth*, 77; Jüngel, "Barth, Karl, " 258–9.
41 Barth, *The Epistle to the Romans*, 30.

42 Ibid., 29.

43 Ibid., 98–9.

44 Torrance, *Karl Barth*, 44; McCormack, *Karl Barth's … Theology*, 243–44.

45 Torrance, *Karl Barth*, 42–3; cf. McCormack, *Karl Barth's … Theology*, 226–33.

46 Mahlmann, "Herrmann, Wilhelm," esp. 170–1.

47 Torrance, *Karl Barth*, 52. Cf. Barth, *The Epistle to the Romans*, 386: "We proclaim that God is free. The Gospel is the glad tidings, precisely because all human conjunctions and adjustments and presuppositions – however transcendentally conceived of – are there confronted by the sovereignty of God."

48 Barth, *The Epistle to the Romans*, 509.

49 McCormack, *Karl Barth's … Theology*, 155; Ebeling, "Barths Ringen mit Luther," 438–40.

50 Torrance, *Karl Barth*, 44, 63. Barth, in a reminiscence about the factors that had moved him to produce the Romans commentary, acknowledges these influences: "Was it the aspect of the world, so suddenly darkened just then, compared with the preceding long peace of our youth, which made us note that man's distress might be too great for him to find in the advice to turn to his religious possibilities a word that brought comfort and direction? Was it – and for me personally this played a decisive role – the failure of the ethics of modern theology at the outbreak of the First World War which led to our discontent with its exegesis, its conception of history and its dogmatics? Or, positively, was it the Blumhardt message of the Kingdom of God, which was only then, strange to relate, becoming actual? Was it Kierkegaard, Dostoevsky, Overbeck, read as commentaries to that message, through whom we found ourselves summoned to search out and make for new shores?" (cited in Torrance, *Karl Barth*, 39). McCormack, *Karl Barth's … Theology*, 218–26, stresses the influence of Barth's younger brother.

51 Urs von Balthasar, *Karl Barth*, 75, 90.

52 Barth, *The Word of God and the Word of Man*, 195–6.

53 Ibid.

54 Barth, *The Epistle to the Romans*, 123.

55 Cf. the argument of Sonderegger, *That Jesus Christ Was Born a Jew*, 24.

56 Stupperich, "Briefe Karl Holls an Adolf Schlatter," 231.

57 Barth, *Die Theologie Calvins 1922*. The translations that follow are my own; cf. Barth, *The Theology of John Calvin*.

58 Barth, *Die Theologie Calvins 1922*, 23, 25, 27, 29.

59 Ibid., 26, 29.

60 Ibid., 20, 23 (emphasis in original).

61 Ibid., 22.

62 Ibid., 51 (emphasis in original).

63 Ibid., 53.

64 Ibid., 54.

65 Ibid., 54–60.
66 Ibid., 32–50, esp. 41.
67 Ibid., 43.
68 Ibid., 51.
69 Ibid., 58–9, 62.
70 Ibid., 64.
71 Ibid., 91–2.
72 Ibid., 68.
73 Ibid., 67–9; cf. 24 for a more guarded assessment of Augustine's impor-
    tance for Luther.
74 Ibid., 69–77, esp. 69, 74.
75 Ibid., 77–86.
76 Ibid., 79.
77 Ibid., 86–90.
78 Ibid., 90.
79 Ibid., 95.
80 Ibid., 95–6.
81 Ibid., 99 (emphasis in original).
82 Ibid., 100.
83 Ibid., 101.
84 Ibid., 104 (emphasis in original).
85 Ibid., 104–5.
86 Ibid., 109 (emphasis in original).
87 Ibid., 52.
88 Ibid., 88.
89 Ibid., 95.
90 Cf. ibid., 111–13.
91 Morgan, "Ernst Troeltsch and the Dialectical Theology," 55–6: "The early
    dialectical theology was stronger in criticism than concrete proposals,
    and the weapon of their theological criticism was Paul's polemical doc-
    trine of justification on the basis of faith alone."
92 Gogarten, "Luther als Gestalt und Symbol?"
93 Thyssen, *Begegnung und Verantwortung,* 15–28, 34.
94 Ibid., 13, 29.
95 Ibid., 16–20.
96 Ibid., 29–47.
97 Gogarten, "Zwischen den Zeiten."
98 Ibid., 100.
99 Ibid., 96–7.
100 Duensing, *Gesetz als Gericht,* 78.
101 Thyssen, *Begegnung and Verantwortung,* 14.
102 Ibid., 44n52; Luther, WA, 7: 566; Gogarten, "Vom heiligen Egoismus des
    Christen."

103 Thyssen, *Begegnung und Verantwortung*, 72–4.
104 Gogarten, "Protestantismus und Wirklichkeit."
105 Nowak, *Evangelische Kirche und Weimarer Republik*, 238–40.
106 Gogarten, "Protestantismus und Wirklichkeit," 193.
107 Ibid., 194.
108 Ibid., 196.
109 Ibid., 198.
110 Ibid., 197.
111 Ibid., 194–5, 198.
112 Ibid., 201.
113 Ibid., 202–5.
114 Ibid., 206–7.
115 Ibid., 208–11, esp. 208.
116 Ibid., 216.
117 Troeltsch, "Ein Apfel vom Baume Kierkegaards," 135–7.
118 Duensing, *Gesetz als Gericht*, 80n52, 82.
119 Ratschow, "Gogarten," 1684: "Die theologische Arbeit G.s kann in metho-
    discher Hinsicht darin gesehen werden, daß G. unablässig als theologi-
    scher Vollzieher philosophischer Entwürfe auftritt. Er handelt hierbei
    sowohl abwehrend (z.B. gegenüber dem Idealismus und Troeltsch) als
    auch aufnehmend (z.B. bei Grisebach und Heidegger)."
120 Cf. above, 44.
121 Stupperich, "Briefe Karl Holls an Adolf Schlatter," 231.
122 Gogarten, *Illusionen*, 25.
123 Ibid., 34.
124 Ibid., 37n1.
125 Ibid., 38–9.
126 Gogarten, "Martin Luther, 1483–1546."
127 Barth, *Die Theologie Calvins 1922*, 23: "[Luther] ist sich auch seiner
    eigenen persönlichen Bedeutung … durchaus bewußt gewesen, viel-
    leicht nur zu gut."
128 Gogarten, "Martin Luther, 1483–1546," 428.
129 Ibid., 420.
130 Ibid., 426.
131 Ibid., 424.
132 Troeltsch, "Ein Apfel vom Baume Kierkegaards," 137.
133 Gogarten, "Martin Luther, 1483–1546," 424–5.
134 McCormack, *Karl Barth's … Theology*, 242.
135 Ibid., 334–7.
136 Ibid., 356.
137 Ibid., 328; Ebeling, "Über die Reformation hinaus?" 37; Ebeling, "Karl
    Barths Ringen mit Luther," 449.
138 Ebeling, "Über die Reformation hinaus?" 37.

139 McCormack, *Karl Barth's ... Theology*, 337–67; Ebeling, "Barths Ringen mit Luther," 446–7.

140 Ebeling, "Über die Reformation hinaus?" 37n19.

141 Ibid., 37–8.

142 McCormack, *Karl Barth's ... Theology*, 314.

143 Ibid., 213–14.

144 Ibid., 238: "Barth was never committed to a truly Kierkegaardian 'dialectic of existence.' From the very beginning, this set him apart from three men who would very soon be numbered among his closest theological allies: Friedrich Gogarten, Rudolf Bultmann and Emil Brunner."

145 Ibid., 391–411; Thyssen, *Begegnung und Verantwortung*, 270–81.

146 Cited in McCormack, *Karl Barth's ... Theology*, 325 (his translation).

147 Ebeling, "Karl Barths Ringen mit Luther," 454–9.

148 Ibid., 451.

149 Ebeling, "Über die Reformation hinaus?" 34.

150 Ibid., 39.

151 Ebeling, "Karl Barths Ringen mit Luther," 468–9.

152 Cf. the excellent, albeit polemical, monographic essay of Gerhard Ebeling, "Karl Barths Ringen mit Luther," passim.

CHAPTER FOUR

1   Conversation with Professor Stupperich.

2   Elert, *Die Lehre des Luthertums im Abriß*, 156–7.

3   Ibid., 32, 105–20, 147–9.

4   Ibid., 116.

5   Ibid., 119.

6   Peters, "Elert, Werner," 494.

7   Elert, *Der Kampf um das Christentum.*

8   Ibid., 210–12.

9   Peters, "Elert, Werner," 494.

10 Duensing, *Gesetz als Gericht*, 24–6.

11 Ibid., 13.

12 Elert, *Die Lehre des Luthertums im Abriß*, 147–8.

13 Peters, "Elert, Werner," 496–7; Ericksen, *Theologians under Hitler*, 98–104.

14 Elert, *Die Lehre des Luthertums im Abriß*, 3, 42.

15 Ibid., 4.

16 Ibid., 5–8.

17 Ibid., 6.

18 Ibid., 9–15.

19 Ibid., 21–2.

20 Ibid., 12.

21 Duensing, *Gesetz als Gericht*, 27.

22 Ibid., 27–35.
23 Elert, *Die Lehre des Luthertums im Abriß*, 93.
24 Ibid., 82–97.
25 Ibid., 84.
26 Ibid., 96.
27 Ibid., 87–8, 94–5.
28 Ibid., 140–2.
29 Ibid., 33–4.
30 Ibid., 142.
31 Ibid., 141.
32 Rupp, *The Righteousness of God*, 248.
33 Peters, "Elert, Werner," 495.
34 Elert, *Die Lehre des Luthertums im Abriß*, 42: "Wir sind nicht mehr Feinde (Kol. 1: 21), auch nicht mehr Knechte, sondern Freunde (Joh. 15: 15). Gott selbst will unsere Freiheit (Gal. 5: 13)."
35 Ibid., 50–1.
36 Ibid., 146, 151, 153–5.
37 Ibid., 151.
38 Ibid., 150.
39 Graß, "Althaus, Paul," 330: "Zusammen mit Werner Elert, mit dem er seit seiner Berufung in einer gewissen Konkurrenz stand, hat er Erlanger Theologie zu hohem Ansehen verholfen."
40 Ericksen, *Theologians under Hitler*, 79–119, 214–18.
41 Assel, *Der andere Aufbruch*, 22–31. Assel defines the Luther Renaissance as the group of scholars who published in the *Zeitschrift für systematische Theologie*. I have preferred to follow the usual convention of calling the Holl school the Luther Renaissance and distinguishing its members from others with different agendas in Luther research. My effort in this chapter to situate Althaus between and beyond the contending schools is a test of that approach.
42 Ibid., 23–4.
43 Althaus, "Zum Verständnis der Rechtfertigung," 727.
44 Althaus, *Unsterblichkeit und ewiges Sterben bei Luther*.
45 Graß, "Althaus, Paul," 330.
46 Ibid., 329–30.
47 Ericksen, *Theologians under Hitler*, 83: "He did not believe former Germans could be 're-Germanized,' but he insisted that further 'de-Germanization' should be opposed."
48 Ibid., 83–4.
49 Althaus, *Religiöser Sozialismus*; cf. Forstman, *Christian Faith in Dark Times*, 121–30, for a summary of the controversies between Althaus and Barth.
50 Barth, *Vorträge und kleinere Arbeiten*, 39–55.
51 Frostin, *Luther's Two Kingdoms Doctrine*, 1: "Although the Two Kingdoms Doctrine has played a central role for decades in the debate of Lutheran

identity it should not be forgotten that it is a relatively young concept, not more than fifty years old"; and 7–8: "As *terminus a quo* is proposed the year of 1922, when Karl Barth coined the phrase '[die] lutherische Lösung, die paradoxe Lehre von den zwei Reichen' in a critical analysis of the Lutheran ethos, specifically in the debate with Paul Althaus about religious socialism. In 1929 Emanuel Hirsch uses the phrase 'the doctrine of the two kingdoms' and some years later, after Hitler's *Machtübernahme*, the term is given prominence in the debate between different Lutheran attitudes to National Socialism. As *terminus ad quem* the year of 1938 usually is quoted, when the first monograph about the Two Kingdoms doctrine – Harold Diem's dissertation '*Luthers Lehre von den zwei Reichen*' – is published."

52 Barth, *Vorträge und kleinere Arbeiten*, 46–7.
53 Ibid., 52 (emphasis in original).
54 Frostin, *Luther's Two Kingdoms Doctrine*, 3.
55 Ericksen, *Theologians under Hitler*, 100.
56 Althaus, "Theologie und Geschichte," esp. 754.
57 Ibid., 755.
58 Ibid., 743.
59 Ibid., 755.
60 Ibid., 775.
61 Ibid., 750.
62 Ibid., 751.
63 Ibid.
64 Graß, "Althaus, Paul, " 332; Althaus, "Werner Elerts theologisches Werk," 407. The two uncontested "uses of the law" in Lutheran theology were (1) the law as a basis of civil authority and (2) the law as an unattainable moral standard that convinces the believer of his sinfulness and need of redemption.
65 Althaus, "Theologie und Geschichte," 781.
66 Ibid., 779–80.
67 Ibid., 781.
68 Ibid., 763.
69 Ibid., 770–1.
70 Moeller, "Problems of Reformation Research," 8.
71 Althaus, "Theologie und Geschichte," 786.
72 Graß, "Althaus, Paul," 330: "[Karl Holl] verdankt Althaus für sein Lutherverständnis am meisten."
73 Althaus, "Werner Elerts theologisches Werk," 404.
74 Althaus, "Zum Verständnis der Rechtfertigung," 727–8.
75 Ibid., 730.
76 Ibid., 734–7.
77 Ibid., 738.

78 Althaus, "Das Kreuz Christi als Maßstab aller Religion," 64.
79 Althaus, "Die Frage des Evangeliums an das moderne Judentum," 196: "Beide Fragen sind voneinander wesentlich verschieden. Die theologische hören heißt nicht: die völkische verneinen, humanitär-liberal das völkische Problem, das uns durch das Wohnen jüdischen Volkstums unter uns gestellt ist, übersehen."
80 Ibid., 203.
81 Althaus, "Das Kreuz Christi als Maßstab aller Religion," 74.
82 Ericksen, *Theologians under Hitler*, 85: "This sentiment is far removed from radical *völkisch* ideology. It illustrates Althaus' insistence upon honesty and moderation."
83 Althaus, "Die Bedeutung des Kreuzes im Denken Luthers."
84 Ibid., 56.
85 Ibid., 52, 57.
86 Ibid., 56.
87 Ibid., 54–5.
88 Erikson, *Young Man Luther*, 213.
89 Althaus, "Die Bedeutung des Kreuzes im Denken Luthers," 54, 58.
90 Ibid., 55.
91 Ibid., 60.
92 Ibid., 57.
93 Martin Luther, *The Bondage of the Will*, in WA, 18: 633, ll. 21–3: "Nunc cum id comprehendi non potest, fit locus exercendae fidei, dum talia praedicantur et invulgantur."
94 Althaus, "Luthers Haltung im Bauernkrieg."
95 Ibid., 160.
96 Ibid.
97 Ibid., 161, 164–5.
98 Ibid., 165.
99 Ibid., 166.
100 Ibid., 179.
101 Ibid., 166.
102 Ibid., 179.
103 Ibid., 174.
104 Ibid., 157.
105 Ibid., 158.
106 Ibid., 165–6.

CHAPTER FIVE

1 Birkner, "Hirsch, Emanuel," 391–2.
2 Ericksen, *Theologians under Hitler*, 124.
3 Trillhaas, *Aufgehobene Vergangenheit*, 52.

4 Birkner, "Hirsch, Emanuel," 390–2; Reimer, *The Emanuel Hirsch and Paul Tillich Debate*, 5–12.

5 Ericksen, *Theologians under Hitler*, 124–6, 162.

6 Birkner, "Hirsch, Emanuel," 391–3.

7 Ericksen, *Theologians under Hitler*, 218n6.

8 Assel, *Der andere Aufbruch*, 167.

9 Ibid., 166.

10 Ibid., 169.

11 Ibid., 167.

12 Stroup, "Political Theology and Secularization Theory in Germany," 339.

13 Birkner, "Hirsch, Emanuel," 392: "Als seinen theologischen Lehrer hat Hirsch in exklusiver Weise den Kirchenhistoriker Karl Holl genannt."

14 Assel, *Der andere Aufbruch*, 164.

15 Ibid,. 169n24.

16 Hirsch, "Nietzsche und Luther," 168–81. The argument about Janssen's influence on Nietzsche is refuted in Blum, "Nietzsche's Idea of Luther in Menschliches, Allzumenschliches."

17 Stroup, "Political Theology and Secularization Theory in Germany," 345–6.

18 Hirsch, "Nietzsche und Luther," 184.

19 Ibid., 193: "Zerstörung und Schaffen, Grausamkeit und höchste segnende Güte."

20 Ibid., 193–4.

21 Ibid, 201.

22 Ibid., 202.

23 Hirsch, *Luthers Gottesanschauung*.

24 Ibid., 4.

25 Ibid., 3–4: "Einmal hat mir starke Anregungen gegeben Theodosius Harnack durch seine noch immer nicht veraltete *Theologie Luthers*. In besonderem Maße aber bin ich abhängig von den Luther-Forschungen Karl Holls, vor allem in seinem Aufsatz über die Rechtfertigungslehre in Luthers Römerbriefvorlesung." The republication of Theodosius Harnack's book in 1926 gave him a particularly strong posthumous voice in the Weimar-era discussions about Luther.

26 This continues to be the approach of Gerhard Ebeling's influential *Luther: An Introduction to his Thought*, 258: "*De servo arbitrio* ... could equally be called *De Deo*."

27 Hirsch, *Luthers Gottesanschauung*, 8.

28 Ibid., 13.

29 Ibid., 15.

30 Ibid., 19.

31 Ibid., 21.

32 Ibid., 7.

33 Ibid., 20.

34 Ibid., 26.
35 Ibid., 23.
36 Ibid., 25.
37 Ibid., 29.
38 Ibid., 6–7.
39 Ibid., 19.
40 Hirsch, "Initium theologiae Lutheri," 28n1.
41 Ibid.
42 Ibid., 21.
43 Ibid., 22.
44 Ibid., 13–18, esp. 15.
45 Ibid., 28.
46 Ibid., 26–27, 26n5.
47 Cf. the detailed discussion in Vogelsang, *Die Anfänge von Luthers Christologie*, 16–22. Vogelsang is tendentious in the usual Protestant way by not emphasizing the centrality of the literal meaning.
48 Hirsch, "Initium theologiae Lutheri," 30.
49 Ibid., 31.
50 Ibid., 30n5.
51 Ibid., 28.
52 Cf. above, 32–3.
53 Hirsch, "Initium theologiae Lutheri," 35n1; Holl, *Luther*, 163–5, esp. 163.
54 Cited in Greschat, *Der deutsche Protestantismus im Revolutionsjahr 1918–19*, 81.
55 Assel, *Der andere Aufbruch*, 167.
56 Ericksen, *Theologians under Hitler*, 127–41, presents a good summary of the book; cf. also Forstman, *Christian Faith in Dark Times*, 51–71.
57 Cited in Assel, *Der andere Aufbruch*, 169: "Ich lese gerade Hirschs neue Schrift: Deutschlands Schicksal. Das ist ein Treffer."
58 Stroup, "Political Theology and Secularization Theory in Germany," 346, refers to Hirsch's discussion of "Luther's dualistic doctrine of the Kingdom of God (what we now call Two Kingdoms)"; Reimer, *The Emanuel Hirsch and Paul Tillich Debate*, 150–4, applies the "two kingdoms" label from current discussion of Luther's political ethic to Hirsch's ideas of the Weimar era. I am disposed to accept the finding of Frostin (see chap 4, note 51) that Hirsch uses the "two kingdoms" term only in 1929. Earlier, in his 1925 edition of *Deutschlands Schicksal*, 125, he does, to be sure, draw a contrast between the *Reich der Welt* and the *unsichtbaren Gottesreich*.
59 Cf. Reimer, *The Emanuel Hirsch and Paul Tillich Debate*, 142–59.
60 Cited ibid., 156.
61 Ibid., 158–9.
62 Ericksen, *Theologians under Hitler*, 146.
63 Hirsch, *Lutherstudien*, 1: 7: "In 1926 I was given a highly gifted disciple, the student Erich Vogelsang, to whom I could entrust one of my most

cherished topics, the emergence of Luther's Christology, particularly with reference to Luther's image of the conflicted human being, Jesus … The Second World War then tore Vogelsang away from the preparations for his Luther book, and the great battles of 1944, so fateful for us all, devoured his life, together with the hopes for scholarly accomplishment that we attached to it" (my translation).

64 Vogelsang, *Die Anfänge von Luthers Christologie*, dedication: "Dem Gedächtnis meiner beiden im Weltkrieg gefallenen Brüder: Leutnant d.R. Friedrich Vogelsang Dr. phil. et cand. min. + am 12. September 1916 an der Somme, Fahnenjunker Adolf Vogelsang + am 24. Oktober 1917 vor Verdun."

65 E.g. Rupp, *The Righteousness of God*, esp. 134–7; Erikson, *Young Man Luther*, esp. 201–4.

66 Vogelsang, *Die Anfänge von Luthers Christologie*, foreword.

67 Ibid., 1.

68 Ibid., foreword: "Grundlegend – auch für die Christologie – bekenne ich von Karl Holl gelernt zu haben."

69 Ibid., 9.

70 Ibid., 4–10; McGrath, *Luther's Theology of the Cross*, 74–5n8.

71 Vogelsang, *Die Anfänge von Luthers Christologie*, 33n2, on the scholia to Psalm 30 (31): "Das Schriftbild ist äußerst unruhig und verworren; zahlreiche Unterstreichungen kommen hinzu … Daß wir hier den Niederschlag einer bedeutsamen Stunde aus Luthers eigenem Leben haben, keinesfalls einen im Hinblick auf den Kollegvortrag mit Bedacht konzipierten Text, ist mir unzweifelhaft."

72 Ibid., 9.

73 Ibid., 40–61.

74 Febvre, *Un destin*.

75 Vogelsang, *Die Anfänge von Luthers Christologie*, 58n2.

76 Ibid., 25: "Wie so oft ist auch hier das Überlieferte für ihn zu einem Gefäß geworden, das er mit einem neuen Inhalt füllt"; ibid., 58n1: "Man spürt, wie Luther die überlieferten Denkformen mit ganz eigentümlich neuem Inhalt füllt." See also Rupp, *The Righteousness of God*, 138: "Luther continues to use traditional words and categories, long after he has ceased to use them in their former sense, and after the background of his thought has changed their meaning."

77 Vogelsang, *Die Anfänge von Luthers Christologie*, 33n2.

78 Ibid., 43–4.

79 Ibid., 45–61.

80 Ibid., 56.

81 Ibid., 60.

82 Ibid., 59.

83 Ibid., 165.

84 Ibid., 91n2: "Luther deutet nicht mehr auf die Gottheit, sondern auf die Menschheit, das Kreuz Christi."

85 Ibid., 23, 167.

86 Ibid., 62–76.

87 Ibid., 164–5.

88 Ibid., 66.

89 Ibid., 75n4, 76: "Der allzu beliebte Ausdruck 'Christusmystik' ist bei Luther nur mit größten Vorbehalten zu verwenden. Ich vermeide ihn deshalb lieber."

90 Ibid., 75.

91 Ibid., 74.

92 Ibid., 79.

93 Ibid., 81.

94 Ibid., 82–4, esp. 83.

95 Ibid., 88.

96 Ibid., 88n3.

97 Psalm 21 (22): 1, 7–8, 16–18.

98 Vogelsang, *Die Anfänge von Luthers Christologie*, 91: "die betende und zitternde Angst Christi von Gott – um unserer Sünde willen – selbst verworfen zu sein."

99 Ibid., 95, 97.

100 Ibid., 96.

101 Erikson, *Young Man Luther*, 213: "The artist closest to Luther in spirit was Dürer, who etched his own face into Christ's countenance."

102 Vogelsang, *Die Anfänge von Luthers Christologie*, 98.

103 Ibid., 100.

104 Ibid., 114.

105 Ibid., 110.

106 Ibid., 117.

107 Ibid., 86–7n2, 106.

108 Ibid., 2–3: "Hatte man früher alles vor 1517 als einen zwar interessanten, aber schließlich entbehrlichen Vorhof zu [Luthers] Theologie betrachtet, so sind heute – entscheidend erst seit Karl Holl – eben diese Schriften zum methodischen Ausgangspunkt der Forschung, zum eigentlichen Schlüssel für das Verständnis der Theologie Luthers geworden."

109 Runestam, *Viljans frihet och den kristna friheten*.

110 Vogelsang, *Die Anfänge von Luthers Christologie*, 123.

111 Ibid., 124.

112 McGrath, *Luther's Theology of the Cross*, 128–47.

113 Bizer, *Fides ex auditu*; Saarnivaara, *Luther Discovers the Gospel*.

114 Vogelsang, *Luthers Kampf gegen die Juden*.

115 Ibid., 5.

116 Ibid., 5–6: "Welch merkwürdige Überschneidung Verstehens und Nicht-
      verstehens!"; "erscheint unser heutiger volksnotwendiger Antisemitis-
      mus noch viel zu elementar, noch viel zu wenig begrifflich faßbar."
117 Ibid., 25, cf. 6–7.
118 Ibid., 7–9.
119 Ibid., 21–2.
120 Ibid., 9–12, 16, 20–1.
121 Ibid., 15.
122 Ibid., 25–7.
123 Ibid., 29.
124 Ibid., 33: "Während die heutigen Ausleger sich weithin darüber einig
      sind, daß Paulus Röm 11, 25 ff. an eine Bekehrung von *ganz* Israel am
      Ende aller Tage denkt, und während auch das Mittelalter den Text ge-
      meinhin so verstand, ist Luther stets anderer Meinung gewesen. Schon
      in seiner ersten Vorlesung 1513 wendet er sich gegen die hergebrachte
      Deutung." By the end of his discussion (34), Vogelsang's clear implica-
      tion is that Luther's exegesis is not only original; it is correct.
125 Ibid., 14.
126 Ibid., 31.
127 Ibid., 18; cf. 10–11, 12, esp. 16: "Eine dämonische Macht muß dahinter
      [the Jews' rejection of Christ] stehen, die unerklärbare Macht, die nur für
      den alles erklärenden Rationalismus nicht vorhanden: die Macht des
      Teufels." After 1945 the superiority of Luther's teaching about the devil
      to superficial liberal rationalism was proved not by the diabolical posses-
      sion of the Jews but by the diabolical possession of Hitler! At any rate,
      that was the viewpoint of a Protestant free-church pastor whom I en-
      countered as a student in Freiburg in 1961–62.

CONCLUSION

1 McCormack, *Karl Barth's ... Theology*, 466.

EPILOGUE

1 Cited in Ericksen, *Theologians under Hitler*, 146.
2 Ibid., 166.
3 Ibid., 146.
4 Cited in Mehlhausen, "Nationalsozialismus und Kirchen," 48–9.
5 Cited in Scholder, *Die Kirchen und das Dritte Reich*, 1: 529.
6 Mehlhausen, "Nationalsozialismus und Kirchen," 47–8, 50, esp. 52.
7 Meier, *Der Evangelische Kirchenkampf*, 1: 27: In 1933 most Holl students
   "sich ... dem Konservativen Flügel der Deutschen Christen anschlossen
   (Emanuel Hirsch, Hermann Wolfgang Beyer, Heinrich Bornkamm, Erich
   Vogelsang u.a.)."

8 Scholder, *Die Kirchen und das Dritte Reich*, 392–3, 533; Ericksen, *Theologians under Hitler*, 167.
9 Mehlhausen, "Nationalsozialismus und Kirchen," 50–1.
10 Ibid., 52–3.
11 Ibid., 53; Vogelsang, *Luthers Kampf gegen die Juden*, dedication page, unnumbered.
12 Mehlhausen, "Nationalsozialismus und Kirchen," 54; Greschat, *Christentumsgeschichte*, 2: 239.
13 Meier, *Der Evangelische Kirchenkampf*, 286, 578n740.
14 Cited in Scholder, *Die Kirchen und das Dritte Reich*, 536–8, esp. 537.
15 Ibid., 538.
16 McCormack, *Karl Barth's ... Theology*, 412, 420.
17 Green, *Karl Barth*, 148.
18 Mehlhausen, "Nationalsozialismus und Kirchen," 55.
19 Green, *Karl Barth*, 148.
20 Text in Green, *Karl Barth*, 148–51; implications elaborated from a Catholic standpoint by J.P. Michael in "Bekennende Kirche." The Michael commentary illuminates the distinctly Protestant, as well as anti-Nazi, implications of the Barmen Declaration.
21 Mehlhausen, "Nationalsozialismus und Kirchen," 56. The synod referred "diese Erklärung den Bekenntniskonventen zur Erarbeitung verantwortlicher Auslegung von ihren Bekenntnissen aus." Greschat, *Christentumsgeschichte*, 2: 241: "In wesentlichen hatte Karl Barth diesen Text formuliert, allerdings in der Absicht, daß er von Reformierten, Unierten und Lutheranern akzeptiert werden könnte. Das fiel letzteren jedoch dauerhaft schwer, weil das 'Christus allein' in These I die lutherische Unterscheidung von Gesetz und Evangelium beiseite schob und die Proklamation der Königsherrschaft Christi in These II die Zwei-Regimentenlehre Luthers zurückwies, freilich nicht prinzipiell, wie These V mit den Ausführungen zum Verhältnis von Staat und Kirche zeigt."
22 Niemöller, *Die erste Bekenntnissynode der Deutschen Evangelischen Kirche zu Barmen*, introduction and text, 142–6; summary of Elert's article "Confessio Barmensis," 146–8; cf. Forstman, *Christian Faith in Dark Times*, 197–202.
23 Ibid., 151–5.
24 Cited in Ericksen, *Theologians under Hitler*, 85.
25 Ibid., 216n105.
26 Ibid., 97.
27 Ibid., 88–9.
28 Assel, *Der andere Aufbruch*, 165n1; Meier, *Der Evangelische Kirchenkampf*, 212, 259–60: Hirsch cited Luther's co-operation with the state at the initiation of the Saxon Visitation.
29 See above, 41.
30 Mehlhausen, "Nationalsozialismus und Kirchen," 57.

31 Assel, *Der andere Aufbruch*, 164n3.

32 Mehlhausen, "Nationalsozialismus und Kirchen," 60.

33 Ericksen, *Theologians under Hitler*, 167–71.

34 McCormack, *Karl Barth's ... Theology*, 449; Forstman, *Christian Faith in Dark Times*, 203–9.

35 Ericksen, *Theologians under Hitler*, 151, 156.

36 Ibid., 176, 222n246.

37 Ibid., 164. Ericksen comments (165): "The issue illustrates the difficulty of judging Hirsch's work. First, his interpretations obviously fit in with Nazi propaganda and his interest in the subject was certainly occasioned by the unacceptability of the Jew in Nazi Germany. But were his conclusions wrong? ... Although experts would have to judge each step in the case Hirsch builds, the steps appear logical and could possibly be the simplest explanation of the various enigmas in the story of Jesus' family tree."

38 See above, 102–5.

39 Brady, "Luther Renaissance," 475.

40 Bornkamm, "Zur Frage der Iustitia Dei beim jungen Luther."

Bibliography

PRIMARY LITERATURE

Althaus, Paul. "Die Bedeutung des Kreuzes im Denken Luthers." In *Evangelium und Leben: Gesammelte Vorträge*, 51–62. Gütersloh: Bertelsmann 1927.
– *Evangelium und Leben: Gesammelte Vorträge*. Gütersloh: Bertelsmann 1927.
– "Die Frage des Evangeliums an das moderne Judentum." *Zeitschrift für systematische Theologie* 7 (1929): 195–215.
– "Das Kreuz Christi als Maßstab aller Religion." In *Evangelium und Leben: Gesammelte Vorträge*, 63–76. Gütersloh: Bertelsmann 1927.
– "Luthers Haltung im Bauernkrieg: Ein Beitrag zur lutherischen Sozialethik." In *Evangelium und Leben: Gesammelte Vorträge*, 144–81. Gütersloh: Bertelsmann 1927.
– *Religiöser Sozialismus: Grundfragen der christlichen Sozialethik*. Studien des Apologetischen Seminars in Wernigerode, 5. Gütersloh, 1921.
– "Theologie und Geschichte: Zur Auseinandersetzung mit der dialektischen Theologie." *Zeitschrift für systematische Theologie* 1 (1923): 741–86.
– *Unsterblichkeit und ewiges Sterben bei Luther: Zur Auseinandersetzung mit Carl Stange*. Studien des apologetischen Seminars, 30. Gütersloh, 1930.
– "Werner Elerts theologisches Werk." In *Gedenkschrift für D. Werner Elert*, ed. Friedrich Hübner, 400–10. Berlin: Lutherisches Verlagshaus 1955.
– "Zum Verständnis der Rechtfertigung." *Zeitschrift für systematische Theologie* 7 (1929): 727–41.
Barth, Karl. "Ansatz und Absicht in Luthers Abendmahlslehre" (1923). In *Die Theologie und die Kirche*, 26–75. Munich: Christian Kaiser 1928.

- *Die christliche Dogmatik im Entwurf.* Vol. 1, ed. Gerhard Sauter. Zurich: Theologischer Verlag 1982.
- *The Epistle to the Romans.* 2nd ed. (1922). Trans. Edwyn C. Hoskyns. London: Oxford University Press 1933.
- "Evangelical Theology in the 19th century." In *The Humanity of God*, 11–33. Richmond: John Knox Press 1960.
- *Evangelische Theologie im 19. Jahrhundert.* Theologische Studien, no. 49, ed. Karl Barth and Max Geiger. Zollikon: Evangelischer Verlag 1957.
- *Der Römerbrief (Erste Fassung) 1919.* Ed. Hermann Schmidt. Zurich: Theologischer Verlag 1985.
- *Der Römerbrief, 1922.* Zurich: Theologischer Verlag 1940.
- *Die Theologie Calvins 1922. Karl Barth: Gesamtausgabe,* vol. 2, *Akademische Werke 1922.* Zurich: Theologischer Verlag 1993.
- *Theology and Church.* Trans. Louise Pettibone Smith. London: SCM Press 1962.
- *The Theology of John Calvin.* Trans. Geoffrey W. Bromiley. Grand Rapids: Eerdmans 1995.
- *Vorträge und kleinere Arbeiten, 1922–25.* Ed. Holger Finze. Zurich: Theologischer Verlag 1990.
- *The Word of God and the Word of Man.* Trans. Douglas Horton. [Boston, Chicago]: Pilgrim Press 1928.
Baur, Ferdinand Christian. *Ausgewählte Werke in Einzelausgaben.* Ed. Klaus Scholder. Vol. 1. Stuttgart-Bad Cannstadt: Friedrich Frommann 1963.
Brunner, Emil. *Die Mystik und das Wort: Der Gegensatz zwischen moderner Religionsauffassung und christlichem Glauben dargestellt an der Theologie Schleiermachers.* Tübingen: J.C.B. Mohr [Paul Siebeck] 1924.
Denifle, Heinrich. *Luther und Luthertum in der ersten Entwicklung.* Vol. 1. 2nd ed. Mainz: Franz Kirkheim 1904.
- and Albert Maria Weiß. *Luther und Luthertum in der ersten Entwicklung.* Vol. 2. Mainz: Franz Kirkheim 1909.
Elert, Werner. *Der Kampf um das Christentum: Geschichte der Beziehungen zwischen dem evangelischen Christentum und dem allgemeinen Denken seit Schleiermacher und Hegel.* Munich: C.H. Beck 1921.
- *Die Lehre des Luthertums im Abriß.* 2nd ed. Munich: C.H. Beck 1926.
Gogarten, Friedrich. *Illusionen: Eine Auseinandersetzung mit dem Kulturidealismus.* Jena: Eugen Diederichs 1926.
- "Luther als Gestalt und Symbol? Zu Gerhard Ritters Lutherbuch." *Theologische Blätter* 5 (1926): 169–73.
- "Martin Luther, 1483–1546." In *Die großen Deutschen: Neue deutsche Biographie,* 1: 419–33. Berlin, 1935.
- "Protestantismus und Wirklichkeit: Nachwort zu Martin Luthers 'Vom unfreien Willen.'" In *Anfänge der dialektischen Theologie,* ed. Jürgen Moltmann, 2: 191–218. Munich: Christian Kaiser 1967.

– *Religion und Volkstum*. Jena: Eugen Diederichs 1915.
– "Theologie und Wissenschaft: Grundsätzliche Bemerkungen zu Karl Holls 'Luther.' " *Die Christliche Welt* 38 (1924): cols. 34–42.
– "Vom heiligen Egoismus des Christen: Eine Antwort auf Jülichers Aufsatz: 'Ein moderner Paulusausleger.' " In *Anfänge der dialektischen Theologie*, ed. Jürgen Moltmann, 1: 99–105. Munich: Christian Kaiser 1977.
– "Zur Frage der authentischen Lutherpredigt." *Theologische Blätter* 6 (1927): 224–5.
– "Zwischen den Zeiten." In *Anfänge der dialektischen Theologie*, ed. Jürgen Moltmann, 2: 95–101. Munich: Christian Kaiser 1967.
Grisar, Hartmann. *Der deutsche Luther im Weltkrieg und in der Gegenwart*. Augsburg: Haas & Grabherr 1924.
– *Luther*. 3 vols. Freiburg: Herder 1911–12.
Harnack, Adolf von. *Lehrbuch der Dogmengeschichte*. Vol. 3. Tübingen: J.C.B. Mohr [Paul Siebeck] 1932.
– "Die Lutherbiographie Grisars." In *Aus Wissenschaft und Leben*, 1: 332–40. Giessen: Töpelmann 1911.
– "Pater Denifle, Pater Weiß und Luther." In *Aus Wissenschaft und Leben*, 1: 298–332. Giessen: Töpelmann 1911.
– *Das Wesen des Christentums*. 3rd ed. Leipzig: Heinrichs 1900.
– *What Is Christianity?* Trans. Thomas Bailey Saunders; intro. Rudolf Bultmann. New York and Evanston: Harper 1957.
Herrmann, Wilhelm. "Albrecht Ritschl, seine Größe und seine Schranke." In *Festgabe … A. von Harnack zum siebzigsten Geburtstag*, 405–6. Tübingen: J.C.B. Mohr [Paul Siebeck] 1921.
Hirsch, Emanuel. *Deutschlands Schicksal: Staat, Volk und Menschheit im Lichte einer ethischen Geschichtsansicht*. 2nd ed. Göttingen: Vandenhoeck & Ruprecht 1922.
– "Initium theologiae Lutheri." In *Lutherstudien*, 2: 9–35. Gütersloh: Bertelsmann 1954.
– *Luthers Gottesanschauung*. Göttingen: Vandenhoeck & Ruprecht 1918.
– "Luthers Rechtfertigungslehre bei Kant." In *Lutherstudien*, 2: 104–21. Gütersloh: Bertelsmann 1954.
– "Nietzsche und Luther." In *Lutherstudien*, 2: 168–206. Gütersloh: Bertelsmann 1954.
Holl, Karl. *Christliche Reden*. Gütersloh: Bertelsmann 1926.
– *Kleine Schriften*. Ed. Robert Stupperich. Tübingen: J.C.B. Mohr [Paul Siebeck] 1966.
– *Luther*. In *Gesammelte Aufsätze zur Kirchengeschichte*, vol. 1. Tübingen: J.C.B. Mohr [Paul Siebeck] 1921.
– "Luther und die Schwärmer." In *Luther*, 4th and 5th eds., 420–67. Tübingen: J.C.B. Mohr [Paul Siebeck] 1927.

- "Die Rechtfertigungslehre im Licht der Geschichte des Protestantismus: Vortrag gehalten auf der Versammlung der Freunde der Christlichen Welt am 17. Oktober 1905."1st ed. Tübingen, 1906.
- "Urchristentum und Religionsgeschichte." In *Gesammelte Aufsätze zur Kirchengeschichte: Der Osten*, 2: 1–32. Tübingen: J.C.B. Mohr [Paul Siebeck] 1928.
- *Der Westen*. In *Gesammelte Aufsätze sur Kirchengeschichte*, vol. 3. 6th ed. Tübingen: J.C.B. Mohr [Paul Siebeck] 1932.
- *What Did Luther Understand by Religion?* Ed. James Luther Adams and Walter F. Bense. Philadelphia: Fortress 1977.
Jülicher, Adolf. "Ein Moderner Paulus-Ausleger." In *Anfänge der dialektischen Theologie*, ed. Jürgen Moltmann, 1: 87–98. Munich: Christian Kaiser 1977.
Kähler, Martin. *The So-Called Historical Jesus and the Historic, Biblical Christ*. Philadelphia: Fortress Press 1964.
Karpp, Heinrich, ed. *Karl Holl: Briefwechsel mit Adolf von Harnack*. Tübingen: J.C.B. Mohr [Paul Siebeck] 1966.
Luther, Martin. *D. Martin Luthers Werke: Kritische Gesammtausgabe*. 63 vols. Weimar, 1883– . (Conventional abbreviation: WA)
Niemöller, Gerhard. *Die erste Bekenntnissynode der Deutschen Evangelischen Kirche zu Barmen*. Göttingen: Vandenhoeck & Ruprecht 1959.
Schweitzer, Albert. *Mystik des Apostels Paulus*. Munich: C.H. Beck 1974.
Stupperich, Robert, ed. "Briefe Karl Holls an Adolf Schlatter (1897–1925)." *Zeitschrift für Theologie und Kirche* 64 (1967): 169–240.
Troeltsch, Ernst. "Adolf v. Harnack und Ferd. Christ. v. Baur." In *Festgabe ... A. von Harnack zum siebzigsten Geburtstag*, 282–91. Tübingen: J.C.B. Mohr [Paul Siebeck] 1921.
- "Ein Apfel vom Baume Kierkegaards." In *Anfänge der dialektischen Theologie*, ed. Jürgen Moltmann, 2: 134–40. Munich: Christian Kaiser 1967.
- *Die Bedeutung des Protestantismus für die Entstehung der modernen Welt*. Munich and Berlin: Oldenbourg 1911.
Vogelsang, Erich. *Die Anfänge von Luthers Christologie nach der ersten Psalmenvorlesung*. Berlin and Leipzig: Walter de Gruyter 1929.
- *Luthers Kampf gegen die Juden*. Sammlung Gemeinverständlicher Vorträge und Schriften aus dem Gebiet der Theologie und Religionsgeschichte, 168. Tübingen: J.C.B. Mohr [Paul Siebeck] 1933.
Weiß, Johannes. *Die Predigt Jesu vom Reiche Gottes*. 2nd ed. Göttingen: Vandenhoeck & Ruprecht 1900.

CONTEXTUAL AND INTERPRETIVE LITERATURE

Assel, Heinrich. *Der andere Aufbruch: Die Lutherrenaissance – Ursprünge, Aporien und Wege: Karl Holl, Emanuel Hirsch, Rudolf Hermann (1910–1935)*. Göttingen: Vandenhoeck & Ruprecht 1993.

Bainton, Roland H. *Here I Stand*. New York: Abingdon-Cokesbury 1950.

– "Luther: A Psychiatric Portrait." *Yale Review* 48 (1958–59): 405–10.

Bauer, Karl. "Luther bei Troeltsch und bei Holl." *Theologische Blätter* 2 (1923): col. 36–9.

Birkner, Hans Joachim. "Hirsch, Emanuel." In *Theologische Realenzyklopädie*, 15: 390–4.

Bizer, Ernst. *Fides ex auditu: Eine Untersuchung über die Entdeckung der Gerechtigkeit Gottes durch Martin Luther*. 3rd ed. Neukirchen: Neukirchner Verlag 1966.

Bloch, Ernst. *Thomas Münzer als Theologe der Revolution*. Munich: Kurt Wolff 1922.

Blum, Heinz. "Nietzsche's Idea of Luther in Menschliches, Allzumenschliches." *Zeitschrift für Kirchengeschichte* 65 (1950): 1053–68.

Bodenstein, Walter. "Karl Holl (1866–1926)." In *Theologen des Protestantismus im 19. und 20. Jahrhundert*, ed. Martin Greschat, 256–73. Stuttgart: Kohlhammer 1978.

– *Die Theologie Karl Holls im Spiegel des antiken und reformatorischen Christentums*. Berlin: Walter de Gruyter 1968.

Bornkamm, Heinrich. *Luther im Spiegel der deutschen Geistesgeschichte*. Heidelberg: Quelle & Meyer 1955.

– ."Zur Frage der Iustitia Dei beim jungen Luther." *Archiv für Reformationsgeschichte* 52 (1961): 16–29; 53 (1962): 1–60.

Brady, Thomas. A., Jr. "Luther Renaissance." In *The Oxford Encyclopedia of the Reformation*, 2: 473–6. New York: Oxford University Press 1996.

Brakelmann, Günter, ed. *Der deutsche Protestantismus im Epochenjahr 1917*. Witten: Luther Verlag 1974.

Duensing, Friedrich. *Gesetz als Gericht: Eine luthersche Kategorie in der Theologie Werner Elerts und Friedrich Gogartens*. Munich: Christian Kaiser 1970.

Ebeling, Gerhard. "Karl Barths Ringen mit Luther." In *Lutherstudien*, vol. 3, *Begriffsuntersuchungen, Textinterpretationen, Wirkungsgeschichtliches*, 428–573. Tübingen: J.C.B. Mohr [Paul Siebeck] 1985.

– *Luther: An Introduction to His Thought*. Philadelphia: Fortress Press 1970.

– "Über die Reformation hinaus? Zur Luther-Kritik Karl Barths." In *Zeitschrift für Theologie und Kirche*, Beiheft 6, *Zur Theologie Karl Barths: Beiträge aus Anlaß seines 100. Geburtstags*, ed. Eberhard Jüngel, 33–75. Tübingen: J.C.B. Mohr [Paul Siebeck] 1986.

Eisenman, Robert. *James the Brother of Jesus*. Vol. 1, *The Cup of the Lord*. London: Faber and Faber 1997.

Ericksen, Robert P. *Theologians under Hitler: Gerhard Kittel, Paul Althaus and Emanuel Hirsch*. New Haven and London: Yale University Press 1985.

Erikson, Erik H. *Young Man Luther: A Study in Psychoanalysis and History*. New York: Norton 1958.

Febvre, Lucien. *Un destin: Martin Luther*. Paris: Rieder 1928.

Forstman, Jack. *Christian Faith in Dark Times: Theological Conflicts in the Shadow of Hitler.* Louisville: Westminster/John Knox Press 1992.

Frostin, Per. *Luther's Two Kingdoms Doctrine: A Critical Study.* Studia Theologica Lundensia, 48. Lund: Lund University Press 1994.

Graß, Hans. "Althaus, Paul." In *Theologische Realenzyklopädie*, 2: 329–36.

Grässer, Eric. "Albert Schweitzer." In *Protestanten von Martin Luther bis Dietrich Bonhoeffer*, ed. Klaus Scholder and Dieter Kleinmann, 2nd ed., 307–27. Frankfurt: Anton Hain 1992.

Green, Clifford. *Karl Barth: Theologian of Freedom.* Glasgow: Clark 1989.

Greschat, Martin. *Christentumsgeschichte.* Vol. 2, *Von der Reformation bis zur Gegenwart.* Stuttgart: W. Kohlhammer 1997.

– ed. *Der deutsche Protestantismus im Revolutionsjahr 1918–19.* Witten: Luther Verlag 1974.

– *Martin Bucer, Ein Reformator und seine Zeit, 1491–1551.* Munich: C.H. Beck 1990.

– *Melanchthon neben Luther.* Witten: Luther-Verlag 1965.

Hakamies, Ahti. *"Eigengesetzlichkeit" der natürlichen Ordnungen als Grundproblem der neueren Lutherdeutung: Studien zur Geschichte und Problematik der Zwei-Reiche-Lehre Luthers.* Witten: Luther-Verlag 1971.

Härle, Wilfried. "Die Aufruf der 93 Intellektuellen und Karl Barths Bruch mit der liberalen Theologie." *Zeitschrift für Theologie und Kirche* 72 (1975): 207–24.

Hashagen, Justus. "Die apologetische Tendenz der Lutherforschung und die sogenannte Lutherrenaissance." *Historische Vierteljahrschrift* 31 (1936): 625–50.

Hermelink, Heinrich. *Das Christentum in der Menschheitsgeschichte von der Französischen Revolution bis zur Gegenwart.* Vol. 3. Stuttgart: Metzler; Tübingen: Wunderlich 1955.

Herte, Adolf. *Das katholische Lutherbild im Bann der Lutherkommentare des Cochläus.* Münster: Aschendorf 1943.

Hoffmann, Heinrich. "Ernst Troeltsch zum Gedächtnis." *Theologische Blätter* 2 (1923): col. 77–83.

Jülicher, Adolf. "Holl, Karl." In *Die Religion in Geschichte und Gegenwart*, 3rd ed., 3: 432–3. Tübingen: J.C.B. Mohr [Paul Siebeck] 1957–65.

Jüngel, Eberhard. "Barth, Karl." In *Theologische Realenzyklopädie*, 5: 251–68.

Kantzenbach, Friedrich Wilhelm. "Harnack, Adolf von." In *Theologische Realenzyklopädie*, 14: 450–8.

Korsch, Dietrich. *Glaubensgewißheit und Selbstbewußtsein: Vier systematische Variationen über Gesetz und Evangelium.* Tübingen: J.C.B. Mohr [Paul Siebeck] 1989.

Krüger, Gustav. "The Theology of Crisis." In *European Intellectual History since Marx and Darwin*, ed. W. Warren Wagar, 135–58. New York: Harper 1967.

Künneth, Walter, and Joest, Wilfried, eds. *Dank an Paul Althaus: Eine Festgabe zum 70. Geburtstag, dargebracht von Freunden, Kollegen und Schülern.* Gütersloh: Carl Bertelsmann 1958.

Loewenich, Walter von. *Von Augustin zu Luther: Beiträge zur Kirchengeschichte.* Witten: Luther Verlag 1959.

Lohse, Bernhard. "Auf dem Wege zu einem neuen Müntzer-Bild." *Luther* 41 (1970): 100–32.

Lotz, David W. *Ritschl and Luther: A Fresh Perspective on Albrecht Ritschl's Theology in the Light of his Luther Study.* Nashville and New York: Abingdon 1974.

McCormack, Bruce L. *Karl Barth's Critically Realistic Dialectical Theology: Its Genesis and Development, 1909–1936.* Oxford: Clarendon Press 1995.

McGrath, Alister E. *Luther's Theology of the Cross.* Oxford: Basil Blackwell 1985.

Macquarrie, John. "Jesus Christus, VI." In *Theologische Realenzyklopädie*, 17: 16–42.

Mahlmann, Theodor. "Herrmann, Wilhelm." In *Theologische Realenzyklopädie*, 15: 165–72.

Mehlhausen, Joachim. "Nationalsozialismus und Kirchen." In *Theologische Realenzyklopädie*, 24: 43–74.

Meier, Kurt. *Der Evangelische Kirchenkampf.* Vol. 1, *Der Kampf um die "Reichskirche."* Göttingen: Vandenhoeck & Ruprecht 1976.

Michael, J.P. "Bekennende Kirche." In *Lexikon für Theologie und Kirche*, 12: 138–42. Freiburg: Herder 1957–65.

Moeller, Bernd. "Problems of Reformation Research." In *Imperial Cities and the Reformation*, ed. and trans. H.C. Erik Midelfort and Mark U. Edwards Jr, 3–16. Durham: Labyrinth Press 1982.

Moltmann, Jürgen, ed. *Anfänge der dialektischen Theologie.* 2 vols. Munich: Christian Kaiser 1967–77.

Morgan, Robert. "Ernst Troeltsch and the Dialectical Theology." In *Ernst Troeltsch and the Future of Theology*, ed. John Powell Clayton, 33–77. Cambridge: Cambridge University Press 1976.

Müntzer, Thomas. *The Collected Works of Thomas Müntzer.* Ed. and trans. Peter Matheson. Edinburgh: T. & T. Clark 1988.

Niebuhr, Reinhold. *Moral Man and Immoral Society.* New York: Scribner's 1932.

Nowak, Kurt. *Evangelische Kirche und Weimarer Republik: Zum politischen Weg des deutschen Protestantismus zwischen 1918 und 1932.* 2nd ed. Göttingen: Vandenhoeck & Ruprecht 1988.

Ozment, Steven E. *The Reformation in the Cities: The Appeal of Protestantism to Sixteenth-Century Germany and Switzerland.* New Haven and London: Yale University Press 1975.

Peters, Albrecht. "Elert, Werner." In *Theologische Realenzyklopädie*, 9: 493–7.

Rathje, Johannes. *Die Welt des freien Protestantismus: Ein Beitrag zur deutsch-evangelischen Geistesgeschichte, dargestellt an Leben und Werk von Martin Rade.* Stuttgart: Ehrenfried Klotz Verlag 1953.

Ratschow, C.H. "Gogarten." In *Religion in Geschichte und Gegenwart*, 3rd ed., 2: 1684–5. Tübingen: J.C.B. Mohr [Paul Siebeck] 1957–65.

Reimer, A. James. *The Emanuel Hirsch and Paul Tillich Debate: A Study in the Political Ramifications of Theology.* Queenston: Edwin Mellen Press 1989.

Reumann, John. *Variety and Unity in New Testament Thought.* Oxford: Oxford University Press 1991.

Riddoch, Sonia A. "The Ernst Troeltsch–Karl Holl Controversy and the Writing of Reformation History." PhD dissertation, Queen's University 1996.

Ritter, Gerhard. *Luther: Gestalt und Symbol.* Munich: Bruckmann 1925.

Rückert, Hanns. *Vorträge und Aufsätze zur historischen Theologie.* Tübingen: J.C.B. Mohr [Paul Siebeck] 1972.

Runestam, Arvid. *Viljans frihet och den kristna friheten: En undersökning i Luthers theologi.* Upsala, 1921.

Rupp, E. Gordon. *The Righteousness of God: Luther Studies.* London: Hodder & Stoughton 1953.

Saarnivaara, Uuras. *Luther Discovers the Gospel: New Light upon Luther's Way from Medieval Catholicism to Evangelical Faith.* St Louis, 1951.

Scholder, Klaus. "Eugenio Pacelli und Karl Barth." In *Die Kirchen zwischen Republik und Gewaltherrschaft*, 98–110. Berlin: Siedler Verlag 1988.

– *Die Kirchen und das Dritte Reich.* Vol. 1, *Vorgeschichte und Zeit der Illusionen, 1918–1934.* Frankfort: Propyläen Verlag 1977.

– "Neuere deutsche Geschichte und protestantische Theologie." In *Die Kirchen zwischen Republik und Gewaltherrschaft*, 75–97. Berlin: Siedler Verlag 1988.

Schott, E. "Ritschl, Albrecht." In *Die Religion in Geschichte und Gegenwart*, 3rd ed., 5: 1114–17. Tübingen: J.C.B. Mohr [Paul Siebeck] 1957–65.

– "Ritschlianer." In *Die Religion in Geschichte und Gegenwart*, 3rd ed., 5: 1117–19. Tübingen: J.C.B. Mohr [Paul Siebeck] 1957–65.

Seebaß, Gottfried. "Politisches Denken im Spätwerk Karl Holls." Vorgetragen Heidelberg Kirchengesch. Societät 3.2. 1981 (unpublished).

Seeberg, Erich. "Karl Holl in memoriam." *Theologische Blätter* 5 (1926): 165–9.

Sonderegger, Katherine. *That Jesus Christ Was Born a Jew: Karl Barth's "Doctrine of Israel."* University Park: Pennsylvania State University Press 1992.

Stendhal, Krister. "The Apostle Paul and the Introspective Conscience of the West." *Harvard Theological Review* 56 (1963): 199–215.

Stroup, John. "Political Theology and Secularization Theory in Germany, 1918–1939: Emanuel Hirsch as a Phenomenon of His Time." *Harvard Theological Review* 80 (1987): 321–68.

Theologische Realenzyklopädie. Berlin: Walter de Gryuyter, 1976– .

Thyssen, Karl-Wilhelm. *Begegnung und Verantwortung: Der Weg der Theologie Friedrich Gogartens von den Anfängen bis zum Zweiten Weltkrieg.* Tübingen: J.C.B. Mohr [Paul Siebeck] 1970.

Torrance, Thomas F. *Karl Barth: An Introduction to His Early Theology, 1910–1931.* London: SCM Press 1962.

Trillhaus, Wolfgang. "Albrecht Ritschl (1822–1889)." In *Theologen des Protestantismus im 19, und 20. Jahrhundert*, ed. Martin Greschat, 113–29. Stuttgart: Kohlhammer 1978.

– *Aufgehobene Vergangenheit: Aus meinem Leben*. Göttingen: Vandenhoeck & Ruprecht 1976.

– "Die Evangelische Theologie im 20. Jahrhundert." In *Bilanz der Theologie im 20. Jahrhundert*, ed. Herbert Vorgrimler and Robert van der Gucht, 2: 88–124. Freiburg: Herder 1969.

Urs von Balthasar, Hans. *Karl Barth: Darstellung und Deutung seiner Theologie*. Cologne: Jakob Hegner 1951.

Wallmann, Johannes. "Holl, Karl." In *Theologische Realenzyklopädie*, 15: 514–18.

– "Karl Holl und seine Schule." In *Zeitschrift für Theologie und Kirche*, Beiheft 4, *Tübinger Theologie im 20. Jahrhundert*, ed. Eberhard Jüngel, 1–33. Tübingen: J.C.B. Mohr [Paul Siebeck] 1978.

Wirth, Jean. *Luther: Étude d'histoire religieuse*. Geneva: Droz 1981.

Wolff, Otto. *Die Haupttypen der neueren Lutherdeutung*. Stuttgart: W. Kohlhammer 1938.

Index